SPORTING REALITIES

SPORTS, MEDIA, AND SOCIETY

SPORTING REALITIES

CRITICAL READINGS OF THE SPORTS DOCUMENTARY

*Edited by Samantha N. Sheppard
and Travis Vogan*

UNIVERSITY OF NEBRASKA PRESS | LINCOLN

Chapter 3 was previously published as "No Girls
Allowed! Female Reporters as Threats to the Male
Domain of Sports," *Journal of Sports Media* 10, no.
2 (Fall 2015): 17–29. Published by the University
of Nebraska Press. Used with permission.

Library of Congress Cataloging-in-Publication Data
Names: Sheppard, Samantha N.,
editor. | Vogan, Travis, editor.
Title: Sporting realities: critical readings
of the sports documentary / edited by
Samantha N. Sheppard and Travis Vogan.
Description: Lincoln: University of Nebraska
Press, [2020] | Series: Sports, media, and society
| Includes bibliographical references and index.
Identifiers: LCCN 2019044482
ISBN 9781496217578 (hardback)
ISBN 9781496221797 (paperback)
ISBN 9781496222459 (epub)
ISBN 9781496222466 (mobi)
ISBN 9781496222473 (pdf)
Subjects: LCSH: Television broadcasting of sports.
| Documentary television programs—History and
criticism. | Sports films—History and criticism.
| Documentary films—History and criticism.
Classification: LCC GV742.3 .S666
2020 | DDC 070.4/49796—dc23
LC record available at
https://lccn.loc.gov/2019044482

Set in Adobe Text by Laura Buis.
Designed by N. Putens.

CONTENTS

SPORTING REALITIES

Introduction

SAMANTHA N. SHEPPARD AND TRAVIS VOGAN

Sports documentaries have never been more popular, prestigious, or visible. Such films won the Academy Award for Best Documentary Feature in 2017 (*O.J.: Made in America*, Ezra Edelman, 2016), 2018 (*Icarus*, Bryan Fogel, 2017), and 2019 (*Free Solo*, Jimmy Chin and Elizabeth Chai Vasarhelyi, 2018). Academy Awards, of course, are no necessary marker of artistic quality. But the sudden concentration of lauded sports documentaries suggests we are in something of a moment—one that various popular commentators have dubbed a "golden age" for the genre.[1]

Like all documentaries, sports documentaries are allied with what Bill Nichols calls the "discourses of sobriety" (law, science, and so forth), which are principally concerned with making an argument about the world they endeavor to reveal.[2] But sports documentaries—unlike, say, educational films about photosynthesis or hydroelectricity—take as their topic an unusually popular site of culture. As a result, they have the potential to attract the outsize audience that comes along with sport—and the global brands and celebrities that make it up. Moreover, they often (though certainly not always) contrast the promotionally driven register through which sport is commonly depicted via game broadcasts and advertisements. They can therefore usefully reposition sport from a site of leisurely consumption into an occasion to consider the cultural attitudes and intersecting forces than inform them. Sports documentaries, for instance, offer some of popular culture's most enduring investigations of identity politics. George Butler's *Pumping Iron* (1977) and *Pumping Iron II: The Women* (1985) use

1

bodybuilding to illustrate the very different standards by which male and female athletes' bodies, genders, and sexualities are judged. Steve James's *Hoop Dreams* (1994) explores the intersection of race, class, and masculinity through inner-city basketball. Henry Alex Rubin and Dana Adam Shapiro's *Murderball* (2005) considers ability and disability by focusing on wheelchair rugby. More recently, documentaries like *The Armstrong Lie* (Alex Gibney, 2013), *Happy Valley* (Amir Bar-Lev, 2014), and *League of Denial* (PBS Frontline, 2013) have contributed to the discourses surrounding sporting controversies like performance-enhancing drugs, sex abuse, and head injuries. *League of Denial*'s exposure of the National Football League's efforts to suppress information about the long-term health effects of the concussions its players routinely sustain, for example, informed lawsuits, settlements, and rule changes. These documentaries' use of sport to ask pressing questions has made them handy teaching tools for those who offer courses across the humanities and social sciences.

While cinematic markers of achievement like awards and film-festival selections powerfully illustrate sports documentaries' recent renown, the genre's surge has been driven largely by television. Most prominently, in 2009 the ESPN subsidiary ESPN Films launched *30 for 30*, a series on which several of this anthology's chapters turn a critical eye. ESPN used documentary's prestige within the context of television to cultivate a sense of refinement among sports media outlets and to help it compete for market share of the sports documentary.[3] The gambit seemed to work; *30 for 30*'s initial run gathered a Peabody Award as well as the International Documentary Award for Distinguished Continuing Series.

Beyond the respectability they built, ESPN's *30 for 30* documentaries served as cost-effective promotional devices that fuel the very commercial motives that the stereotypically edifying documentary often suppresses. The films cost less to produce than the rights to broadcast even marginally popular live sporting events. They can also be flexibly scheduled to complement related programming and can be used in perpetuity by the channel and its various offshoots. ESPN thus extended its critically acclaimed and economical documentary series with spin-offs organized around specific events and properties, such as *SEC Storied*, which it used to help launch the SEC Network; *Nine for IX*, a complement to its women-centered ESPNW website; *Soccer Stories*, made to support ESPN's and ABC's coverage of the 2014 World Cup; and *30 for 30 Shorts*, brief documentaries that live primarily online instead of on TV. As of this writing, ESPN Films has created more than two hundred documentaries under its various banners. The *New York Times* described *30 for 30* as "a thunderclap in the industry" that established the sports documentary as sports television's most prominent genre outside of live event coverage and instituted ESPN as the form's unquestioned leader.[4]

ESPN's success with sports documentaries motivated other TV outlets to start participating in the genre, such as the NBC Sports Group and Fox Sports, which respectively established documentary film units in 2015 and 2018. Streaming services like Netflix also began producing original sports documentaries that include *The Battered Bastards of Baseball* (Chapman Way and Maclain Way, 2014), *Team Foxcatcher* (Jon Greenhalgh, 2016), and *Icarus*. Even current sport superstars have taken to the genre. LeBron James's production company SpringHill Entertainment has produced several documentaries, including *More than a Game* (Kristopher Belman, 2009), *Shut Up and Dribble* (Showtime, 2018), *Student Athlete* (HBO, 2018), and the Muhammad Ali documentary *What's My Name?* (Antoine Fuqua, 2019). The genre's rise coincides with and embodies the move from traditional film and television to digital streaming and on-demand media culture. Though they screened theatrically and gathered Academy Awards, the multipart *O.J.: Made in America* was principally designed to drive consumers to ESPN's streaming application, *Icarus* sought to boost Netflix's subscribership, and *Free Solo* was made with the understanding that it would ultimately live on Nat Geo and increase traffic to the cable channel's app.[5] The sports documentary, then, is on the front wave of a broader intermingling of television, cinema, and streaming that fictional films like *Roma* (Alfonso Cuarón, 2018) and *The Irishman* (Martin Scorsese, 2019) are beginning to normalize.

While they often do important work, sports documentaries also merit close critical scrutiny. As Nichols points out, documentaries are separated from fictional films principally because they do not present *a* world, but rather *the* world—a "shared historical construct." They are, as Carl Plantinga puts it, "asserted veridical representations," or, perspectives on reality that use indexical images to make their points.[6] As such, they carry with them significant epistemological weight, and perhaps even responsibility.

Documentaries, as asserted representations, are necessarily selective. And this selectivity is shaped by a variety of aesthetic, ideological, technological, and economic factors. Documentaries, for instance, often round off their political edges in favor of building dramatic narratives that might attract a bigger audience. Many of the most popular sports documentaries, in fact, sacrifice nuance to make way for more immediately salable drama that reflects the often inspirational fictional sports film. *Hoop Dreams*, for example, both critiques the naive notion that basketball offers a reliable corridor through which inner-city African American men can improve their economic circumstances and adopts a triumphalist competition narrative that reinforces the very American Dream mythos it ostensibly sets out to interrogate.[7] Along different lines, ESPN's and Netflix's sports documentaries are as invested in branding these media entities and promoting their other corporate properties as they are in illuminating or critiquing their subjects.[8]

This is where scholars can come in handy. Despite the sports documentary's prominence, it has received little critical attention. Most of the scholarship on the sports documentary—such as Dan Streible's *Fight Pictures: A History of Boxing and Early Cinema* (2008) and Travis Vogan's *ESPN: The Making of a Sports Media Empire* (2015)—only partially focuses on the genre and considers it within very specific historical and industrial parameters. An exception is Zachary Ingle and David W. Sutera's pair of anthologies, *Identity and Myth in Sports Documentaries: Critical Essays* (2012) and *Gender and Genre in Sports Documentaries: Critical Essays* (2012), which explore the sports documentary's engagement with identity politics. More recently, the *Journal of Sport History* (41, no. 2 [2014]) published a forum on the sports documentary, and the *Journal of Sport & Social Issues* (41, no. 6 [2017]) published a special issue on it. But these works are still only beginning to establish a conversation about the sports documentary as its "golden age" flourishes. Work on the genre—particularly given its narrative-inspired and entertainment-driven tendencies—also complements scholarship on the sports film, such as Deborah Tudor's *Hollywood's Vision of Team Sports: Heroes, Race, and Gender* (1997), Aaron Baker's *Contesting Identities: Sports in American Film* (2003), Bruce Babington's *The Sports Film: Games People Play* (2014), and Seán Crosson's *Sport and Film* (2013).

This anthology brings together a collection of scholars to probe the sports documentary's cultural meanings, aesthetic practices, business imperatives, and political contours. In particular, the chapters' focus on the industrial and commercial elements informing the sports documentary's ideologically loaded depictions sets this collection apart from already published material on the topic. The ten chapters assembled consider and critique the sports documentary's increasingly visible and powerful position in contemporary culture and forge novel connections between the study of nonfiction media and sport. And they do so by exploring a diverse and important collection of sports documentaries, many of which have not yet received scholarly treatment.

We open the volume with Branden Buehler's "The Documentary as 'Quality' Sports Television," which explores, pushes against, and expands the common identification of documentary programming as "quality" sports TV. Buehler considers precisely how documentary has been positioned as exceptional and the various forces that shape the genre's vaunted image in the media industry and in popular culture. He also argues that the discursive positioning of documentary as high quality devalues both sports television and its audience as unsophisticated by centering understandings of aesthetic merit on filmic texts that are, ironically, not representative of sports TV more generally.

The following two chapters build on Buehler by focusing on documentaries from ESPN Films' *Nine for IX* (2013)—a series of nine documentaries about and directed by women that were made to commemorate the fortieth anniversary of Title IX. Aaron Baker's "Intersectionality in *Venus Vs.*" examines how Ava DuVernay's *Venus Vs.*—the first and highest-profile *Nine for IX* film—exemplifies intersectional analysis by linking the roles that race and gender played in Venus Williams's struggle to secure equal prize money for women in professional tennis. DuVernay, Baker contends, complements the documentary's thematic intersectionality with formal intersectionality that melds the conventions of the documentary and the melodramatic sports film to get its point across.

Korryn D. Mozisek's chapter "No Girls Allowed! Documenting Female Reporters as Threats in *Let Them Wear Towels*" (a revision and update of a 2015 article published in the *Journal of Sports Media*) focuses on Ricki

Stern and Annie Sundberg's *Let Them Wear Towels*, a *Nine for IX* documentary that complements *Venus Vs.*'s focus on activism by charting female journalists' decades-long struggle to gain access to male locker rooms. Mozisek notes the documentary's interrogation of the sexist culture that prohibited female journalists from doing their jobs but argues that the documentary's ultimately optimistic conclusion misses a crucial opportunity to urge for greater structural changes in the still overwhelmingly male sports media industry.

Evan Brody's "Documenting Difference: Gay Athletes of Color, Binary Representation, and the Sports Documentary" critiques a series of sports documentaries about gay athletes of color. Brody explains how these documentaries at once offer increased visibility for gay athletes of color and participate in the production of stereotypes surrounding sexuality, gender, and race. He does this by focusing on these documentaries' reliance on three easily digestible and normative binaries that simplify their subjects' complex sexual, gender, and racial identities. Brody also explains how future documentaries about gay athletes of color might productively push against such restrictive molds.

Justin Hudson deepens the exploration of how sports documentaries mediate race and gender with "To the (Black) Athlete Dying Young: Documenting and Mythologizing Len Bias and Ben Wilson." Hudson focuses on the *30 for 30* documentaries *Without Bias* (Kirk Fraser, 2009) and *Benji* (Coodie and Chike, 2012). The films respectively center on Len Bias and Ben Wilson, young black basketball phenoms who died tragically and without fulfilling their considerable promise. Hudson explains how these documentaries both challenge stereotypes surrounding urban African American men and—echoing *Hoop Dreams* and the narrative template it established—reinforce an ethos of individualism that de-emphasizes the economic and racial conditions that shaped Bias's and Wilson's stories and that continues to impact popular depictions of urban black basketball players.

Emily Plec and Shaun M. Anderson's "Protest and Public Memory: Documenting the 1968 Summer Olympic Games" compares an American and an Australian documentary about the famous raised-fist demonstration at the 1968 Mexico City Olympics that involved the black American sprinters Tommie Smith and John Carlos and the white Australian runner

Peter Norman. Their critiques complement and offer some historical context for Hudson's focus on race and masculinity. Plec and Anderson also add a transnational component by pointing out how these documentaries differently depict the protesting athletes and how these representational variances map onto their subjects' national identities. The chapter shows the importance of documentary to remembering iconic sporting moments like the 1968 protest and explains how these commemorations sometimes trade in stereotypes—a common practice in sports documentaries that the following chapter also probes.

Dario Brentin and David Brown's "Of Friends and Foes: Remembering Yugoslavia in Sports Documentaries" considers how five documentaries reflect on the former Yugoslavia through sport. Brentin and Brown identify key tropes through which these documentaries narrate the former Yugoslavia and the important roles sport played in it—and continue to play in how it is remembered. The chapter also complements Plec and Anderson's focus on masculinity and transnationalism. In particular, it explains how the *30 for 30* documentary *Once Brothers* (Michael Tolajian, 2010), which covers the fraught relationship between the basketball players Vlade Divac and Drazen Petrovic, compares to documentaries about Yugoslavian sport that were produced in the former Yugoslavia.

Ray Gamache's "'Measuring Up': Fathers, Sons, and the Economy of Death in Mountain Film Documentaries" turns a critical eye on William A. Kerig's *The Edge of Never* (2009) and Stephen Judson's *The Alps* (2007). The chapter extends Brentin and Brown's analyses by explaining how these transnational and cross-cultural mountain film documentaries utilize an "economy of death" to memorialize two men killed on mountains and to dramatize how their respective sons sought to honor and redeem their fallen fathers by conquering the same feats they died attempting. These little-known and provocative films, Gamache explains, both dangle the titillating prospect of death and navigate the relationship between risk and masculinity in mountain sports.

The anthology's final two chapters engage the long and largely unexplored history of sports documentaries in broadcast and cable television before *30 for 30*. Alex Kupfer's "*Sports Album*'s Replay: Newsreel Compilation, Early Television, and the Recirculation of Sport History" investigates the syndicated compilation series *Sports Album*, which was made by Frederic W. Ziv Productions and distributed from 1948 to 1956. Kupfer shows how *Sports Album* exemplifies many of the aesthetic and commercial characteristics against which recent sports documentaries often position themselves to fashion their exceptional status in sports TV. The chapter offers the first scholarly examination of *Sports Album* and uses the largely forgotten program to historicize the discourses of aesthetic quality surrounding contemporary sports television documentaries.

Finally, Travis Vogan's "HBO Sports: Docu-Branding Boxing's Past and Present" explores how the premium cable channel HBO used documentaries and other docu-branding efforts—docudramas, product placements, and so on—to build its association with boxing. The combination of boxing with documentary helped HBO to establish the subscribership that eventually fueled its original series and the respected institutional image they signal. Vogan shows how boxing documentaries and other practices that mediate the sport's reality not only contribute to HBO's efforts to craft a prestigious brand but also helped to build the infrastructure through which it established its coveted identity.

The chapters assembled in this anthology combine to show the various and important purposes sports documentaries serve in media and popular culture—and they offer some explanation as to why the genre has recently achieved such prominence in film, TV, and online. They also, we hope, provide critical inquiries that will encourage more investigation of the sports documentary's history, politics, and economics as the genre continues to serve as a key—though often problematic—form through which sport is remembered, explained, and challenged.

NOTES

1. Barney Ronay, "Dramatic Victory: Are We Entering a Golden Age for the Sports Documentary?," *Guardian*, November 20, 2017, www.theguardian.com.

2. Bill Nichols, *Representing Reality: Issues and Concepts in Documentary* (Bloomington: Indiana University Press, 1992), 3.

3. See Travis Vogan, *ESPN: The Making of a Sports Media Empire* (Urbana: University of Illinois Press, 2015), 121–45.

4. Richard Sandomir, "Documentaries Are the Go-to Players of Sports Television," *New York Times*, March 21, 2015, SP5.

5. Travis Vogan, "ESPN: Live Sports, Documentary Prestige, and On-Demand Culture," in *From Networks to Netflix: A Guide to Changing Channels*, ed. Derek Johnson, 107–16 (New York: Routledge, 2018).

6. Nichols, *Representing Reality*, 109; Carl Plantinga, "What a Documentary Is, After All," *Journal of Aesthetics and Art Criticism* 63, no. 2 (2005): 105–17.

7. Murray Sperber, "Hoop Dreams, Hollywood Dreams," *Jump Cut* 40 (March 1996): 3–7; bell hooks, "Neo-colonial Fantasies of Conquest: *Hoop Dreams*," in *Reel to Real: Race, Sex, and Class at the Movies*, 77–82 (New York: Routledge, 1996).

8. Travis Vogan, "Chronicling Sport, Branding Institutions: The Television Sports Documentary from Broadcast to Cable," in *Routledge Handbook of Sport Communication*, ed. Paul Pedersen, 128–35 (New York: Routledge, 2013).

The Documentary as "Quality" Sports Television

BRANDEN BUEHLER

In the 1990s and 2000s, American television entered what a variety of critics referred to as a new "golden age of television," largely spearheaded by prestige cable series like *The Sopranos* (HBO, 1999–2007) and *Mad Men* (AMC, 2007–15). Critics hailed such shows for their intricate narratives, complex characterization, dense thematic undertones, and technical precision. Following this discursive shift, a number of scholars either began or continued exploring similar terrain, not just by analyzing how television's form and content may have evolved in recent decades, but also by asking how certain shows came to be labeled as "quality" and, more broadly, by examining how media industries and media audiences construct discourses of value.

Despite its cultural and financial import, sports television has largely been missing from the popular and academic conversations surrounding this new "golden age of television" and, as Travis Vogan has noted, the related questions of "quality." This chapter suggests that sports television's absence from these conversations is largely a product of the sports television industry's unique structure and economics, as well as its idiosyncratic place within the broader American media landscape. As Philip Sewell argues, "quality television" is perhaps best understood as a discursive construct uniting "network executives, producers, creative personnel, critics, regulators, and audiences" around shared interests, as in the desire by networks to positively spin ratings numbers and the impulse of television critics to legitimate their object of analysis. Quality has thus primarily been linked to certain narrative series—particularly hour-long dramas—not because these series are necessarily aesthetically superior, but rather because of their "ability to serve as a contingent rallying point where disparate needs, uses, and values can be rendered culturally and/or economically productive."[1]

As Sewell suggests, then, the discursive alignments that have continually equated the hour-long drama with quality have largely been a product of both the financial imperatives and the cultural contexts of prime-time narrative television programming. In the case of sports television, though, these financial imperatives and cultural contexts vary. Sports television is not only composed of different forces from prime-time television—lacking, for instance, the highly visible creative personnel often found in prime time—but those forces also have had different interests from those in other sectors of television. For example, broadcast networks have typically aimed their sports offerings at different audiences than much of their prime-time narrative programming traditionally associated with quality television.

That sports television's absence from discussions of television quality is primarily a product of its distinct place within the broader television landscape is further confirmed by the discourses that have recently surrounded the sports television documentary. Over the past several years, a number of sports television documentaries have received great praise and, in the process, been explicitly highlighted as unusual examples of quality sports television. Significantly, the sports television documentary has been the rare instance in which a wide range of forces within and surrounding the sports television industry have shared an interest in promoting sports television as quality. Much as most of sports television has been absent from quality discussions because of the industry's unique financial imperatives and cultural contexts, the documentary has been positioned as quality because these imperatives and contexts more closely mirror those of prime-time narrative television.

By exploring the relationship between quality and sports television, this chapter works to expand the understanding of how quality discourses operate and further illustrates how sports media industries define and position themselves. Moreover, in specifically analyzing how and why the sports documentary has been positioned as quality television, the chapter examines the larger stakes involved in these discursive constructions. The positioning of the sports television documentary as quality has had several consequences that extend beyond the intended effect of creating an aura of prestige around the documentary genre and its producers. The discursive binary that elevates the documentary not only devalues sports television and its viewers by implicitly treating most sports television as pedestrian, lowbrow fare in need of transcending, but also flattens the critical discourse surrounding sports television by disproportionately emphasizing filmic texts largely unrepresentative of the multifarious genre.

"Quality" Boundaries

The reasons for television's absence from "quality television" discourses appear, at first, to be relatively straightforward. Quality television has largely been associated with narrative television series, particularly dramas. To that point, in *Television's Second Golden Age*, Robert Thompson limits his discussion of quality television to the "hour-long dramatic form," arguing that quality "has come to be associated in the minds of many with the 'quality drama.'"[2] Most sports television programming, of course, shares few formal conventions with the drama. Moreover, sports television largely operates in its own separate sphere of the television landscape. Television networks, for instance, tend to house their sports programming, like their news programming, in independent departments. The sports television industry, too, has separate trade groups and its own awards.

Undoubtedly, sports television's relatively unique formal properties and general remove from narrative television contribute to its omission from quality discourses. However, sports television's exclusion from these discourses also has a more complex background rooted in the history of the television industry and how concepts of quality emerged out of specific economic and cultural contexts. As Mark Alvey details, American television broadcasters initially gauged the success of their programming solely by measuring audience size. However, as the television industry grew more established in midcentury, broadcasters began to broaden their focus. As Alvey explains, major ratings services started offering demographic breakdowns of audiences in the 1950s, and networks began to take heed of not just how many people were watching but also who was watching. Significantly, as networks started conceiving of audiences in terms of demographics, they also started conceiving of audiences in terms of "quality" demographics—that is, "younger, more affluent, better-educated adults" likely to appeal to advertisers. As Alvey notes, too, there was also a racial component to this rhetorical shift. He comments, "The unstated but implicit word in every network construction of 'young adult' or 'urban, educated' was, of course, 'white.'"[3]

Unsurprisingly, networks soon began touting to advertisers their ability to attract the newly conceived quality audiences. As Alvey details, though, the networks' recognition and promotion of quality audiences began largely as a "defensive" rhetorical strategy. Initially, he writes, the networks continued to prioritize attracting the largest audiences possible and primarily used the new demographic data to spin low ratings as successes, strategically claiming that poorly performing programs were nevertheless attracting particularly desirable viewers. However, the rise of "demographic thinking" eventually moved beyond rhetoric. As the 1960s progressed, the "quest for the upper audience slant" started to influence the selection and development of programming. In 1966, for example, CBS canceled a number of shows whose audiences skewed older, such as *Candid Camera* (1960–67). A few years later, the network similarly eliminated several rural-themed shows, as in *The Beverly Hillbillies* (CBS, 1962–71), which were particularly popular with older rural viewers. NBC, meanwhile, pointed to "quality" demographics in deciding to renew several series with "marginal audience share," such as *Star Trek* (1966–69).[4] NBC vice president Paul Klein commented, "A quality audience—lots of young adult buyers—provides a high level that may make it worth holding onto a program despite low over-all ratings."[5]

While the 1950s and 1960s marked the beginning of "demographic thinking" that began to prioritize programming able to attract quality audiences, ensuing decades would see quality television emerge as an even more potent idea. As Jane Feuer documents, the 1970s and 1980s saw the growing success of MTM Enterprises, a production company known for quality shows such as *The Mary Tyler Moore Show* (CBS, 1970–77) and *Hill Street Blues* (NBC, 1981–87). As she writes, too, networks increasingly marketed themselves as homes to quality programming. To that point, Sewell notes that NBC, the most aggressive promoter of quality, ran ads proclaiming, "NBC, Quality Television." According to Sewell, quality television began to emerge as a more prominent concept in this period because of its power to unite a number of competing concerns, as "the interests of network executives, producers, creative personnel, critics, regulators, and audiences are not necessarily congruent."[6] The concept of quality, though, unified these often competing forces. It was, of course, logical for a production company like MTM to brand itself apart from competitors, but the appeal of highlighting "quality" stretched well beyond producers. Sewell details:

> The discourse of quality facilitated a relatively efficient system of cultural and economic exchange. NBC made a profit selling value-added audiences while enhancing its prestige and arguably serving the public interest mandated by law. Advertisers marketed upscale products without having to pay for the chaff of the mass audience. Critics who had long decried much popular television saw validation for their assertions that television could be better. The FCC [Federal Communications Commission], which had taken a decidedly deregulatory turn under the chairmanship of Reagan appointee Mark Fowler, could point to the programs and critical acclaim as evidence of the workings of the market. Viewers of programs hailed as quality could enjoy a sense of distinction along with the other pleasures of the program.[7]

Sewell further explains that quality's status as a discursive alignment means it is flexible and, as such, open to change. To that point, the concept of quality television has undergone a slight transformation since the 1980s.

As a number of scholars have noted, quality has largely shifted from broadcast television to cable, with quality becoming particularly associated with HBO and its "Not TV" branding.[8] Significantly, an embrace of quality has offered cable networks a way to separate themselves from their competitors and, again, to lure upscale audiences. For a pay network like HBO, quality has been a particularly helpful concept, as it has allowed the network to market itself as offering programming unavailable on broadcast networks and basic cable. Quality continues to serve other interests, too. Creative personnel, for instance, use quality as a way to position themselves as offering distinctively artistic products. Meanwhile, Avi Santo suggests the concept of quality also allows audiences to understand themselves as uniquely elevated, able to understand and appreciate the exclusive, supposedly sophisticated programming on offer on networks like HBO. He comments, "Pay cable sells cultural capital to its subscribers, who are elevated above the riffraff that merely consume television."[9]

With quality television understood less as a set of formal attributes and more as a series of discursive alignments, sports television's exclusion from discussions of quality can be understood in a new light. For a number of reasons, sports television is unlikely to produce a discursive alignment around quality. On the most basic level, discourses surrounding sports television are typically composed of different forces from discourses surrounding prime-time narrative television. Notably, the sports television industry is structured much differently from other segments of the television industry. In the 1970s, the FCC sought to reduce the power of broadcast networks over both television distribution and production, introducing the Financial Interest and Syndication Rules (Fin-Syn Rules). These rules, which had the effect of limiting networks' ability to produce their own prime-time programming, helped spur the growing success of independent television producers, like MTM and Norman Lear's Tandem Productions.[10] Part of the reason quality emerged as a salient idea was that it allowed broadcast networks and independent producers to articulate themselves in a way that connected their intersecting commercial and cultural interests.

Sports television, however, largely fell outside of the Fin-Syn Rules. Networks may have partnered with independent firms to provide production facilities and other services for their sports programming, but this programming was—and continues to be—largely internally produced. As such, networks have not been as wedded to outside producers for sports television programming as they have been in the case of prime-time programming. Rather, the networks' closest partners in sports programming have arguably been sports rights holders, as in the International Olympic Committee and professional leagues like the National Basketball Association (NBA).

Sports television is largely absent of not just independent producers but also visible creative personnel. Historically, some of the strongest proponents of quality have been showrunners and writers. Many of the creators of HBO dramas, for instance, have been prone to grand statements about their programs. David Simon, creator of *The Wire* (HBO, 2002–8), has loftily compared the show to Greek tragedy, while Nic Pizzolatto, creator of *True Detective* (HBO, 2014–), has been eager to celebrate his creative process and the depth of his storytelling, extolling the "multiple associations, multiple layers" written into the show.[11] Although sports television has certainly not been absent publicly visible creative forces, as in Roone Arledge of ABC Sports and Steve Sabol of NFL Films, the vast majority of sports television is produced with comparative anonymity. Thus, there are neither independent producers nor creative personnel available to tout the aesthetic merits of sports television programming.

Further speaking to the idiosyncratic discourses surrounding the different realms of television, sports television has typically been missing from popular and scholarly analysis of television aesthetics. As Toby Miller and Linda J. Kim remarked in explaining the lack of popular commentary on HBO's sports programming, "In the world of press engagement with TV, sport is usually relegated to issues of access; reviews of content are largely restricted" to narrative television. This phenomenon stretches back decades, with major newspapers like *USA Today* having featured sports media columnists primarily focused on the business of sports media rather than its form and content. Relatedly, sports television content has rarely been recognized by awarding bodies. To some degree, this is a function of sports television having its own set of awards, the Sports Emmys. However, sports television has also been largely missing from awards meant to cast wider nets, such as the Peabody Awards. Furthermore, sports television has long been absent from scholarly discussions of television, with Miller and Kim writing that "in the world of TV scholarship, sport is generally a poor cousin," and Vogan similarly noting that sports media, in general, has been a topic "neglected in academe."[12]

The discourses surrounding sports television, then, have been mostly absent some of the primary forces that have historically rallied around the quality television concept, including producers, creative personnel, and critics. However, the primary reason sports television is unlikely to produce a discursive alignment around quality revolves around demographics. As mentioned, the concept of quality television has its roots in its association with the affluent quality audiences in high demand by advertisers—an association that lingers today. As Andrew J. Bottomley writes, "The 'quality' in Quality TV" still primarily refers "to the audience itself—it is programming that the networks produce to attract an audience with optimal age, education, occupation, and income demographic characteristics," typically defined, much as it was in the 1950s, as "wealthy ($100,000 household income), well-educated (some college), and young (18–49), as well as living in urban areas." The term has continued to carry other connotations, too. As Michael Z. Newman and Elana Levine suggest, the "quality demographic the television industry and its advertisers crave" is still often associated with attributes such as "straight," "white," and "married."[13]

To a certain degree, sports television programming has been aimed at exactly the sorts of "quality" audiences more typically associated with other realms of television. For instance, Deborah L. Jaramillo argues NBCSN (NBC Sports Network) has attempted to appeal to "valuable 'quality'" audiences by emphasizing "sports attractive to followers of European sports and sports like hockey and polo assumed to be more popular with educated and wealthier viewers." Similarly, Garry Whannel notes that "sports with an upmarket profile," such as golf and tennis, have held particular appeal to advertisers. Unsurprisingly, then, both the Golf Channel and the Tennis Channel have promoted themselves as having the same sorts of affluent audiences linked to prestige prime-time programming. An executive at the Tennis Channel boasts, "The audience is just premium. . . . [T]hey're upscale, they spend a lot of money." Similarly, a Golf Channel executive argues, "Golf fans are some of the most affluent and highly engaged viewers." The channel bills itself as "the No. 1 most-affluent ad-supported television network."[14]

More typically, though, sports television has not been linked with these sorts of "quality" viewers. Rather, sports television has routinely been associated with large, wide-ranging mass audiences. As Victoria E. Johnson details, sports television—even through the fragmentation of the multinetwork era—has carried with it the connotation of "the communal, 'mass' audience, shared cultural experience," thus providing American culture with increasingly rare "water cooler talk." That said, sports television has long been specifically coveted by advertisers for its particular ability to attract large numbers of young adults, especially young men. Richard Sandomir, the longtime sports media writer for the *New York Times*, comments, "For advertisers, sports remains the strongest avenue to reach men 18 to 34, a demographic group that is still forming its brand loyalties and is especially valuable to companies marketing themselves to sports viewers." He quotes an Anheuser-Busch executive who says, "The stability of that demographic is very comforting to us. It's more of a male field." Indeed, longtime ESPN anchor Bob Ley jokingly refers to young males as "that targeted—and blessed—demographic." Such demographic targeting in mind, discourses surrounding sports television have often taken on their own unique contours. Rights holders, for instance, have been quick to declare their sports' power to attract young men to television sets. Following a new television deal in the mid-1990s, National Hockey League (NHL) commissioner Gary Bettman boasted of the league's "ability to sell advertising efficiently because of our strong demographics, particularly among males 18 to 49." In the early 2000s, amid declining ratings across the television industry, NBA commissioner David Stern declared, "The young males that everybody is writing about abandoning the networks are not abandoning the NBA on ESPN and TNT."[15]

Unsurprisingly, though, the strongest proponents of sports television's valuable, young male demographic have been the networks. Indeed, the young male demographic even fueled the creation of an entirely new sports league at the turn of the century, as NBC partnered with the World Wrestling Federation to create the XFL football league. Dick Ebersol, head of NBC Sports, explained, "NBC's greatest interest in this new league is the ability to attract the most elusive audience in all of television, to get young males to the television." Particularly illuminating are the back-and-forth comments between the heads of the networks' sports departments. As Sewell explains, the parameters of quality television in the 1980s were made especially apparent in the verbal sparring of network programming executives struggling to lay claim to the valuable "mantle of quality." Over the course of the past few decades, the heads of the networks' sports departments have often butted heads, too. Especially intense were the rhetorical battles between Fox and NBC as Fox emerged as a major force in sports television in the 1990s and 2000s, offering up unprecedented sums for sports rights. Sometimes these verbal duels were matters of name-calling. In 1995, for instance, Fox won the rights to Major League Baseball (MLB), thus supplanting previous rights holders ABC and NBC. Ebersol reacted with anger. Taking a dig at Fox, he commented that MLB was "trading the promotion of the No. 1 and 2 networks for a pushcart." David Hill, head of Fox Sports, responded by bashing Ebersol, remarking, "I just see it as Little Dickie thrashing about. . . . [H]e's being puerile."[16]

As in the case of prime-time narrative programming, these sorts of rhetorical clashes between the networks have often centered on demographics. In the case of sports television, however, networks have typically promoted their ability to appeal to large numbers of young adults, particularly young men. In 1994, for instance, Fox took over the rights to the NHL. Chase Carey, the president of Fox Television, commented, "It is a sport with demographics that match up tremendously well with Fox in the young-adult market."[17] Ebersol responded with skepticism, stating, "It's terrific for the NHL, but I cannot fathom how the dollars will work for Fox."[18] In 2001 baseball was again at the center of controversy. That year Fox placed full-page newspaper advertisements touting the favorable demographics of its World Series coverage, boasting that it had outperformed NBC's Olympics coverage among men eighteen to thirty-four. Hill commented, "To quote Jack Webb, we just wanted to get the facts out, to show how well baseball has done." In response Ebersol critiqued Fox's ad campaign as disingenuous, saying of the Olympics, "They're sold as the biggest event in sports television for the family, not just women, not just young men, and not just children." He added, "This is all rather sad, silly and desperate."[19]

Sports television's absence from quality television discourses, then, has not been solely a matter of its formal differences from prestige narrative programming. As Sewell argues, quality can best be understood "in terms of contingent stability and the multiple material and cultural investments that give utterances substance."[20] As the idea of quality television has been articulated and defined over the past several decades, there have been few "material and cultural" reasons for sports television to be included. Most significantly, much of the industry has remained focused on articulating its power to lure young male viewers rather than sketching out ways it could entice the affluent viewers associated with quality television. For sports television to enter quality television conversations, then, the economic and cultural contexts of sports television would require a shift.

The Sports Documentary as Quality Television

Although sports television was rarely associated with quality television as the quality concept emerged and evolved over the past several decades, it has recently entered the quality conversation by way of the sports television documentary. As Vogan documents, the sports television documentary—like quality programming found in other areas of television—has been framed as transcending the supposedly pedestrian fare more typical of television. More specifically, he details how the sports documentary has been frequently lauded for operating in a different register from the rest of sports television, framed as offering something of greater depth and artistry. For instance, Vogan notes how director Jonathan Hock, who has created four documentaries for ESPN's *30 for 30* (2009–), praised "the series for bringing an element of quality and contemplativeness to the traditionally unrefined context of sports television." Similarly, Kevin Connolly, director of the *30 for 30* film *Big Shot* (2013), commented, "The quality and brand of the ESPN *30 for 30* series can make people go, 'Oh, OK . . . I know that they do work on a certain level of quality.'"[21]

Documentarians, though, have not been the only ones to tout the quality of sports television documentaries. Critics have made comparable claims. *Deadspin*'s Tim Grierson, for instance, contrasted the shallow nature of ESPN's everyday programming with the complexity offered by the *30 for 30* series, arguing the *30 for 30* documentaries do more than just tell "old stories," but rather get "at something deeper: that mysterious hold that sports have on us." "Sports are another way to think about the issues that make us human," he opined. "ESPN's endless har-har-har, whoop-whoop-whoop misses that. The films of *30 for 30* understand that to their core." Ken Fang of *Awful Announcing* likewise chimed in, "There are many areas where ESPN has fallen short, but *30 for 30* is the network's star. It's quality television." Alan Sepinwall, writing for the *Newark Star-Ledger*, similarly cited "the quality and sweep" of *30 for 30* films.[22]

Critics have also singled out certain sports television documentaries as exemplary texts. Vogan documents, for instance, how ESPN's *O.J.: Made in America* (Ezra Edelman, 2016), an atypically extensive seven-and-a-half-hour entry into the *30 for 30* series that perhaps represents the network's most visible reach toward prestige, "garnered nearly universal praise after its debut—often from arts and culture commentators who seldom pay attention to ESPN's programming." He notes, for example, that *Rolling Stone* dubbed the documentary a "major cultural event" and that *New York Times* film critic A. O. Scott suggested it "has the grandeur and authority of the best long-form nonfiction." Significantly, *O.J.: Made in America* also marked the rare occasion in which television critics have explicitly grouped a sports media text alongside the programs more commonly associated with quality. Daniel Fienberg of the *Hollywood Reporter* ranked *O.J.: Made in America* as the "best TV" of 2016, putting it ahead of quality standard-bearers like *The Americans* (AMC, 2013–18), *Atlanta* (FX, 2016–), and *Veep* (HBO, 2012–). *Washington Post* television critic Hank Stuever similarly cited the documentary as "the best thing on TV" in a 2016 year-end list, while NPR's Eric Deggans called it "one of the best TV shows of the year." The unusually lengthy *O.J.: Made in America* has not been the only sports documentary to receive such critical adoration, though. Both the *Atlantic* and the *Village Voice* placed *30 for 30* documentary *The Price of Gold* (Nanette Burstein, 2014) on their end-of-year "Best Television" lists in 2014, while the next year saw Neil Genzlinger of the *New York Times* put *30 for 30* film *Of Miracles and Men* (Jonathan Hock, 2015) on his top ten "Best TV" list.[23] Again, these lists marked rare instances in which television critics have grouped sports television texts alongside—and even above—the comedies and dramas emblematic of quality television.

On a similar note, too, sports television documentaries have been showered with awards generally not bestowed upon sports television. In 1998, for instance, HBO was awarded a Peabody Award for its sports documentaries, which the Peabody board described as "consistently playing at a higher level." The next year, in 1999, ESPN won its first Peabody Award for its *SportsCentury* (1999–2007) documentaries, which were similarly praised for their "overall excellence." A decade later, the *30 for 30* series was also awarded a Peabody, with the board hailing "its rich and textured storytelling" that elevates "sport beyond its role as entertainment or diversion."[24] Even more recently, *O.J.: Made in America* was honored with the Academy Award for Best Documentary Feature.

As Vogan documents, sports television networks have also worked to celebrate the quality of the sports television documentary, publicly extolling the many virtues of the genre. Recently, for instance, following the creation of a new *Sports Illustrated* video channel on Amazon, *Sports Illustrated* executive producer Josh Oshinsky announced the company's plans to emphasize documentaries, stating that documentaries offer "high-end storytelling." ESPN has been even more aggressive in boosting the documentary genre. Vogan mentions how ESPN executives like Connor Schell and Keith Clinkscales have touted the *30 for 30* series as being able to "provide a layer of intimacy that you just can't get from the normal way sports are covered" and, in contrast to the rest of the television landscape, being "intellectual and smart."[25] ESPN executives, too, have not hesitated to invoke the language of quality. Following *O.J.: Made in America*'s Academy Award, ESPN president John Skipper argued the win stood as "a reflection of years of hard work that has gone into building the *30 for 30* brand and setting that high expectation of quality among our fans."[26] Similarly, Schell suggested the win cemented ESPN's reputation as a "home for really high-quality, non-fiction sports storytelling."[27]

Much as Sewell observes in the case of 1980s prime-time narrative programming, the sports television documentary has come to represent a site for discursive alignment around quality. There are several reasons the documentary has defied the sports television norm. On a basic level, the discourses surrounding the documentary have been composed of different forces than is typical of sports television. While the majority of sports television lacks visible creative personnel, sports documentaries have often been publicly touted by their creators. Although this is certainly not a uniform phenomenon—sports documentaries are often still produced with relative anonymity, as in ESPN's *SportsCentury* series—documentaries are increasingly produced and marketed as authored texts. To that point, whereas most sports television is internally produced, networks have often partnered with outside producers and filmmakers for their documentaries. ESPN, for example, has worked with a number of independent filmmakers, like Hock and Connolly, in producing the *30 for 30* series. HBO, appearing to follow the lead of ESPN, has recently teamed with LeBron James and Maverick Carter's production company, SpringHill Entertainment, for the documentary projects *Student Athlete* (Sharmeen Obaid-Chinoy and Trish Dalton, 2018) and *What's My Name? Muhammad Ali* (Antoine Fuqua, 2019), with Bill Simmons's production company, Ringer Films, for the documentary *Andre the Giant* (Jason Hehir, 2018), and with sports agency IMG for the docuseries *Being Serena* (2018). Moreover, the network has worked with several prominent filmmakers for their recent sports documentaries, including Jeff Zimbalist and Michael Zimbalist for *Momentum Generation* (2018) and Antoine Fuqua for *What's My Name? Muhammad Ali*. Just as significantly, networks—particularly ESPN—have worked to make these sorts of creative partners highly visible. This not only provides the films additional mouthpieces, but also serves to position the films as pieces of auteurist art.[28]

The discourses surrounding the sports television documentary, too, differ from the discourses surrounding the rest of sports television in that they feature critics and, relatedly, awarding bodies. As mentioned in the previous section, critics have generally paid little attention to the form and content of sports television. That has changed, though, with the rise of the sports television documentary. The above quotes reveal how critics and awarding bodies have approached many sports television documentaries through deliberative, interpretive frameworks—treating these films as significant texts to be studied in terms of their aesthetics and how they historicize sports, media, and culture. Indeed, these groups have touted the prestigious credentials of sports television documentaries, explicitly praising their quality and positioning them, as the Peabody Awards have done, as transcending sports television's typical "role as entertainment or diversion." Speaking to this sort of phenomenon, Joshua Malitsky argues that the genre's "associations with seriousness, rigorous analysis, and topics of public importance provide cultural capital . . . to sponsoring institutions." Although Malitsky is describing networks like ESPN, it would appear critics and awarding bodies—who might otherwise be reluctant to praise sports television given its low-culture connotations—are similarly leaning on the genre to protect their cultural capital. Notably, this rhetorical strategy fits within the larger history of attempts to legitimate television. As Michael Curtin notes, documentaries have long been "characterized as the key genre for transcending the superficial and commercial aspects" of television.[29]

Most notably, though, it has been in the interest of networks to promote sports documentaries as quality television. Again, it is a matter of audiences and their demographic profiles. As with other segments of sports television, executives have trumpeted the ability of their documentaries to attract young adults. Schell, for instance, has boasted to journalists that the *30 for 30* series has done particularly well with eighteen- to thirty-four-year-olds.[30] Ross Greenburg, formerly the head of HBO Sports and now a documentary producer, has similarly commented of sports documentaries that "younger demographics eat this up, not just the 50-somethings who've lived a life in sports."[31] In fact, rhetorical battles have been waged over sports documentary demographics. As ESPN launched *30 for 30*, Greenburg positioned the HBO documentaries as superior, saying, "It's like walking into a gallery and seeing a David as opposed to something I chipped out when I was 10. . . . [ESPN will] do what they do. We're always going to feel like we own this category." Simmons, who was instrumental in creating *30 for 30*, replied on Twitter: "Yes, ages 55–90. You still do."[32] Responding back, Greenburg defended the youth appeal of HBO's documentaries on subjects like Vince Lombardi, saying, "If it's a story we feel needs to be told, we think all ages will come to the television set and watch." He continued, "I think a lot of times, people underestimate the minds of a younger generation, and their thirst for knowledge and entertainment."[33]

However, the networks' positioning has not solely focused on sports documentaries' ability to appeal to the eighteen-to-thirty-four demographic. As Vogan explains, a network like ESPN might have a number of reasons for incorporating sports documentaries into their brands. He describes, for example, how sports documentaries have allowed ESPN to reinforce its status as the "Worldwide Leader in Sports" by illustrating the network's ability to serve as an authority on sport's history. The specific emphasis on quality, though, is undoubtedly wrapped up in the pursuit of quality viewers. Again, quality programming has long been synonymous with quality audiences. Bottomley, for instance, describes how quality has come to "operate in a double sense, meaning both a socioeconomic category (class) and a particular aesthetic form (taste)." Similarly, Sewell notes that networks' emphasis on quality in the 1980s "relied on an economic and discursive sleight of hand, in which the quality of a program, the audience it draws, and the goods and services pitched to that audience" became commingled. To that point, Vogan notes how ESPN's marketing of the *30 for 30* series aims to "satisfy viewers who yearn for more refined programming."[34]

While the above quotes indicate that young men—that "blessed" demographic—remain the most coveted demographic, the documentary push reflects a desire to target new niches. Indeed, Vogan suggests ESPN's *SportsCentury* documentaries represented an attempt by the network to "broaden its demographic reach." Dawn Heinecken, meanwhile, argues ESPN's *Nine for IX* (2013) documentaries, which the network described as "stories of women in sports told through the lens of female filmmakers," were marketed as being "particularly consequential for women viewers" and reflected an attempt by the network "to appeal to women."[35] Executives' comments explicitly reflect such demographic strategizing. ESPN executive John Dahl, for instance, has touted the ability of the *30 for 30* documentaries to reach beyond sports television's usual male-dominated audience and to draw in new viewers to the network. He comments, "They'll tell me I'm not much of a sports fan, but I love the stories you tell."[36] Schell, meanwhile, says in one interview that the *30 for 30* series is "great complementary programming to what is core to the network."[37] In another interview, he appears to comment on the desire to use the *30 for 30* films to attract a new group of viewers while still appealing to young men, saying, "We try and strike that right balance between nostalgia and discovery." He continues, "I remember Jimmy Connors' epic run at the '91 Open. For a whole generation of ESPN's audience, that's completely new. This happened 22 years ago, and for our key demographic of men 18–34, they may not even have been aware of it."[38]

The sports documentary, then, has done something relatively novel within the sports television landscape. Although the documentary has not represented the first time sports television has been aimed beyond its core demographic, it has represented the rare occasion when the networks have found themselves in sync with several other forces in promoting the idea of sports television quality.[39]

Quality Stakes

The discursive alignment around the documentary that has brought sports television into the quality television conversation is atypical, reflecting the unique financial imperatives and cultural contexts surrounding the genre. Few other instances of sports television, for example, are likely to involve public-facing filmmakers touting the depth of their work. For the foreseeable future, then, to speak of sports television quality will be to conjure up the sports television documentary. This narrow association is more than semantic, though, and has larger ramifications for how sports television is discussed and positioned within American culture.

For one, the limited equation of the documentary with sports television quality has the effect of reinforcing the reputation of sports television as uncultured fare watched by those looking for a distraction from serious thought. Vogan explains, "Sports media have a reputation for not providing much in the way of credibility, complexity, or edification" and, even more specifically, argues sports television has frequently been depicted as "a mundane excuse to avoid thinking (along with spouses, kids, and jobs) rather than a site that provokes thought." Significantly, these criticisms have also been attached to sports media consumers. As Vogan continues, "Those who consume sports media have a reputation for not demanding" qualities like complexity.[40] The elevation of the sports documentary, rather than subverting these reputations, reifies them.

Newman and Levine explain that discourses of television legitimation—as in discussions of quality television—have long operated by invoking hierarchies. Acclaimed quality shows like *Deadwood* (HBO, 2004–6) and *Breaking Bad* (AMC, 2008–13), for instance, are praised by critics not just for their ability to stand alongside the finest works of cinema, but also for being so unlike the rest of television. As they write, too, legitimating "more respectable" forms of television has meant not only separating television supposedly more worthy of "admiring, critical appraisal," but also distancing that television from "less valued" audiences. Similarly, sports documentaries have been positioned as transcending the usual mire of sports television to better serve quality audiences. Such positioning reentrenches the belief that sports television is unremarkable fare best enjoyed by indiscriminating, "nonquality" audiences. As Charlotte Howell writes, judgments of quality "always carry a political implication." Similarly, Charlotte Brunsdon argues, "There are always issues of power at stake in notions such as quality and judgement." She continues, "Quality for whom? Judgement by whom? On whose behalf?" In the case of sports television, the concept of quality has been used to again mark most sports television programming and audiences as lowbrow, thereby reproducing what Newman and Levine term "class-based hierarchies of cultural value."[41]

The limited equation of sports television quality with the documentary has the effect not just of producing a problematic binary that devalues sports television and its viewers, but also of restricting the critical imagination around sports television. Although sports television documentaries represent but a minuscule portion of the sports television programming available to viewers, they have been disproportionately singled out for praise by critics and awarding bodies. The critical discourse surrounding sports television, then, has been oddly dominated by filmic texts and terminology that are largely unrepresentative of sports television. For instance, in commending television documentaries like HBO's *Journey of the African-American Athlete* (1996) and *Ali-Frazier 1: One Nation . . . Divisible* (2000), the Peabody Awards have often reverted to language reminiscent of the film review, highlighting, for instance, "sharp, fast-paced" editing and skillfully "smooth" narration—plaudits only loosely applicable to most sports television.[42]

This critical imbalance surrounding sports television speaks to debates that have previously surrounded quality discourses. As the concept of quality television became a central point of debate within television studies in the 2000s, Michael Kackman intervened to remind television scholars the increasing focus on quality programming—as typified by critical explorations of "narratively complex" programs like *Lost* (ABC, 2004–10) and *The Wire*—was not necessarily to the field's benefit. As he explained, television studies has its roots in feminist analysis, with scholars originally looking to "television's low cultural value as a provocative starting point, exploring the overt gendering of its pathologized, culturally subordinate viewers." He continued, "Many of the medium's most compelling possibilities lay not in its aesthetic sophistication, but precisely its low status." He argued, then, that the interest in quality television represented something of an abandonment of the field's roots and, instead, "a return to elitist aesthetics."[43]

Although Kackman was speaking primarily of scholarly interventions, especially those related to the "gendered hierarchies" that have long denigrated the melodrama, there is much to be gained by heeding his call in analyzing sports television.[44] In a variety of ways, sports television represents unique territory within the television landscape, featuring unusual attributes that range from a pronounced emphasis on the human body to a frequent commingling of text and image. Because of these distinctive attributes, sports television often eludes the language regularly used to critically analyze television and film. This slipperiness may contribute to sports television's "low cultural value" by ensuring sports television escapes easy comparisons to more prestigious forms of media, but it simultaneously makes sports television fertile ground for novel aesthetic and ideological explorations. For critics and awarding bodies to solely recognize the sports television documentary and its familiar cinematic conventions is to potentially miss much of what makes sports television compelling. Although there might be a temptation to read the association of the sports television documentary with quality as a breakthrough for sports television, representing a newfound ability for sports television to be treated as meaningful and worthy of analysis, this association may ultimately end up continuing to limit how sports television is valued and discussed.

NOTES

1. Travis Vogan, "ESPN Films and the Construction of Prestige in Contemporary Sports Television," *International Journal of Sport Communication* 5, no. 2 (2012): 138; Philip W. Sewell, "From Discourse to Discord: Quality and Dramedy at the End of the Classic Network System," *Television & New Media* 11, no. 4 (July 2010): 238.

2. Robert Thompson, *Television's Second Golden Age: From Hill Street Blues to ER* (Syracuse NY: Syracuse University Press, 1997), 17.

3. Mark Alvey, "'Too Many Kids and Old Ladies': Quality Demographics and 1960s US Television," *Screen* 45, no. 1 (March 2004): 48, 59.

4. Alvey, "'Too Many Kids and Old Ladies,'" 51.

5. Walter Spencer, "TV's Vast Grey Belt," *Television*, August 1967, 74.

6. Jane Feuer, "MTM Enterprises: An Overview," in *MTM: "Quality Television,"* by Jane Feuer, Paul Kerr, and Tise Vahimagi (London: BFI, 1984), 27; Sewell, "From Discourse to Discord," 240, 238.

7. Sewell, "From Discourse to Discord," 239.

8. See, for example, Janet McCabe and Kim Akass, "It's Not TV, It's HBO's Original Programming: Producing Quality TV," in *It's Not TV: Watching HBO in the Post-television Era*, ed. Marc Leverette, Brian L. Ott, and Cara Louise Buckley, 83–94 (New York: Routledge, 2008). See also Avi Santo, "Para-television and Discourses of Distinction: The Culture of Production at HBO," in *It's Not TV*, ed. Leverette, Ott, and Buckley, 19–45.

9. Santo, "Para-television and Discourses of Distinction," 20.

10. Amanda D. Lotz, *The Television Will Be Revolutionized*, 2nd ed. (New York: New York University Press, 2014), 99.

11. "*The Wire*: David Simon Reflects on His Modern Greek Tragedy," *Variety*, March 8, 2008, https://variety.com; Andrew Romano, "Inside the Obsessive, Strange Mind of *True Detective*'s Nic Pizzolatto," *Daily Beast*, February 4, 2014, www.thedailybeast.com.

12. Toby Miller and Linda J. Kim, "Overview: It Isn't TV, It's the 'Real King of the Ring,'" in *The Essential HBO Reader*, ed. Gary R. Edgerton and Jeffrey P. Jones (Lexington: University Press of Kentucky, 2013), 218; Travis Vogan, *ESPN: The Making of a Sports Media Empire* (Urbana: University of Illinois Press, 2015), 5.

13. Andrew J. Bottomley, "Quality TV and the Branding of U.S. Network Television: Marketing and Promoting Friday Night Lights," *Quarterly Review of Film and Video* 32, no. 5 (2015): 485; Michael Z. Newman and Elana Levine, *Legitimating Television: Media Convergence and Cultural Status* (New York: Routledge, 2012), 154.

14. Deborah L. Jaramillo, "NBC Sports Network: Building Elite Audiences from Broadcast Rights," in *From Networks to Netflix*, ed. Derek Johnson (New York: Routledge, 2018), 123; Garry Whannel, "Television and the Transformation of Sport," *ANNALS of the American Academy of Political and Social Science* 625 (September 2009): 215; Jon Lafayette, "New Ad Execs Create Advantage at Expanding Tennis Channel," *Broadcasting & Cable*, April 9, 2018, www.broadcastingcable.com; "NBCUniversal Expands Golf Channel's International Reach with Strategic Agreements within Influential Japanese Golf Market," *NBC Sports Pressbox*, February 28, 2017, http://nbcsportsgrouppressbox.com.

15. Victoria E. Johnson, "Everything New Is Old Again: Sport Television, Innovation, and Tradition for a Multi-platform Era," in *Beyond Prime Time: Television Programming in the Post-Network Era*, ed. Amanda D. Lotz (New York: Routledge, 2009), 123; Richard Sandomir, "The Decline and Fall of Sports Ratings," *New York Times*, September 10, 2003, www.nytimes.com; Dan Caesar, "NFL Reigns Supreme on TV," *St. Louis Post-Dispatch*, October 7, 2004; Prentis Rogers,

"NHL's TV Rights Go for $600 Million," *Atlanta Constitution*, August 26, 1998; Jonathan Feigen, "NBA Commissioner Rolls on through Good Times, Bad," *Houston Chronicle*, February 1, 2004, www.chron.com.

16. Leonard Shapiro, "NBC Gets In on WWF Football," *Washington Post*, March 30, 2000, www.washingtonpost.com; Sewell, "From Discourse to Discord," 249.

17. Steve Zipay, "NHL Believes TV Deal Is Foxy Move," *Newsday*, September 14, 1994.

18. Rudy Martzke, "Fox Makes Hockey Its Newest Surprise," *USA Today*, September 12, 1994.

19. Richard Sandomir, "Truth Twisted as Fox Pats Itself on Back," *New York Times*, May 12, 2001.

20. Sewell, "From Discourse to Discord," 251.

21. Richard Deitsch, "The Stories of Their Time: ESPN's *30 for 30* Fields a Rich Lineup of Documentaries," *Sports Illustrated*, 2010, 26, quoted in Vogan, "ESPN Films and the Construction of Prestige," 149; Christopher Rosen, "Kevin Connolly, *Big Shot* Director, on John Spano's Stranger-than-Fiction True Story," *Huffington Post*, April 25, 2013, www.huffingtonpost.com.

22. Tim Grierson, "Welcome Back, '30 for 30': In Praise of ESPN's Documentary Series," *Deadspin*, September 27, 2012, https://deadspin.com; Ken Fang, "30 for 30's 'Survive & Advance' Elevates ESPN's Documentary Series," *Awful Announcing*, March 18, 2013, http://awfulannouncing.com; Alan Sepinwall, "Review: ESPN Scores with '30 for 30,'" NJ.com, October 6, 2009, www.nj.com.

23. Travis Vogan, "ESPN: Live Sports, Documentary Prestige, and On-Demand Culture," in *From Networks to Netflix*, ed. Johnson, 113; Rob Sheffield, "What *O.J.: Made in America* Says about America Right Now," *Rolling Stone*, June 29, 2016, www.rollingstone.com, and A. O. Scott, "Review: *O.J.: Made in America*, an Unflinching Take on His Rise and Fall," *New York Times*, May 9, 2016, www.nytimes.com, both quoted in Vogan, "ESPN: Live Sports," 113; Daniel Fienberg, "The Best TV of 2016," *Hollywood Reporter*, December 15, 2016, www.hollywoodreporter.com; Hank Stuever, "The Best TV Shows of 2016: *O.J.: Made in America*, *Veep* and *The Americans* Lead the Pack," *Washington Post*, December 8, 2016, www.washingtonpost.com; Eric Deggans, "2016 Had So Much Good TV, It Was Almost Too Much—We Pick Some Standouts," NPR.org, December 19, 2016, www.npr.org; "The Best Television Episodes of 2014," *Atlantic*, December 15, 2014, www.theatlantic.com; Inkoo Kang, "The Ten Best TV Shows of 2014," *Village Voice*, December 24, 2014, www.villagevoice.com; James Poniewozik, Mike Hale, and Neil Genzlinger, "The Best TV Shows of 2015," *New York Times*, December 7, 2015, www.nytimes.com.

24. *HBO Sports Documentaries*, *ESPN SportsCentury*, and *30 for 30*, Peabody Awards, www.peabodyawards.com.

25. Andrew Bucholtz, "New SI Executive Producer of Sports Video Josh Oshinsky on SI TV: 'We Need to Be That Legitimate *30 for 30* Alternative,'" *Awful Announcing*, January 4, 2018, http://awfulannouncing.com; Tim Lemke, "ESPN Documentaries 30 Years in the Making," *Washington Times*, October 6, 2009, quoted in Vogan, "ESPN Films and the Construction of Prestige," 142; Bill Simmons, interview with Connor Schell and John Dahl, quoted in Vogan, "ESPN Films and the Construction of Prestige," 149.

26. Jennifer Cingari Christie, "Academy-Award Winning Documentary *O.J.: Made in America* to Air on ESPN2 over Five Nights," *ESPN MediaZone* U.S., February 27, 2017, https://espnmediazone.com.

27. Neil Best, "ESPN Films at Top of Its Game with Oscar for *O.J.: Made in America*," *Newsday*, March 4, 2017, www.newsday.com.

28. Vogan, *ESPN*, 136.

29. *30 for 30*, Peabody Awards; Joshua Malitsky, "Knowing Sports: The Logic of the Contemporary Sports Documentary," *Journal of Sport History* 41, no. 2 (2014): 213; Michael Curtin, *Redeeming the Wasteland: Television Documentary and Cold War Politics* (New Brunswick NJ: Rutgers University Press, 1995), 24.

30. Marc Tracy, "It Was a Great, Awful Week in ESPN's History," *New Republic*, December 15, 2012, https://newrepublic.com.

31. Richard Sandomir, "Documentaries Are the Go-To Players of Sports Television," *New York Times*, March 21, 2015, www.nytimes.com.

32. Neil Best, "NBC, Then HBO Tweak ESPN; ESPN Tweets Back," *Newsday*, April 29, 2010, www.newsday.com.

33. Paulsen, "SMW Q&A with Ross Greenburg," *Sports Media Watch*, October 29, 2010, www.sportsmediawatch.com.

34. Vogan, *ESPN*, 63, 139; Bottomley, "Quality TV," 486; Sewell, "From Discourse to Discord," 237; Vogan, "ESPN Films and the Construction of Prestige," 146.

35. Travis Vogan, "Institutionalizing and Industrializing Sport History in the Contemporary Sports Television Documentary," *Journal of Sport History* 41, no. 2 (2014): 197; Amanda DeCastro, "ESPN Films and ESPNW's *Nine for IX* Documentary Series Focuses on Female Sports Icons, Issues," *ESPN Front Row* (blog), February 20, 2013, www.espnfrontrow.com; Dawn Heinecken, "For Us All? *Nine for IX* and the Representation of Women in Sport," *Women in Sport and Physical Activity Journal* 26, no. 1 (2018): 23.

36. Selina Chignall, "Realscreen Summit: Scoring with Sports Docs," *Realscreen*, January 24, 2017, http://realscreen.com.

37. Tracy, "It Was a Great, Awful Week in ESPN's History."

38. Alison Willmore, "TCA: Kevin Connolly, Brian Koppelman, David Levien Talk Their *30 for 30* Docs While Keith Olbermann Touts His Return to ESPN," *IndieWire*, July 24, 2013, www.indiewire.com.

39. Travis Vogan, "Chronicling Sport, Branding Institutions: The Television Sports Documentary from Broadcast to Cable," in *Routledge Handbook of Sport Communication*, ed. Paul Mark Pedersen (Routledge, 2013), 129.

40. Vogan, *ESPN*, 2–3.

41. Newman and Levine, *Legitimating Television*, 18, 5, 9; Charlotte E. Howell, "Legitimating Genre: The Discursive Turn to Quality in Early 1990s Science Fiction Television," *Critical Studies in Television* 12, no. 1 (2017): 40; Charlotte Brunsdon, "Problems with Quality," *Screen* 31, no. 1 (1990): 73; Newman and Levine, *Legitimating Television*, 167.

42. *Journey of the African-American Athlete* and *Ali-Frazier 1: One Nation . . . Divisible*, Peabody Awards, www.peabodyawards.com.

43. Michael Kackman, "Quality Television, Melodrama, and Cultural Complexity," *Flow*, October 31, 2008, www.flowjournal.org.

44. Kackman, "Quality Television."

2

Intersectionality in *Venus Vs.*

AARON BAKER

Sports documentaries, especially those made for television, have reached larger audiences in recent years. This is due in part to the increased popularity of the genre in general that Pat Aufderheide describes as the "unprecedented burgeoning of documentary production and consumption" for the past two decades. Sports documentaries offer the kind of "prized" programming that Amanda Lotz argues viewers seek out in the postnetwork or digital era. They draw nothing close to the viewership that live games attract, but because of their relatively small budgets in contrast to the expensive rights fees to show live sporting contests, a number of networks have set up production units specifically to make these films.[1]

Since 2008 the ESPN division ESPN Films has produced nearly two hundred documentaries, and its *30 for 30* series in particular has attracted sizable audiences along with Emmy and Peabody Awards. Using well-credentialed directors from Hollywood and the documentary world such as Barry Levinson, Ron Shelton, John Singleton, Barbara Kopple, Albert Maysles, and Steve James, the *30 for 30* series fits the time-shifting habits of viewers looking to watch what they want when they want it and is available from a variety of streaming applications and on DVD. To bolster the identity of these documentaries as quality TV made by auteur directors and worthy of concentrated viewing, *30 for 30* films were originally shown on ESPN with limited commercials and without the network's usual line of scores, statistics, and news headlines running at the bottom of the screen.[2] By positioning the makers of *30 for 30* documentaries as visionary authors,

ESPN followed the practice that John Caldwell has described as aiming to "cut through the televised clutter" and reach audiences with a promise of the kind of esteemed content that gets noticed in today's crowded media marketplace.[3]

The subsequent expansion of *30 for 30* diluted the brand somewhat, but ESPN documentaries have nonetheless helped the network define itself as a major voice in public discourse on the history of sports. Yet while the *30 for 30* series got credit for the cultural diversity of its subjects and for its auteur filmmakers—including in its first season a number of films about black and Latino athletes made by directors such as Singleton, Reggie Rock Bythewood, Ice Cube, and Cruz Angeles—its target audience was still largely the white male viewers the network already had watching. ESPN senior vice president Keith Clinkscales referred to this assumption when he announced that the goal of *30 for 30* was to appeal to its core audience rather than to bring in new viewers: "You want to make sure you don't take the ones who come to your party for granted," he commented. About the gender imbalance in *30 for 30* documentaries, Katherine Lavelle writes that "the acclaimed film series . . . featured only three female athletes in its first set of films," a ratio she sees as consistent with the network's practice of underrepresenting women. Lavelle quotes a 2013 study that found only 1.3 percent of the coverage on *SportsCenter*, the network's flagship program, was about female athletes.[4]

To address this underrepresentation of women, in 2013 ESPN Films launched a new documentary series titled *Nine for IX*, named after the landmark federal legislation mandating equal funding for girls and women in publicly supported educational programs. *Nine for IX* was set up by ESPN Films in conjunction with ESPNW, a website and social media platform established in 2010 with articles, blogs, videos, and statistics aimed at women athletes and fans. Before starting ESPNW, the network interviewed four thousand girls and women and found that they saw ESPN as "their father's brand, or husband's brand or boyfriend's brand."[5] *Nine for IX*, like ESPNW, was an attempt by ESPN to respond to this gender imbalance in viewership and to increase its appeal to female media consumers. When the new documentary series was launched, Laura Gentile, vice president of ESPNW, commented that "we are developing new and powerful ways to engage women with compelling stories that live across ESPN's multimedia platforms. . . . Through *Nine for IX* . . . we are spotlighting the athletes, coaches and teams that have defined women's sports."[6] While acknowledging the increased representation of women's sports that Gentile describes in her statement, the smaller scope of the *Nine for IX* series indicates a less ambitious plan than ESPN had for *30 for 30*. Travis Vogan also points out that the *Nine for IX* series was "less aggressively promoted" by the network than its *30 for 30* predecessor.[7]

Part of the lower profile ESPN created for *Nine for IX* involved those hired to direct the documentaries about women athletes. The first *Nine for IX* film was Ava DuVernay's *Venus Vs.* (2013), about professional tennis player Venus Williams, shown initially on July 2, 2013, during that year's Wimbledon tournament that ESPN was televising, having taken over live coverage from NBC in 2012. *Venus Vs.* focuses on the challenges that Williams faced moving from a working-class, African American family into the affluent, largely white world of professional tennis and on her campaign to get equal prize money for women at Wimbledon. In 2014 DuVernay would gain major attention with her Academy Award–nominated film *Selma* about the civil rights movement. She has since made the highly acclaimed documentary *13th* (2016) and a miniseries, *When They See Us* (2019), for Netflix, and a television series, *Queen Sugar* (2016), for Oprah Winfrey's network, OWN. In 2018 DuVernay also completed the first $100 million film directed by a woman of color, the Disney project *A Wrinkle in Time*.[8] However, when DuVernay made *Venus Vs.* she had yet to receive much recognition. After her second feature, *Middle of Nowhere* (2012), won best-director honors at Sundance, DuVernay sarcastically commented that the award "raised my profile from zero to 2.2, maybe."[9] Like DuVernay, the women who directed the other *Nine for IX* documentaries had achieved only modest success, mostly in sports television or documentary or both. The choice of DuVernay exemplified how ESPN chose the directors for the *Nine for IX* series more for their skill as documentarians and in representing women's issues rather than for the high-profile auteur reputations brought by some of the *30 for 30* filmmakers.

But even though ESPN's ambitions were clearly different for the *Nine for IX* films, DuVernay's *Venus Vs.*—like the *30 for 30* documentaries made by more established directors—can be seen in retrospect as a work consistent with the thematic concerns of an auteur filmmaker. Writing about the *30 for 30* series, Vogan points out how "in many cases the films resemble those that made the directors famous."[10] Similarly, DuVernay in *Venus Vs.* presents a documentary about the tennis career of Venus Williams with the same focus on the intersections of racial, class, and gender identities that have typified all her film work.

Although *Venus Vs.* foregrounds the story of Williams successfully pushing to win equal prize money, it also examines how race was another barrier in her career that both compounded the gender disadvantage she faced and also created for her an outsider position from which she could challenge the discrimination and sexist thinking in women's professional tennis. The linkage in *Venus Vs.* of racial bias with gender inequality constitutes an example of the kind of intersectional analysis that Patricia Hill Collins and Sirma Bilge posit as an important tool for understanding how concepts of identity, and practices of social power, impact lives. Collins and Bilge state that inequality is "better understood as being shaped not by a single axis of social division, be it race or gender or class, but by many axes that work together and influence each other," in what they call "mutually constructing systems of power." Critical race theory scholar Kimberlé Williams Crenshaw refers to the importance of such intersectional analysis when she writes of "the need to account for the multiple grounds of identity when considering how the social world is constructed."[11] In addition to the use of intersectional analysis of social identity in how her film shows Venus Williams's tennis career, DuVernay establishes formal intersectionality in its use of genre, combining conventions from documentary with those from melodrama and the sports film. This hybrid mix of genres builds viewer identification on an emotional level by documenting Williams's experience in confronting racism and sexism, yet it also celebrates her achievement on the tennis court as a sports hero who overcame these barriers. Because of its representation of an important female athlete and the analysis of gender inequality in sports and media that it offers, *Venus Vs.* is one successful example of ESPN addressing with the *Nine for IX* series its prior overemphasis on men. The complex link that DuVernay's documentary makes between gender and racial issues also shows clearly that her film presents social insight at the same level of significance as the *30 for 30* films by other black and Latino directors.

DuVernay establishes such an intersectional approach to understanding Venus Williams's career in professional tennis in the director's statement that accompanies the DVD of her film—another effort ESPN Films uses to mark its documentaries as products of directors' distinct creative visions. She links gender and racial discrimination by describing *Venus Vs.* as a film about Williams responding to "the politics of patriarchy" and the questions "Why is there racism?" and "Why does it take so long for people to understand there should be equality across the board?"

The documentary begins by laying out the backstory of how the former number-one-ranked women's player, Billie Jean King, fought successfully in 1970 to gain equal prize money for women at the U.S. Open, even while other major tournaments such as Wimbledon and the French and Australian Opens still paid male players more. This opening sequence establishes that Williams's campaign for equal pay at Wimbledon stands on the shoulders of King's earlier activism. As historian Susan Cahn notes, "The late 1960s and early 1970s . . . were a period of tremendous gains and even greater hopes for women athletes," and "women's professional sport experienced a similar boom, led by tennis." In 1970 King became the first woman tennis player to earn $100,000 in prize money, yet even that was only one-third of what the number-one male player, Rod Laver, earned by playing in fewer tournaments. That same year King led a boycott to protest such pay inequality, and over the next three years she also worked to establish a separate women's procircuit and organized the Women's Tennis Association to represent female players. Fifty-five-year-old former men's champion Bobby Riggs sensed the opportunity to profit off challenging King after her successes building women's tennis. Their much-publicized "Battle of the Sexes" match took place in September 1973 and saw King defeat Riggs in straight sets in the Houston Astrodome before thirty thousand fans and an estimated forty-eight million television viewers.[12]

DuVernay invokes the "Battle of the Sexes" match between King and Riggs to reinforce its importance in the fight for equality in women's tennis that Venus Williams took up three decades later. However, just as Williams experienced both sexism and racism, King had to confront discrimination on multiple fronts: not just gender inequality but also bias against her sexuality. Cahn explains how athletes who acknowledge their lesbian sexuality create what the corporations that invest in women's sports regard as "a death blow to popular acceptance" and therefore a barrier to profits. As a historical example of this problem, Cahn points out that "when tennis superstars Billie Jean King and Martina Navratilova admitted to lesbian relationships in the 1980s, each lost millions of dollars in endorsement money."[13] King's experience of both homophobia and sexism therefore represents a combination of intersectional social and economic barriers similar to those we see Venus Williams confront in DuVernay's film.

With King's pioneering work for equal pay in women's professional tennis established in the film's first few minutes, DuVernay shifts the focus to telling how racial and class biases positioned Venus Williams as an outsider in the sport. We see and hear about her growing up in Compton in South Central Los Angeles, learning to play under the tutelage of her father, Richard, and how she changed women's tennis with what ESPN commentator Howard Bryant describes as her unprecedented "speed, power, height, [and] athleticism." Former men's champion John McEnroe acknowledges that tennis is "an elitist sport, and a rich man's game," and therefore "a lot of people wanted to see them [Venus and her sister Serena] fail." The reaction that McEnroe describes exemplifies an "anxiety about the undermining of white racial domination" that Delia Douglas shows the success of the Williams sisters as having evoked. McEnroe's comment also illustrates Nicole Fleetwood's observation that "tennis . . . has historically been associated with the leisure and genteel classes, private clubs and racial exclusivity," and the training away from the world of tennis academies and junior competitions that Richard Williams chose for his daughters can therefore be interpreted as a response to what Fleetwood describes as "the challenges that the girls [Venus and Serena] endured as teens because of their racial and class differences from the majority of participants in tennis schools and tournaments."[14]

To document the hostility with which the world of professional tennis viewed Williams, the film shows an incident when she was penalized by an umpire at a 1999 Australian Open match after some of the hair beads she was wearing fell on the court. African American studies scholar Jelani Cobb describes this action by the white umpire as a symbolic rejection of Williams because she foregrounded her racial difference with her hairstyle. Cobb characterizes the penalty as "a metaphor . . . saying who you are . . . is not exactly fitting in with this sport and in this case you will literally be penalized for that." In addition to how this incident demonstrated the lack of racial inclusion in women's professional tennis, Williams was also viewed as challenging accepted gender norms. Nowhere is this latter challenge more apparent than in the sequence showing her winning her first Wimbledon title against Lindsay Davenport. Bryant states that "in that match . . . you saw the future. Davenport, six foot three, against Venus, six foot one. . . . This is a new era of power." Former *Sports Illustrated* columnist Selena Roberts describes Williams and Davenport as creating a new image of strong femininity: "You had sluggers out there for the first time." Moreover, Bryant connects the revisionist idea of gender with which Williams challenged women's tennis to the racial difference she represented when he comments that "the game wasn't just reacting to a player with height and speed and power, it was reacting to a black woman with height and speed and power who was not going to defer to the cultural mores of time because that culture did not accept [her]." While the clothing worn by women tennis players had traditionally been "restrained and dainty," consistent with what Fleetwood views as race and class-defined ideas of "feminine constraint," Venus and later Serena Williams "moved away from the conventions of tennis fashion with bolder colors . . . and black accessories," like the hair beads at the center of the incident during the Australian Open.[15]

The majority of DuVernay's film employs what Bill Nichols calls the expository mode typical of mainstream documentary to lay out an argument about an issue or problem, in this case the racial, class, and sexist barriers Williams faced in her tennis career. Interviews, archival footage, and evidentiary editing construct a position on the injustice Williams experienced and build the sort of "discourse of sobriety" that, in Nichols's view, defines the role of documentary to illuminate the world it indexes and advocate for social change within it. The following statement by Collins and Bilge—written in reference to the world of sports but with larger implications for social relations in general—describes the thinking at the center of this discourse for change in *Venus Vs.*: "Competition is not bad. People accept the concept of winners and losers if the game itself is fair. Yet fairness is elusive in unequal societies where the rules may seem fair, but are differentially enforced through discriminatory practices."[16]

After establishing the racial and class barriers that Williams faced, DuVernay shifts the focus of the documentary back to the issue of equal pay for women in professional tennis. *Venus Vs.* explains that ticket sales are comparable for men's and women's tournaments and that in fact TV audiences have at times been higher for the women. The documentary also points to the $40 million endorsement deal that Venus Williams signed with Reebok in 2000 as evidence of the economic viability of the women's game.

But in addition to such evidence-based expository arguments for equal prize money, DuVernay engages the audience by combining her film's documentary form with conventions from melodrama. This mixture of genres exemplifies the recent tendency that Chris Cagle describes toward hybrid documentaries that balance their expository construction of arguments with what he calls "the emotional identification of narrative film."[17] At several points *Venus Vs.* emphasizes an emotional response from Williams to the racial and gender discrimination she faced. One example of such emotion occurs in the scene described earlier when she was assessed a point penalty because the umpire determined that her hair beads were a distraction.

The commentary by Cobb and ESPN's Bryant casts this incident as evidence of the racial intolerance in professional tennis. However, DuVernay also emphasizes the emotional reaction by Williams as, almost in tears and with her voice straining, she tells umpire Denis Overberg, "No one was distracted [by the beads]." Several shots move in closer on Williams to show her exasperation with the ruling, and then the film cuts away to her family watching in silence from the stands, creating a scene that shows racial intolerance but also aims to evoke a sympathetic reaction from the viewer regarding the unfairness of the penalty.

Another point at which the film emphasizes melodramatic emotion is when it recalls Williams making an impassioned call for equal prize money at a 2005 meeting of Grand Slam representatives on the eve of her Wimbledon final. This was the first time a player had addressed the tournament representatives, and she made a very personal appeal to them by asking everyone in the room to close their eyes and imagine "being a young girl . . . with dreams and aspirations" and "then one day someone tells you . . . you can't reach the same level as a boy." Women's Tennis Association chairman Larry Scott remembers that Williams's words in this meeting made the issue of less prize money for women players "personal for every single person in the room that day."

While the focus on female protagonists and the emphasis on emotions generated by Williams's experience are effective narrative devices taken from melodrama and aimed at engaging the audience, DuVernay avoids what Mary Ann Doane describes as the victimization of women typical of that genre. The scenes in which she is penalized for her hair beads and in which Williams makes an impassioned plea to representatives of Grand Slam tournaments both engage the sympathy of the viewer but end in disappointment for Williams and therefore fit Cagle's statement that "films may qualify as melodramas largely because their narratives center on emotional conflicts and they do not have . . . happy resolution to these conflicts."[18]

To depart from that disempowered outcome, DuVernay inflects the narrative of *Venus Vs.* with a third film genre, the sports movie, to steer Williams's story from racial and gender discrimination to active resistance. Venus Williams as the victim of discrimination therefore gives way to action sequences that highlight her success on the tennis court. From the public courts of Compton we see her rise to win both the 2000 and the 2001 Wimbledon finals, suffer a period of injury, grief (her sister Yetunde was killed in 2003), and subpar play under the pressures of celebrity and the grind of maintaining her position at the top of the sport, but then come back to win Wimbledon again in 2005 and 2007. This narrative roller coaster is typical of the sports film, particularly biopics of star athletes, which often tell of a rise from modest beginnings, a fall from grace often due to health or family problems or simply the seduction of wealth and fame, and then redemption in the third act.

Another convention of the fictional sports film used in *Venus Vs.* is the importance of showing action sequences to invoke the enjoyment that fans get from watching real athletic events. In preparation for the final section of the documentary in which she will show Williams address the issue of gender and unequal pay head-on, DuVernay builds up her subject's heroic stature by presenting several scenes from her victories at Wimbledon. The most extended of these action sequences showcases the 2005 final against Davenport, who had been Williams's primary rival in reaching the number-one ranking earlier in her career. The buildup for the match includes Venus remembering how this was a major moment that would determine her legacy: "Everybody wrote me off," she recalls. "[I had] something to prove . . . that I'm a Grand Slam champion." The Wimbledon final in 2005 would be the longest women's championship match in that tournament's history. To show it DuVernay employs another convention of the sports movie: the climactic competition that cements the heroic status of the star athlete. This is the longest section in the fifty-two-minute documentary devoted to tennis action, and it includes footage of one rally between Williams and Davenport that by itself lasts for thirty-six seconds.

DuVernay's attention to barriers that Venus Williams faced in her career, her forceful critique of such discrimination, and the film's emphasis on the tennis star's success despite it all suggest *Venus Vs.* fits the category of what Phyllis Klotman and Janet Cutler define as the African American documentary. Specific to this kind of documentary is a focus on what Klotman and Cutler describe as "the economic, historical, political and social forces that shape the lives of black Americans, as seen from their perspectives . . . opportunities for African Americans to define a sense of self and place in their own voices." DuVernay, as a black filmmaker whose main interviewee in her documentary is Venus Williams herself, exemplifies such foregrounding of the perspective of African Americans articulated by "their own voices" in response to the "distorted representations" that pervade "mass media television and film productions."[19]

When *Venus Vs.* was released in 2013 such "distorted representations" and the marginalization of nonwhites in American film and television were documented by the annual diversity report from the Ralph J. Bunch Center for African American Studies at the University of California–Los Angeles. The report showed that while nearly 40 percent of the population of the United States was nonwhite, only 16.7 percent of film leads were minorities and only 19.7 percent of primary roles in programming on cable outlets like ESPN went to nonwhites. Behind the camera, just 17.8 percent of film directors were minorities and just 6.3 percent were women like DuVernay. In the center's 2016 report, after those numbers dropped even further, the lead author, Dr. Darnell Hunt, commented on exactly the exclusion and "distorted representations" to which a film like *Venus Vs.*, as a black documentary, is responding when he stated that "to the extent that whole populations are absent in media or are placed exclusively in stereotypical roles, you tend to normalize certain types of hierarchical structures that are already in place in society and reinforce prejudices."[20]

This activist response in *Venus Vs.* to the misrepresentations and exclusion facing black media makers like Venus Williams impacts its documentary form in regard to the usual expectation that all perspectives on an issue are equally represented. Clyde Taylor has written that black documentarians feel pressure to employ "journalistic even-handedness" that limits what they can show about issues that face African Americans because "they are heavily influenced by the need to shield the defensive sensibilities of white viewers."[21] In the section of her film that focuses on how racial attitudes limited Williams's career, DuVernay gives voice to a number of white commentators, but their statements generally avoid identifying race specifically and several of them focus instead on Williams choosing an outsider status. Steven Flink from *Tennis Week Magazine* characterizes her training methods as "unorthodox" and "unconventional," and Christopher Clarey from the *New York Times* explains Williams's separation from other players on the tour as her being "introverted." The film also includes audio clips of a number of white commentators from sports media describing Williams in a discourse that Jelani Cobb says placed her as "the black girl in the hood who is now in the country club sport." While the white voices in *Venus Vs.* either avoid race or fall into stereotypical modes of representing Williams as black and therefore disadvantaged, the analysis from African American commentators such as Cori Murray, Bryant, Cobb and especially Venus Williams herself either describes her cultural identity as a source of strength and support or speaks directly about the barriers created for her by whites.

Venus Vs. ends with an extended sequence showing how tournament officials at Wimbledon finally agreed to pay women the same prize money in 2007 soon after Williams had published an impassioned op-ed essay in the *Times* of London in which she wrote, "It is a shame that the greatest tournament in tennis . . . is tarnished" and "on the wrong side of history." She summed up by stating that "I intend to keep doing everything that I can until Billie Jean King's original dream of equal pay is made true." This opinion piece spurred a member of the House of Commons, Janet Anderson, to raise the issue on the floor of the British Parliament. Two days later Prime Minister Tony Blair made a statement of support in Parliament for equal prize money for women. The following February the Lawn Tennis Association, the national governing body of tennis in Great Britain, finally equalized the prize money for men and women at Wimbledon. Jelani Cobb observes that the outsider status Venus Williams occupied because of her racial identity allowed her to see clearly the unfairness of lesser pay for the women players and push to end it. "Sometimes it takes an outsider," Cobb states, "to step outside the sport and say this is wrong and it needs to change."

Looking at *Venus Vs.* from the perspective of intersectional analysis shows the links between issues of gender and race in the professional tennis career of Venus Williams. Intersectionality illustrates that social identities are defined through their ideological and structural interrelationships, and only by seeing that larger pattern can we understand the influences and choices that confront athletes. Early in *Venus Vs.* Selena Roberts explains that Venus Williams took the lead in pushing for equal pay for women because when she entered professional tennis, "there weren't a lot of strong, powerful voices fighting for the women." We then hear Chris Evert, a former number-one-ranked player and eighteen-time Grand Slam champion, comment that she had trouble speaking up for equal prize money because "deep down inside" she didn't really believe women deserved it. Evert's comment implies a core belief that Collins and Bilge describe as neoliberalism, which rejects intersectional analysis of inequality in favor of a belief that individual self-reliance alone determines one's opportunities and achievements. By contrast, *Venus Vs.* shows that Venus Williams, like Billie Jean King before her, understood the limitations of regarding her identity and position in society as determined just by her own actions. The *Nine for IX* documentary skillfully foregrounds an analysis woven from examinations of how gender, race, and class impacted her experience, and it employs a similar mixture of film genres to effectively tell her story.

In the world of commercial sports in which the bodies of black athletes like Venus Williams are commodified, struggles over fair distribution of the revenue those bodies create are inevitable. As Fleetwood reminds us, such commodification of African American sports stars also invokes the larger social problem of the control of the black body. This theme of how blacks are positioned to their disadvantage links DuVernay's work from *The Middle of Nowhere*, *13th*, and *When They See Us*, which focus on disproportionate rates of African American incarceration, to *Selma*, in which intimidation and violence are used to keep blacks out of the voting booth. In *Venus Vs.* as well, control of the black—and specifically female—body is at the center of the story. But in the tradition of African American documentary, DuVernay's *Nine for IX* film foregrounds black voices to reposition Venus Williams and celebrate the ability, courage, and resolve to overcome the barriers that stood in the way of her success in women's tennis.

NOTES

1. Pat Aufderheide, "Mainstream Documentary since 1999," in *American Film History: Selected Readings, 1960 to the Present*, ed. Cynthia Luca, Roy Grundmann, and Art Simon (Boston: Wiley Blackwell, 2015), 376–77; Amanda D. Lotz, *The Television Will Be Revolutionized*, 2nd ed. (New York: New York University Press, 2014), 28; Richard Sandomir, "Documentaries Are the Go-to Players of Sports Television," *New York Times*, March 21, 2015, www.nytimes.com.

2. Travis Vogan, *ESPN: The Making of a Sports Media Empire* (Urbana: University of Illinois Press, 2015), 134.

3. John Caldwell, *Televisuality: Style, Crisis and Authority in American Television* (New Brunswick NJ: Rutgers University Press, 1995), 105.

4. Jamin Brophy-Warren, "Documentaries: A New Style of Sports Films," *Wall Street Journal*, October 2, 2009, W4; Katherine L. Lavelle, "As Venus Turns: A Feminist Soap Opera Analysis of *Venus Vs.*," *Journal of Sports Media* 10, no. 2 (2015): 127–28; Cheryl Cooky, Michael Messner, and Robin H. Hextrum, "Women Play Sport, but Not on TV: A Longitudinal Study of Televised News Media," *Communication & Sport* 1, no. 3 (2013): 8.

5. Sarah Wolter, "It Just Makes Good Business Sense: A Media Political Economy Analysis of ESPNW," *Journal of Sports Media* 9, no. 2 (2014): 1.

6. Jennifer Cingari Christie, "ESPN Films and ESPNW Announce *Nine for IX*," *ESPN Press Room*, February 19, 2013, https://espnpressroom.com.

7. Vogan, *ESPN*, 143.

8. Britni Danielle, "Ava DuVernay on *Queen Sugar*'s Ratings Success & Changing Hollywood," *Ebony*, December 8, 2016, http://ebony.com/entertainment-culture; Tracey Brown, "Ava DuVernay's *A Wrinkle in Time* Begins Production," *Los Angeles Times*, November 2, 2016, www.latimes.com.

9. Jada Yuan, "Ava DuVernay, Directing History," *New York Magazine*, December 1–14, 2014, 94.

10. Vogan, *ESPN*, 134.

11. Patricia Hill Collins and Sirma Bilge, *Intersectionality* (Malden MA: Polity Press, 2016), 2, 27; Kimberlé Williams Crenshaw, "Mapping the Margins: Intersectionality, Identity Politics and Violence against Women of Color," in *The Feminist Philosophy Reader*, ed. Alison Bailey and Chris Cuomo, 279–309 (New York: McGraw-Hill, 2008).

12. Susan K. Cahn, *Coming on Strong Gender and Sexuality in Women's Sport*, 2nd ed. (Urbana: University of Illinois Press, 2015), 246, 250, 251–52.

13. Cahn, *Coming on Strong*, 266.

14. Delia Douglas, "Venus, Serena, and the Inconspicuous Consumption of Blackness: A Commentary on Surveillance, Race Talk and the New Racism(s)," *Journal of Black Studies* 43, no. 2 (2012): 128; Nicole R. Fleetwood, *On Racial Icons: Blackness and the Public Imagination* (New Brunswick NJ: Rutgers University Press, 2015), 98–99.

15. Fleetwood, *On Racial Icons*, 100.

16. Bill Nichols, *Introduction to Documentary* (Bloomington: Indiana University Press, 2001), 33, 39; Collins and Bilge, *Intersectionality*, 29.

17. Chris Cagle, *Sociology on Film* (New Brunswick NJ: Rutgers University Press, 2016), 47.

18. Mary Ann Doane, *The Desire to Desire; The Woman's Film of the 1940s* (Bloomington: Indiana University Press, 1987), 73; Cagle, *Sociology on Film*, 142.

19. Phyllis Klotman and Janet Cutler, introduction to *Struggles for Representation: African American Documentary Film and Video* (Bloomington: Indiana University Press, 1999), xiv–xv, xvi.

20. *2016 Hollywood Diversity Report: Business as Usual?*, Ralph J. Bunch Center for African American Studies at the University of California–Los Angeles, http://www.bunchecenter.ucla.edu.

21. Clyde Taylor, "Paths of Enlightenment: Heroes, Rebels and Thinkers," in *Struggles for Representation*, ed. Klotman and Cutler, 137.

No Girls Allowed!

Documenting Female Reporters as Threats in *Let Them Wear Towels*

KORRYN D. MOZISEK

In the opening scenes of the ESPN *Nine for IX* documentary *Let Them Wear Towels* (Ricki Sten and Annie Sundberg, 2013), the audience sees highlights from baseball, football, and hockey games as an unnamed narrator compares big-time sports to the childhood tree house: no girls allowed! Why the opposition to female sports reporters? The answer is quite simple—masculinity. And, as the film importantly chronicles, the fight over masculinity and the locker room was often hostile and unseemly.

In *Female Masculinity* Judith Halberstam writes, "Masculinity, one must conclude, has been reserved for people with male bodies and actively denied to people with female bodies. And this is not to say that all things being equal, all female-bodied people would desire masculinity, only that the protection of masculinity from women bears examination." Even though the women's movement was making progress in the arenas of employment, education, and even sports, doors to men's locker rooms remained firmly barred in the 1970s to female journalists. As women made advances toward social equality, the men's locker room became the last bastion of masculinity and, as the film examines, had to be protected by any means necessary. This portrayal aligns with a point made by Mariah Burton Nelson, in her book *The Stronger Women Get, the More Men Love Football*, regarding the "invasion" of locker rooms by female journalists: "Male locker rooms are shrines to masculine might. Traditionally, women have entered only as men's fantasies and fabrications, as body parts. . . . When mentioned at all, women tend to be discussed in derogatory and often sexualized terms.

When a real woman does enter this shrine, she automatically challenges the male bonding process. Having defined masculinity as sexually aggressive and not feminine, many male athletes seem to feel they must subjugate this woman to an inferior role. In order for them to continue feeling like men, she must become Other."[1] Through this Othering process, female journalists are sexualized by players (and other men) so as to establish authority and power over them.

Prior research by academic sport scholars has critiqued the institution of sports media and sports more generally as disenfranchising women and, thus, hastening their marginalization.[2] Yet the ways that sports media and various sports marginalize women are not at the forefront of public discussion, which is one of the reasons the documentary is important culturally. This reality is created in part, as academic research documents, because female journalists do not want to rock the boat and would rather assimilate to masculine norms than expose their mistreatment.[3] The torments of the locker room's masculine culture, then, remain largely unseen. Burton points out that film is one medium where women have power and can reveal the ugly layers of bullying within an industry: "Most women don't have the opportunity to make men look bad. Journalists do. Filmmakers, authors, and radio and television reporters do. They can record male behavior and disseminate their observations and interpretations to large audiences. They can name names. They can interrupt a daily discourse that tells readers and viewers how heroic men are."[4]

Let Them Wear Towels offers an interruption, albeit a historical one, that unmasks the domination and inequality that female reporters (regardless of their race) faced by being excluded from the locker room and their continued discrimination within the sports media industry. And while the documentary illuminates prior hardships in ways that alter public consciousness about the behavior and acceptance of male athletes, the positive tone at the end limits the film's ability to advocate or enable changes to what remains an unequal industry for women.

Researching the Female Sports Reporter

In December 1969 Elinor Kaine wrote an article titled "A Woman's Right to Write and Sit with Men in the Press Box," which documented how she was treated after requesting a credential for a Jets-Giants game at the Yale Bowl. Her story recounts how she received a seat in a press "area" (a room previously used for newsreel cameras with no way to take notes) while many seats in the traditional press box sat empty and how she was ostracized by her male peers. Kaine's article is but the first rendition of such poor treatment by the sports media and sporting institutions to a female sports reporter. Kaine was the subject of news articles at the time, including those filled with humorous jabs, as the fight over the rights for female sports reporters was just getting started.[5]

Since Kaine's foray into sport reporting in 1969, the number of female journalists on sports beats has increased dramatically. But as Phyllis Miller and Randy Miller point out, "Even though their numbers are growing, once they are on the payroll, female sports reporters say that they are, for all practical purposes, ignored." The long-held belief was that as more women entered into the field, the criticism and ostracism that Kaine faced would transform into acceptance and respect. As Miller and Miller found, though, this level of acceptance has not materialized. Instead, women are frustrated by not being taken seriously (by either male counterparts or readers) and by being viewed as less knowledgeable, thus limiting their beat and promotions, all while facing sexist comments.[6] This frustration from female sports reporters is in part the result of "butting against a glass ceiling, a hierarchical system that prefers men for the top jobs."[7]

In their work studying the status and conditions of employment for women and minorities in sports departments, Marie Hardin and Erin Whiteside found that the newspaper industry believes that it upholds values of social responsibility, but that does not extend to creating diversity in the sports department by hiring women and minorities. Within their report Hardin and Whiteside advocate for newspapers to hire, promote, and retain women in part because the newsroom does not match its demographic.[8] Even as bosses don't feel an obligation to diversify the sports department, Hardin and Stacie Shain found that women are optimistic regarding opportunities to enter the sports-media industry. That optimism is tempered, though, by an overwhelming majority of women who believe sexual discrimination remains pervasive in the industry, whether it be in the form of harassment, not being taken seriously, or having a tougher job than male counterparts. Hardin and Shain offer the following conclusions regarding female sportswriters and the work environment: "Respondents reported satisfaction while also reporting discrimination and abuse; they also reported concerns about advancement. . . . They are resilient enough to face down a sometimes-hostile workplace to pursue their career goals until other obstacles wear down their resolve. *Respondents seem to accept discrimination and harassment as 'par for the course'—as something they must endure as they go about their job duties.*"[9] In addition, research has found that those in the industry believe that while discrimination occurs, efforts are being enacted so as to achieve equity in sports media.[10]

Some might ask whether female sportswriters have an ability to fight back or negate this pervasive environment of discrimination. But as Toni Bruce argues, female sportswriters have historically lacked such power to alter the locker room's boys-will-be-boys culture or its acceptance more widely in culture. This lack of power occurs because women gain acceptance and are less likely to be bullied if they assimilate by acting like just another one of the guys. While academic research has studied the workplace experiences of female sports reporters, "there have been virtually no attempts to understand the locker room from an insider's perspective—that of women sports writers," for public consumption.[11] Enter the ESPN *Nine for IX* series and its firsthand account of female sportswriters entering the locker room in *Let Them Wear Towels*.

Critical Rhetoric as Advocating Change

Raymie McKerrow argued that discourses by those in power function to dominate and restrict the freedoms of individuals and various groups because they do not adhere to prevailing public norms. In response to such domination and subjugation, McKerrow introduced the perspective of critical rhetoric as a way to "unmask and demystify the discourse of power. The aim is to understand the integration of power/knowledge in society—what possibilities for change the integration invites or inhibits and what intervention strategies might be considered appropriate to effect social change."[12] This critique of domination is an investigation of ideologies, including who is viewed as credible and capable of speaking within culture. The critique of power focuses on how discourses serve to restrict individual rights and participation within culture.

As a mode of inquiry Kent A. Ono and John Sloop argue that critical rhetoric means "paying attention to who speaks, what those who speak assume to be the basis for their claims, and the perspective of the audience to whom they speak." By providing a critique, particularly of the status quo (or of the past, as *Let Them Wear Towels* does), the aim is to "address large-scale and long-standing economic, political, cultural, and historical imbalances of power."[13] There are three implications with a critical rhetoric focus: a critical rhetorician wants to know how and why public knowledge and understandings are created, the investigation aims to alter or change public understandings about an idea or thought, and the investigator wants to think about discourse, like films, as having a material impact on public debates.[14] A documentary like *Let Them Wear Towels*, which works to bring to light the experiences of female reporters from the production arm of the Worldwide Leader in Sports, is a form of critical rhetoric by engaging in these three areas. ESPN, by way of the film, is adding to public knowledge as to how the female sportswriters faced discrimination, including a critique of the masculine culture and requisite exclusion it created, and exploring why change had to occur for these individuals to do their job.

By focusing the documentary's perspective on the past and examining the predominant ideologies for women's exclusion, the film functions as a point of conversation so as to encourage a deliberation about women's treatment within the industry, no matter how ESPN might contribute to it (which goes unaddressed). In this regard *Let Them Wear Towels* is a piece of public argumentation that alters the collective life in the United States. This occurs because, as Michael Calvin McGee points out, "each new vision of the collective life, in other words, represents a movement of ideas (and of 'the people') from one 'world' of attitudes and conditions to another."[15] While the film alters audiences' perceptions of the past, does its representation of the present and future for female sportswriters encourage further changes in the industry or its own production home, ESPN?

Walking through the Locker Room Door And . . .

In offering an exposé of the treatment of female sportswriters, *Let Them Wear Towels* works to alter how publics view the sports and media industries. The film allows female journalists to explain how they got into the sports-media industry and to recall how the negative perceptions (not being smart enough, not knowing sports, and just going there to leer) hindered many from doing their job. It also illustrates how the shoddy treatment of the women cut across racial lines (on the part of the players and the female journalists).

As these women express, they simply wanted to do their job in reporting their assigned sport or game, not to become trailblazers. *Let Them Wear Towels* provides an opportunity to alter perceptions of the sports and media entities like the Worldwide Leader in Sports, but the suggestion that all has been accomplished at the end of the film ignores the continuing ideology of masculinity that aims to undermine women in sport.

Exposing a Boys-Will-Be-Boys Culture

A major focus of the film is on documenting the physical and discursive exclusion that female sportswriters faced while covering various teams and sports. Because of their inability to enter the locker room and their restricted access to athletes, female sportswriters were made to feel as if they were strangers, thus constituting them as Others. Robin Herman recounts that she was not initially given a sports beat when she joined the Princeton student newspaper as a member of the first coeducation class at the university. Of course, she wasn't given one because the newspaper's editor assumed that she wouldn't want to cover sports, but she balked at doing half the work of her male counterparts and covered rugby. Melissa Ludtke "didn't know what to expect" when she was assigned the baseball beat at *Sports Illustrated* and felt "like a stranger in a strange land" with so few women reporters covering games. Jane Gross recounts how she was not allowed to eat in the same room as the male sportswriters at Fenway Park, so she had to eat off a tray on the roof of the park, rain or shine. Lesley Visser remembers that her press credential for the New England Patriots read "No women or children allowed in the press box." And Claire

Smith recalls how Baltimore Orioles manager Earl Weaver had a sign on his office door that read "No Wo-*MEN*" in an attempt to illustrate that the clubhouse did not encourage warm and fuzzy feelings for female journalists.

Interspersed with the interviewees recounting their experiences is faux vintage footage where a female journalist reenacts the experiences the female sportswriters are narrating. In creating such vintage footage the film gains a sense that the audience is reliving these experiences all over with the women. They hurry down the hall with the female journalist in heels but encounter a sign barring the entrance. The viewers pace and tap their notepad with the reporter waiting for a player to be brought to her in a stadium tunnel. The viewers are physically barred from entering the locker room by security. All of this is meant to evoke the ostracism, loneliness, and difficulties female sportswriters faced, thus encouraging the audience to feel as if their rights are also being infringed on. The struggles of female sportswriters are no longer a mystery but rather have been brought to light.

During the 1977 baseball season Melissa Ludtke learned what female sportswriters were missing out on as Billy Martin (manager of the New York Yankees) allowed her in a side door and she sat on his office couch. In the film Ludtke states that the couch was "like a bleacher seat" that "made [her] hunger for more" as she "finally realized what [she] was missing." Even when the players voted to allow female sportswriters into the locker rooms during the 1977 World Series, the baseball commissioner struck down the access because the players' wives had not been polled and the players' children would face ridicule at school. Because of the decision Ludtke missed the opportunity to fully write about Reggie Jackson and the Yankees' World Series win as she waited and waited to meet with Jackson in the hallway until he emerged exhausted and declined to answer questions.

After the 1977 season Ludtke was asked by her editor to write a letter to the baseball commissioner requesting access. When she was denied, *Sports Illustrated* filed suit, and Ludtke was thrust into the middle of a media firestorm. As Ludtke recalls it created a headline field day that was a part of the circus the media "wanted to play so we didn't have to get down to what were the critical issues that had to do with women's equal rights." With Ludtke's recollections the feelings of loneliness, frustration, and resentment are created by such exclusions. The sense of being a stranger shifts from abstract concept to reality impacting an individual's ability to work. In shifting those emotions from the hallways to the screen, the implications of the exclusion are unmasked for the audience in such a way as to see the actions as unjust.

As the film chronicles, the barrier to the locker room extended to all female sportswriters. Lawrie Mifflin recounts her experience being physically picked up and taken out of the Vancouver Canucks locker room in the early 1980s. Claire Smith recalls being pushed out of the San Diego Padres locker room during the playoffs in 1984. After being granted access to the locker room at the National Hockey League All-Star Game in 1975, Robin Herman became the story as she was spotted trying to get quotes for her report. Afterward she got hate mail from fans condemning her actions. As a part of these stories the female journalists often express frustration and anger about their exclusion. What seemed to irk them the most, though, was their need to rely on male colleagues for help and the emotional reactions that such encounters produced. Betty Cunniberti goes so far as to remark that the continued exclusion and restrictions on female journalists' access to players were like "death by a thousand cuts" when they just wanted to do their job and not rock the boat. Assimilation, though, was not an option for these women, which is what the audience is encouraged to find most offensive.

Importantly, the film places the actions of the female journalists in the context of changing social and political conditions, thus recognizing how the locker room became the last masculine space. Robin Herman, Betty Cunniberti, and Michele Himmelberg acknowledge that the locker room became a symbolic last stand where the women's movement advances stopped. In including their commentary, though, the film questions why such bullying tactics were necessary when the women merely wanted to do their job, thus driving home that their exclusion was based on sexual discrimination and nothing else. By including players (Tommy John and Steve Garvey) who were on teams when access became headline news, the film also aims to argue that players understood exclusion and could recognize the access issue, as Claire Smith argued, as "about a right to work." And with this sentiment the viewer has their first encounter with the symbol of the promised land—a light shining through the locker-room door—and a female sportswriter walking through it.

Professional sports leagues may have bowed to legal pressures to allow women in locker rooms, but that didn't mean that players had to roll out the red carpet for them. As the film illustrates, the players' tactics of Othering female sportswriters merely intensified so as to exert masculine power over the women, which is exposed within the film. With the women's entrance players found enjoyment in constantly attempting to embarrass reporters by pulling towels from around other players' waists, by playing with their genitalia in proximity to the women, and by shouting so as to get the female reporters to look up and thus leer at their naked bodies. Jane Gross recounts her experience of being cursed at and then having a bucket of water poured over her head while interviewing a player. As Claire Smith articulates in her interview, such actions "peeled back a layer of real ugliness," as does the film in spotlighting the behavior. The public's good guys become exposed for their childish, sexist behavior as the women reiterate that the locker room was not a sexual place and that they merely wanted to get an interview and be on their way. By placing the female reporters' actions in such context, the film encourages the audience to view the players' behavior negatively while reevaluating whether such players should be viewed as heroes.

With each incident of harassment the women's ability to prove that they could do their job was challenged. In 1990 Lisa Olson was sexually harassed by players in the New England Patriots' locker room, which became public after Olson complained to ownership about the players' behavior. In commenting on the situation Ludtke reveals that she was astonished by the behavior but not surprised, because as female journalists, "there was a lot that you took when you went in this territory." While female journalists knew that they were required to be a little deaf and blind in the locker room, all agree that the Olson incident crossed a line, including the media coverage that blamed Olson for the incident. As Christine Brennan points out, "Bottom line: a woman was doing her job in the locker room, and these players did things that would have had them arrested on a street corner." With Brennan's comment the behavior is cast as criminal, not funny, thus changing the tenor of the players' actions.

In arguing for access Michele Himmelberg acknowledges that the women had not expected to be harassed by fans, players, and management. The harassment of Olson by fans merely intensified when the Patriots' owner called her a "classic bitch," which, as Himmelberg points out, fueled opposition to women in locker rooms. Ultimately, Lisa Olson fled to Australia (a move negotiated by the parent company of her newspaper) after being subjected to multiple death threats, slashing of her tires, and burglarizing of her home. The treatment of Olson had female reporters questioning whether access was worth it. Lawrie Mifflin observes, "Many such incidents happened along the way in the early days to sportswriters that didn't get publicized; people thought it was more important to do your job and stay beneath the radar. Be the reporter, not the story."

In highlighting the Olson incident and others within the narrative, the film exposes the unseemly, bullying behaviors inspired by a fight to preserve masculinity. As such the film encourages the audience to question whether it is just or appropriate, thus severing some cultural approval of the boys-will-be-boys perspective. In demystifying the supposed glamour and sexual nature of the locker room, the film questions why respect and dignity are not extended to women as they would be in other arenas, thus altering the tide of cultural approval of masculine culture.

Arriving at the Promised Land?

The discussion about the Olson incident closes with Claire Smith stating, "The women who went into those locker rooms showed an industry how it should behave. Showed two industries because it showed newspapers that they were complicit in this, too." With such a remark the tone is set that everything has been resolved. Immediately after Smith's comment the music becomes lighter and fast paced, as Brennan remarks that women's sports and female journalists have come a long way. This transition serves to communicate that such incidents in locker rooms are now nonexistent, a sentiment bolstered by remarks about how much progress has been made. Lesley Visser offers the 1999 Women's World Cup as the turning point when both female athletes and sportswriters gain acceptance, thus allowing the event to be symbolic of progress on both fronts.

The film then closes with many of the women reflecting on how far the industry and female sportswriters, in particular, have come since the dark, lonely early days. Ludtke remarks about the locker-room fight in this chapter of the film: "It was about our invasion into the whole world of sports, and the locker room was, I guess, where they decided to take their final stand. And that's where it ended." Immediately after Ludtke's comment Claire Smith concludes the film: "I'd like to think that it mattered what Jackie [Robinson] did, it mattered what Melissa did, not just because of baseball, but because of what it meant to society. It transcended baseball; it transcended sports. Those were steps taken by very brave people, steps that advanced the society, and I will always believe that." At the end of Smith's comment the back-lit locker-room door opens and the viewer (via the camera) walks in as light washes over them, thus entering the promised land and presumably its ensuing acceptance.

This closing message, though, is problematic, as it obscures Jane Gross's point in this section of the film as to how most of her cohorts changed beats because of the relentless torments and loneliness of their jobs. But with the metaphorical entering of the promised land, the film makes it seem as if all is equal and respectful within the industry, thus creating the impression that harassment has ceased or that discrimination no longer occurs. Sports scholars, though, have established that flaws within the industry continue, as there is a revolving door where female journalists change departments so as to advance their career or escape a masculine culture that devalues their contributions.[16] In this regard the film fails to fully critique the masculine culture of sports media, where women's assimilation as just one of the guys is necessary for success and longevity. With such an image of the promised land the film does not continue to critique how women within the industry remain marginalized, thus perpetuating the underlying issue that prevented women's entrance and fueled their harassment in the first place.

Such a positive ending, though, better serves the ESPN brand, which had its own sexual harassment problems recently exposed in a tell-all book, *Those Guys Have All the Fun: Inside the World of ESPN*. Rather than highlight the continued masculine culture of the sports newsroom and the company's contribution to the culture, ESPN is creating a reformed image for itself. This attempt at image repair occurs with *Let Them Wear Towels* and the other *Nine for IX* films, because documentary films "are as invested in building institutional identities as they are in exploring sport's meaning and history." In addition, Travis Vogan observes that the *30 for 30* series, out of which *Nine for IX* grew, serves to solidify being the worldwide leader in sports as ESPN's actual image and not just an organizational slogan of the company.[17] In offering the series and the exposé, ESPN shapes its image as embracing female sportswriters and women's sports, thus rewriting or erasing its own rocky past and present in contributing to the ostracization of female sportswriters and athletes. Such image repair further obscures the necessary cultural and structural changes that are needed in an industry that continues to embrace a frat-house, boys-will-be-boys culture and are illustrated by the recent #metoo movement.

Conclusion

Let Them Wear Towels functions as a public piece of critical rhetoric in exposing and unmasking the sports-media industry and women's treatment as members of it. The documentary offers an insider's view on the legal and cultural push to allow female sportswriters into locker rooms. Importantly, the film criticizes the masculine culture of sports by legitimizing the experiences of these women without engaging in victim blaming, which, as the film highlights, was how the female reporters were portrayed by the media at the time. In this regard, the film seems to aim to right a previous wrong.

The more significant issue is that the film also continues to marginalize female sportswriters. It does this by creating a tone that suggests all has been resolved in terms of access, harassment, and advancement within the industry. In contrast to this conclusion, much research has been done by sports scholars that finds that marginalization of female sportswriters continues. But in not offering such a conclusion, the film (and ESPN) stops short of advocating for changes in an industry that would make it the promised land that the filmmakers and female journalists desire. Viewers are encouraged to view the highly demeaning treatment of female sportswriters as part of the past, not an issue for the present. This serves to neutralize Jane Gross's point as to how the industry continues to push women out of the sports newsroom and into other departments. With such framing the boys-will-be-boys culture continues to reign, and female journalists are forced to continue to assimilate or potentially face ridicule, career suicide, or reassignment.

NOTES

1. Judith Halberstam, *Female Masculinity* (Durham: Duke University Press, 1998), 269–70; Mariah Burton Nelson, *The Stronger Women Get, the More Men Love Football* (New York: Avon Books, 1994), 230.
2. Erin Whiteside, "Gender in the Workplace: Using a Post-structural Approach to Theorize Diversity in Sports Media Organizations," in *Routledge Handbook of Sport Communication*, ed. Paul Pedersen (New York: Routledge, 2013), 32–33.
3. Edward M. Kian, "Gender in Sports Writing by the Print Media: An Exploratory Examination of Writers' Experiences and Attitudes," *SMART Journal* 4, no. 1 (2007): 13; Marie Hardin, Stacie Shain, and Kelly Shultz-Poniatowski, "'There's No Sex Attached to Your Occupation': The Revolving Door for Young Women in Sports Journalism," *Women in Sport and Physical Activity Journal* 17, no. 1 (2008): 76–77.
4. Nelson, *The Stronger Women Get, the More Men Love Football*, 227.
5. Elinor Kaine, "A Woman's Right to Write and Sit with Men in the Press Box," *Quill*, December 1969–March 2009, 11–12 (originally published December 1969).
6. Phyllis Miller and Randy Miller, "The Invisible Woman: Female Sports Journalists in the Workplace," *Journalism and Mass Communication Quarterly* 72, no. 4 (1995): 883, 884–88.
7. Sherry Ricchiardi, "Offensive Interference," in *Women and Sports in the United States: A Documentary Reader*, ed. Jean O'Reilly and Susan K. Cahn (Boston: Northeastern University Press, 2007), 313.
8. Marie Hardin and Erin Whiteside, "Fewer Women, Minorities Work in Sports Departments," *Newspaper Research Journal* 27, no. 2 (2006): 47–48, 49.
9. Marie Hardin and Stacie Shain, "Strength in Numbers? The Experiences and Attitudes of Women in Sports Media Careers," *Journalism and Mass Communication Quarterly* 82, no. 4 (2005): 813, 814 (emphasis in the original).
10. Kimberly S. Miloch et al., "The Current State of Women Print Journalists: An Analysis of the Status and Careers of Females in Newspapers Sports Departments," *Public Organization Review: A Global Journal* 5, no. 3 (2005): 228–31.
11. Toni Bruce, "Supportive or Hostile? Teasing or Professional? Women Sportswriters Categorize Locker Room Interaction," *Women in Sport and Physical Activity Journal* 11, no. 2 (2002): 51–52.
12. Raymie E. McKerrow, "Critical Rhetoric: Theory and Praxis," *Communication Monographs* 56, no. 2 (1989): 92–94, 91.

13. Kent A. Ono and John M. Sloop, *Shifting Borders: Rhetoric, Immigration, and California's Proposition 187* (Philadelphia: Temple University Press, 2002), 157, 167.

14. John M. Sloop, *Disciplining Gender: Rhetorics of Sex Identity in Contemporary U.S. Culture* (Amherst: University of Massachusetts Press, 2004), 17–23.

15. Michael Calvin McGee, "In Search of 'the People': A Rhetorical Alternative," in *Contemporary Rhetorical Theory: A Reader*, ed. John Louis Lucaites, Celeste Michelle Condit, and Sally Caudil (New York: Guildford Press, 1999), 347.

16. Marie Hardin and Erin Whiteside, "Token Responses to Gendered Newsrooms: Factors in the Career-Related Decisions of Female Newspaper Sports Journalists," *Journalism* 10, no. 5 (2009): 643–44.

17. Travis Vogan, "Chronicling Sport, Branding Institutions: The Television Sports Documentary from Broadcast to Cable," in *Routledge Handbook of Sport Communication*, ed. Pedersen, 129, 135–36.

4

Documenting Difference

Gay Athletes of Color, Binary Representation, and the Sports Documentary

EVAN BRODY

The sports documentary has often served as a way to elevate the symbolic capital of sports and to "construct an aura of refinement" for sports media products and institutions.[1] This understanding of the genre, "as an authenticating agent, imbued with the power to shape social images while validating their cultural meanings," is of particular importance for members of underrepresented groups, such as the lesbian, gay, bisexual, and transgender community.[2] Since "media are the primary site of production for social knowledge of LGBT identities," these communities rely on media texts to circulate understandings and depictions of identities often ignored or devalued within mainstream culture.[3]

A commitment to increased media visibility, and the assumed social and political recognition it engenders, is essential to some forms of activism related to the LGBT community, particularly in the late twentieth century. However, questions have arisen as to whether a proliferation of these visuals assimilate LGBT culture into mainstream frameworks without questioning the dominance of norms related to heterosexuality. As Joshua Gamson argues, "Visibility may be a necessity and a pleasure, but it guarantees nothing more than itself." This questioning of the effectiveness of visibility as a stand-alone strategy for combating collective disadvantage is not unique to LGBT studies. Scholars within critical race studies have also questioned the modern "cultural politics of diversity," which "seeks recognition and visibility as the end itself."[4] For both of these disciplines there is a concern that a focus on the quantity of representations of difference will supplant a more robust engagement with the material consequences of these representations. But there is also a concern as to how difference, made salient through representations of diversity, operates in the service of dominant groups by using a celebration of diversity to supplant critiques of racism or heteronormativity. Put another way, while the presence of LGBT characters, and specifically queers of color, helps to incorporate an underrepresented group within the media landscape, these representations do not automatically work to challenge preconceived stereotypes or question the ways in which the community must reaffirm heteronormative and white values in order to be seen as equal.

Despite these concerns, for some LGBT studies scholars the documentary, as a specific stand-alone format, is essential to gay media representation. It is able to provide a space for gay men to tell their truth because it allows "for the foregrounding of discursive ideas connected to the performer's personal story more than a producer's argument."[5] However, for queer theorists, a gay presence within documentaries alone is not enough to challenge dominant discourses about sexuality. These productions should also work to queer the form through "a stance separate from and critical of the heterosexual hegemony."[6] In this chapter I argue that modern sports documentaries about gay men, such as *Ring of Fire: The Emile Griffith Story* (Ron Berger and Dan Klores, 2005), *Forbidden Games: The Justin Fashanu Story* (Jon Carey and Adam Darke, 2017), *Michael Sam: The Documentary* (Amy Rice, 2014), and *Game Face* (Michiel Thomas, 2015), are not, in fact, open spaces of discursive potential because of their frequent reliance on binaries that promote normative knowledge production about gay men of color.

I focus on normative binaries for two reasons. First, they work to organize knowledge by positioning themselves as the proper way to understand identities and organizations of sexuality. This has particular relevance to documentary films because the genre's "attendant claims to authenticity and presumed indexical relationship to reality is understood to have a privileged relationship to truth."[7] These binaries, through their repetition, entrench themselves as natural. Just as documentaries "recycle familiar narratives that perpetuate sport's stereotypical reinforcement of dominant power relations," a reliance on normative binaries perpetuates axioms about gay men in sports.[8] I argue that the documentaries analyzed for this chapter assist in this normalizing project through their mediated repetition, which in turn makes them seem self-evident, when in fact they are socially constructed.

The second reason I focus on the concept of binaries is because resisting a binary view of the world is a key component to queer modes of inquiry.[9] As Cathy Cohen writes, the power of queerness is "located in its ability to create a space in opposition to dominant norms."[10] Therefore, recognizing and resisting the allure of normative binaries, which are often the only entry point for discussing gay men in athletics, would work to queer documentaries. In this estimation, queerness as a mode of documentary storytelling questions dominant frameworks and heteronormative binaries while illuminating alternative and transformative ways of living. And while I utilize queerness as a way to disrupt normative binaries, I do so with the recognition that queer theory has, historically, used its definitional ambiguity to "reinstall white, male subjectivity as normative."[11] I attend to this critique by recognizing that whiteness often operates as a "privileged and (often) unacknowledged universal referent" within these texts and rely instead on an intersectional approach that recognizes that "race and sexuality are constructed alongside, and inform, one another."[12] This tactic, one that seeks to identify rather than order interlocking marginalized positions, works to illuminate structural inequalities and opens up new possibilities for queer representation.

While there is a significant amount of scholarship focused on sports documentaries, there is less that focuses specifically on sports documentaries of historically underrepresented communities. Previous articles and edited volumes have examined questions of gender, race, religion, and dis/ability, to name but a few marginalized identities.[13] However, Sarah Boslaugh's overview of documentaries that focus on sexual minorities is one of the only sustained engagements with LGBT sports documentaries, albeit one that primarily describes the field.[14]

Since the LGBT community makes up a variety of marginalized sexual and gender identities, this chapter focuses on four twenty-first-century films that concentrate on gay men of color playing, or attempting to participate in, professional sports. It is not my intent to efface women's, nonprofessional, or transgender stories within the world of LGBT athletics, but to honor them by not conflating important differences in identity that contribute to their stories. By focusing this study on gay men of color I am better able to compare texts, unpack the methods used to portray gay athleticism, and understand how normative binaries are utilized as storytelling techniques.

I argue that three binaries become the dominant modes for situating and understanding gay men of color's athletic experiences. The first concerns the way in which coming out serves as the grounding point for discussions of gay identity and reinforces assumptions that closeted individuals are spuriously concealing their identity, while "out" individuals are truly authentic and honest. In my analysis I situate how this reliance on the coming-out narrative establishes it as a single moment of disclosure and ignores the very material ways in which coming out is actually a continual process. The second binary concerns how individualism and community are juxtaposed, particularly in light of neoliberal traits of personal responsibility and individual accomplishment that lend themselves to narratives of athletic achievement and heteronormativity. The last binary concerns the urban and the rural, which has particular relevance for LGBT individuals because of the way it reifies assumptions about the proper, or more "naturally" conducive, environment for LGBT folk. This critical analysis establishes how stories of gay men in athletics are made legible to a wider audience through the use of normative binaries. I also acknowledge how and when these arenas are disrupted by more transgressive or queer storytelling techniques so as to identify the way in which media texts can be vehicles that contain both progressive and regressive moments. I do so in order to highlight the ways in which future documentaries on similar topics might expand their storytelling focus to challenge assumptions about the presumed legibility of gay storytelling, or the necessity for stories of assimilation, thereby pushing the format into antinormative territory.

Coming Out as a Representational Strategy

Since the 1970s coming out has served as one of the key narrative structures for *labeling* gay individuals, though not necessarily for *engaging* with mediated story lines regarding gay identity. Documentaries such as *Word Is Out: Stories of Some of Our Lives* (Peter Adair, Nancy Adai, Andrew Brown,

Rob Epstein, and Lucy Massie Phenix, 1977) worked to establish coming out as "the core narrative of lesbian and gay identity."[15] Additional theatrical documentaries such as *Coming Out! A Documentary Play about Gay Life and Liberation in the U.S.A.* (Jonathan Ned Katz, 1972) and cinematic documentaries like *Out Late* (Beatrice Alda and Jennifer Brooke, 2008) and *Coming Out* (Alden Peters, 2015) further entrenched the coming-out narrative as a media strategy to visualize, locate, and incorporate gay sexualities. The coming-out narrative has thus become an expected and universally accepted stereotype of gay identification and "the most common storyline for queer characters."[16] I follow Amy Villarejo's use of the term *stereotype*, which argues that "stereotypes keep chaos at bay; they are 'an indispensable element in the organization and anticipation of experience.'"[17] The coming-out narrative, in this sense, becomes a way to categorize identity and limit experiences by convincing LGBT folk that this process is the only way to reach happiness and self-acceptance. Reliant on this approach, the majority of the documentaries examined in this chapter entrench the coming-out process as the foundational narrative of gay identification.

Relying on coming out in this manner additionally authorizes the narrative of the tragic gay man. While early nonfiction portrayals, such as the Mike Wallace–hosted CBS *Reports* episode "The Homosexuals" (premiered March 7, 1967), presented homosexuality as a problem to be solved or a disease in need of curing, more modern stories rely on the perils of secrecy associated with the coming-out narrative. Homosexuality is depicted as a secret in need of exposing: gayness itself is not destructive, but keeping a secret about one's sexual identity is. While meant to be a moment of self-liberation, these narratives contribute to assumptions that being "out" is always the better choice. However, as a close reading of these documentaries show, a single-minded focus on the act of coming out not only limits the potential storytelling focus, but also misrepresents it as a single defining moment as opposed to a continual process.

One of the key concerns with focusing the gay male experience around coming out is the narrative's necessary reliance on secrecy and disclosure. It casts homosexuality as a "problem" to be wrestled with. These films are no different in that they situate ideas of authenticity and honesty as resting on the coming-out narrative. Coming out then serves as a moment of unequivocal truth production that necessitates itself as the only way for gay individuals to live honestly. As Michel Foucault argued, the confession was invented to serve as a production of knowledge that would tell the "truth" of sexuality, thereby authorizing the coming-out narrative as the grounding point for sexual authenticity.[18] However, this confession, posited as a voluntary avowal, is actually a one-sided admission, since heterosexuals are never expected to make the same type of explicit announcement to live an "honest" life.[19]

This concept is evident in the competing logics at play in *Forbidden Games*, which centers on Premier League soccer player Justin Fashanu, the first UK black soccer player to be traded for a million pounds. Through archival footage we see Justin Fashanu discussing his decision to come out by stating that he wanted to "to be honest and truthful, not only to myself but to other people as well." However, this same honesty is used to critique his announcement by his brother John, who had at that point eclipsed his brother as the more successful and sought-after British footballer. John stated, "He's come out publicly and said his sexual preferences, you know, I mean what, every footballer doesn't come and say I like women, I like men. That's nobody else's business. So now he'll have to suffer the consequences."

We also see this reliance on ideas of veracity early on in *Michael Sam*, which tells the story of aspiring professional football player Michael Sam with a focus on the events after his coming out in 2014, as Sam poses for a photo shoot for *Out* magazine in the days leading up to the NFL draft. Photographer Richard Phibbs asks Sam if there is one word he can put on his eye black that would "make some sense." Sam replies that he likes the word *truth*. In *Game Face*, which narrates, as part of its focus, aspiring basketball player Terrence Clemens's attempts to restart his collegiate basketball career—as a closeted gay man—after serving time in prison, a school administrator that the student-athletes, including Clemens, lovingly referred to as "Mom" finds out that Clemens is gay while he is still struggling with how and when to tell his teammates and friends at Northeastern Oklahoma A&M College (NEO). She questions why he would want to tell everyone, to which he responds: "It was eating at me. For a while I could deal with people not knowing. But now it eats at me, to not be truthful to people."

These examples show us how the coming-out narrative forces gay individuals to produce a "truth" about their sexuality that is not only a one-sided admission since, as Fashanu's brother noted unintentionally, straight individuals are never expected to make the same type of confession. This forced admission then works to "reward the heterosexual subject rather than the queer one."[20] What is obscured in these moments is the way that this production of truth occurs only because of assumptions that those who are not "out" are somehow hiding something from the world. This approach to the closet as a hidden and isolated experience assumes that a closeted life is a negative one and that the ability to come out provides respite from this despair while also devaluing pre-coming-out experiences. Jeffrey Q. McCune further complicates this notion with regards to race by suggesting that the closet, in particular for nonwhite men, could be read as a space of protection.[21] This should be understood not only in how an acknowledgment of gay sexuality works to further marginalize athletes of color, a consideration that white athletes do not have to contend with, but also forces nonwhite athletes to wrestle with the ways that masculinity and whiteness are yoked to one another.[22] Here again we are brought back to concerns raised by critical race scholars that recognition, through an incitement to visibility, often leads to further prejudice. By staying in the closet, these athletes are often read as deceiving others rather than as protecting themselves from racist institutions and practices.

Positioning of the "coming-out" narrative as a moment of unequivocal truth production relies on an assumption of whiteness and situates preannouncement experiences as somehow less than truthful, and it imagines the coming-out narrative as the only way to exist honestly. It creates a binary surrounding the before and after of the coming-out experience that privileges the period after the announcement.[23] Furthermore, it fails to interrogate the ways in which structural constraints, such as institutionalized homophobia and racism, and the lack of governmental-mandated protections for LGBT folks, might hinder one's ability to come out openly.

This reliance on a coming-out moment to ground LGBT stories also ignores how coming out is a continual process. For example, though Justin Fashanu had already participated in a highly mediated coming out in the United Kingdom, his experiences later in his career showed how coming out must be continually navigated and that this disclosure can still prompt antigay sentiment. As Fashanu's friend A.J. recounts, Fashanu returned to the United States in 1997 to coach the Maryland Mania professional soccer team. However, "when people found out that he was gay here, he went from Justin Fashanu, the great coach and teacher to . . . 'Did you know he was gay?' and 'Do we want that here?'" Fashanu's mediated coming out in the early 1990s was not enough to prevent him from having to continually "come out" and deal with what both that disclosure and the reception of the information meant for his capacity to work and live.

We also see notions of coming out as a process through Sam's narrative. While Sam had come out to his college teammates in the summer of 2013, he discusses how he was continually approached by reporters, agents, and front-office personal after his senior season asking whether he was gay. These efforts to find out his sexuality prompted him to come out in a highly mediated sense in February 2014. However, as Sam soon discovered, his "coming out," or at least the reaction to and discussion of his sexuality, continued, as seemingly "new revelations" about his identity were made. For instance, after his selection during the NFL draft he shared a celebratory kiss with his longtime boyfriend, Vito Cammisano, an act that is commonplace for aspiring players and their opposite-sex partners. The kiss, as documented in *Michael Sam*, became the focus of news reports and commentary about Sam's draft-day accomplishment, with various news and sports outlets weighing in on what the kiss meant and ruminating over whether it was planned by the pair or their handlers. However, as Sam noted in reaction to the shock many expressed at seeing him and his boyfriend kiss, "Did you forget that I was gay?" Even though Sam had explicitly stated his sexuality in a highly mediated manner, as the documentary shows, he still had to continually come out as the practicalities of his announcement became operationalized.

Game Face additionally highlights this continued entrenchment of the closet metaphor and the overimagining of it as a single moment. The documentary follows a "closeted" Clemens for most of the film, since the majority of his friends, teammates, and advisers do not know about his sexuality until the final scene of the documentary when he gathers them all in a classroom at NEO to officially "come out." Even the reasons for the camera crew following Clemens are mysterious. After one friend asks early on in the documentary "Why are you on camera right now?" Clemens replies with a sly, "I'll tell you later." But a closer examination reveals that Clemens had to navigate his coming-out experience over and over. Prior to coming out to his community at NEO, a moment that is dramatized as anxiety producing and the climax of both Clemens's closeted life and the documentary's narrative, we hear about Clemens coming out to his family and high school friends, before coming out to Jason Collins (the first NBA player to announce his gay identity while actively playing), his mother figure at NEO, and a new team of gay men in the National Gay Basketball Association (NGBA). While some of these instances involve the more traditional coming-out announcement, others are more metaphorical. Clemens does not announce his sexuality to the NGBA team, but his joining the team serves as a figurative coming out since it is the first time that Clemens is able to play basketball with teammates who all know about his sexuality.[24] However, despite the fact that this reinforces the notion that coming out is a continual process—one that LGBT folk, in a heteronormative society, must navigate on a daily basis—the traditional coming-out moment still serves as the documentary's grounding point for understanding nonnormative sexualities. Clemens identifies this when he notes that despite the fact that many individuals know that he is gay, he still considers himself a "gay player working on coming out." Through these examples we see that although coming out is posited as a single moment that leads to happier, healthier individuals, the work of "coming out," within a society based on compulsory heterosexuality, never truly ends.

Ring of Fire is the only film that forgoes the traditional coming-out narrative. The documentary focuses on the fatal 1962 fight between Emile Griffith, a welterweight champion boxer, and Benny Paret. While this decision to not rely on coming out as the authorized account of Griffith's story could be read as a queer way to conceptualize documentary storytelling about gay athletes, I argue that it is Griffith's historical context that justifies this narrative approach. In particular, Griffith's athletic career took place during a time when homosexuality was not only classified as a psychiatric disorder by the American Medical Association, but also considered a criminal act under antisodomy laws in every state except Illinois.

The announcement of his sexuality in a mediated manner similar to that of Sam would have been unheard of for these legal concerns, but also because of the symbolic strangeness that would have accompanied such a statement. As historians such as George Chauncey have argued, modern understandings of coming out are rooted in the second half of the twentieth century, since coming out originally referred to early twentieth-century galas in which gay men were formally presented to audiences of mainstream gay partygoers, similar to the presentation of debutantes at cotillion balls. This notion of coming out referred not to exiting a closet, a metaphor fraught with notions of secrecy, but rather to coming out *into* the gay world and is rooted in notions of community absent from many of the films. The historical specificity of the early 1960s matters, then, not just in a legal sense but also in a metaphorical one, since cultural geographies identify the late 1960s as the moment when this shift in understandings of coming out occurred. As Michael Brown writes, the "closet came to mean hidden, covert, or secret somewhere around 1968."[25]

However, Griffith's story is not immune to the shorthands of gay identification. Similar to stereotypes, shorthands do the work of "condensing a lived past into a panoply of signifying data, whether through appearance, costuming, gesture, or dialogue."[26] Griffith's story, as told through *Ring of Fire*, is more representative of coded shorthands that allude to gayness. For instance, the film positions Griffith's road to boxing as out of the ordinary. The documentary goes to great lengths to situate Griffith not as a natural fighter but one who stumbles into the sport as he worked in the fashion industry, first as a delivery person, and then as a designer, prior to beginning a career as a boxer. His boss recommended he take up the sport after seeing him shirtless during a particularly hot day at work (he had removed his shirt since it was soaking with sweat). The film makes clear that Griffith was an outsider in the sport. As Howie Albert, the son of Griffith's garment district boss, states, "He didn't seem like that type of guy. . . . My God, this kid could fight. But he didn't look like a fighter. I mean, he looked like he could kill anybody, but he wasn't that type of guy." We see Albert's rhetorical clumsiness as he tries to reconcile what he knows of Griffith the athlete, that he was a boxing world champion, with what he knows of Griffith the person, that he was not straight. Furthermore, little attention is given to the fact that his movement into design was a function of his need for survival with few options for a person of his race and class. This is particularly relevant because the garment industry became a landing point for many uneducated individuals after World War II. But this is reframed as a failure of masculinity when positioned within the world of sports, since heteronormative culture has erased the history of economic and professional immobility to imagine the fashion business as an enclave for gay men. This shorthand is further evident in the description of Griffith's fighting style. While Griffith was technically superior to Paret, in particular because of his punching power, much of the film's focus is on the fact that he did not like to be hit. Alternatively, Paret is commended as a tough fighter who could take a punch. Rather than recognizing the queer potential of Griffith's unexpected path and sports successes, the film positions his accomplishments as resulting in spite of, rather than because of, his nonnormative body and experiences.

Through these portrayals, the coming-out narrative serves as a prosaic and formulaic process that overimagines the act as a single moment that allows surreptitious individuals access to honesty and authenticity. It forces individuals into a performance that does not necessarily mirror the realities of dealing with sexuality or how coming out furthers compulsory heterosexuality. However, one cannot dismiss the effects of the coming-out narrative completely, since, as we see in *Game Face*, the mediated coming out of Jason Collins served as a vital resource for Clemens. As Clemens states, "Sometimes I may have a plan [about coming out], but then I'm nervous about going through with it. I just . . . I don't know how to go about it. That's another area where I would want to call somebody and get some advice, but who do I call now?" Clemens's ability to find another individual "like him" through Collins's public announcement is important. While coming out limits the potential for transgressive moments, both in narrative and in lived experiences, it also functions as a stereotype that becomes a vehicle "for social participation, exchange, and recognition."[27] Although it is necessary to problematize the coming-out narrative, we must also recognize the way in which this process accomplishes something very real for individuals.

Though the highlighted documentaries differ in the significance they place on the coming-out narrative, they all land in the same spot concerning the acceptable boundaries of gayness within sports culture. For Griffith, Fashanu, Sam, and Clemens, gayness is tolerated when conceptualized theoretically, but not practically. Even when not overtly condemned, we see the way in which Griffith's accomplishments were devalued in response to his nonstraight identity, Fashanu's playing opportunities and sponsorship deals disappeared after "coming out," Sam's draft stock plummeted after his announcement, and Clemens lost a spot on his varsity team once rumors circulated about his sexuality. For all of these individuals gayness is tolerated until sports individuals and institutions are forced to confront the realities of being gay.

The Isolation of Individualism and Community's Proper Place

These documentaries situate gay athletes as individual, isolated figures. In particular, the films often present the LGBT community as antagonistic, or at least as inimical, to athletic achievement. This reliance on individual achievement, and the erasure of community as advantageous and supportive of LGBT athletes, is representative of neoliberalism. However, despite these narrative impulses, one film does provide an opportunity to read the LGBT community as recuperative and restorative for gay athletes.

As Ralph Fevre argues, neoliberalism relies on tropes of individuality to justify inequalities.[28] This understanding echoes other theorists who position neoliberalism as intent on abstracting systemic or structural disparities and placing them within the domain of personal responsibility and choice.[29] Since neoliberalism places complete agency in the individual, their choices define their standing in life, not structural barriers that might either create, circulate, or sustain inequalities of race, sexuality, and class, to name a few. The athletes in these documentaries are disarticulated from a history of gay athletes, and gay athletic achievements, just as their struggles are disassociated from structural constraints that might hinder their ability to succeed. Stories of modern gay athletes that rely on the language of individualism ignore structural inequalities and bias and instead ask the individual to claim responsibility and accountability for their success or failure.

This line of thinking fits into a lineage of both fiction and nonfiction sports films that position individual performance as the best way to overcome the aforementioned disadvantages. In particular, Joshua Malitsky notes that individual expression is a key feature of modern sports documentaries. However, when contextualized within the framework of marginalized positionalities, this individualism does not focus on individual accomplishment that is meant to demonstrate how the featured athlete performs differently from his or her peers.[30] Rather, it highlights how the athletes differ from their peers because of their inability to meet traditional assumptions about male athletes as naturally heterosexual.

This understanding of individualism has additional importance when discussing race and masculinity, since discourses of race are mostly absent from the films. Though *Ring of Fire* and *Forbidden Games* engage with discussions of race, the latter is the only film to connect race and sexuality as mutually informative through a discussion of Fashanu's early life as an outsider in an all-white family and an almost entirely white town. Race as a visual marker can also be connected to ideas of individualism when observing the athletes in their cinematic surroundings. Despite the fact that three of the four athletes play, or played, sports in which the majority of athletes are nonwhite, within the world of the documentaries these athletes are often surrounded by white individuals, whose commentary rarely invokes any structural constraints or racist practices that might have increased barriers to success. The intersectionality of these athletes' identities is lost, and instead they are represented as discrete categories.

For instance, Sam's screen time is most commonly shared with his white publicist, agents, and boyfriend. So too for Clemens, whose teammates, coaches, and friends are predominantly white. For Griffith the majority of those who speak about his experience—his manager, former employer's son, and journalists who covered his career—are white. And for Fashanu much is made of the fact that he is the only nonwhite player in his adopted family (besides his biological brother), in his hometown, and on many of the teams he played for during the height of his career. Echoing Zora Neale Hurston's observations that "I feel most colored when I am thrown against a sharp white background," visualizing these athletes within predominantly white worlds further "others" them.[31]

This reliance on individualism makes sense considering the way in which hegemonic masculinity, as represented in fictional sports films, reifies notions of the heroic individual who "overcomes obstacles and achieves success through determination, self-reliance, and hard work." Tying ideal masculinity to neoliberal tenets of individual accomplishment allows films such as *Ring of Fire*, but especially *Michael Sam* and *Game Face*, to sidestep a direct engagement with the way in which sports culture must redefine its reliance on tropes of masculinity in the presence of transgressive bodies. Instead, it recasts gay athletes as isolated individuals who control their own "destiny by succeeding in free and fair competition offered as representative of an American society that promises rewards to the most deserving individuals."[32] Rather than interrogating the hegemonic norms produced through stereotypes of masculinity in sports, a method of queer inquiry, this cinematic device relies on an assimilationist, or affirmative, approach that works to correct "inequitable outcomes of social arrangements without disturbing the underlying framework that generates them."[33] It brings members into the fold of existing structures and makes them feel included, but only as long as they reproduce existing ways of living.

Furthermore, none of the featured portrayals resist the normative tropes of masculinity in sports, which presents a missed opportunity to queer the form by challenging sports' heterosexual hegemony. This is not surprising, considering that marginalized communities are often less likely to call attention to these oppressive structures, especially when attempting to gain entry to the world that promotes and sustains them. In this manner the documentaries again borrow a common storytelling technique from fictional films: "Nonwhite male athletes in sports films have compromised and fit in with a white-controlled society because of the belief that such cooperation produces progress for—or at least a positive image of—their race."[34] *Forbidden Games* positions Fashanu's success as a way to show that black people were "relevant to society." As Fashanu further describes, "The thing that spurs me on is that I'm playing for black people." Fashanu did not engage in discussions of the racist taunts that were levied at him but rather attempts to recast his blackness within affirmative values. His playing is meant to be a way to uplift his community, not to draw attention to how racism circulated throughout English sports. So too do we see the same ideas of stereotype boost play within the frameworks of gay identity. Rather than using the documentaries as an opportunity to interrogate notions of hegemonic masculinity, players' accomplishments are cast solely as vehicles to inspire their community, but within a framework that promotes homonormativity.

While individual accomplishment, and the need for gay folk to take control of their situation rather than call attention to structural inequalities that might hinder their ability to succeed, receives the bulk of the representational focus, there is also an erasure of community within these documentaries. This is not entirely surprising, since neoliberal narratives of sexual sensibility are cast as a politics that does "not contest dominant heteronormative assumptions and institutions, but upholds and sustains them, while promising the possibility of a demobilized gay constituency."[35] Neoliberalism disarticulates choice from a collective so that it can be refashioned within individual terms, the outcome of which then provides for an isolated subaltern individual as opposed to one connected to the power of a meaningful collective. Despite the fact that Griffith and Fashanu both were members of gay communities while competing at the highest level of professional sports, these associations receive very little consideration. When they do they are visualized as dark places—both literally and figuratively: literally because the viewer only sees nighttime shots of gay communities, which imagine and promote the stereotype of gay culture as solely revolving around seedy bars, hidden in the shadows (again, with no recognition of the political and cultural reasons as to why gay culture might need, or be forced, to operate covertly), and also metaphorically because these same gay communities serve as somber moments in the history narrated by the documentaries. For Fashanu gay culture is the place he disappears into to the detriment of his athletic career. When his team does not know where he is the suspicion is often that he is lost among the young hustlers he found in gay enclaves. The gay community is similarly situated for Griffith. New York City is only briefly mentioned as a source of support, as Griffith discusses that he would go to gay bars to see friends. However, these discussions of gay neighborhoods are foregrounded, similarly to *Forbidden Games*, as sordid spaces full of peep shows and dark movie theaters.

In another missed opportunity to queer the form, to call attention to living otherwise, this cinematic framing lacks a critical discussion of how these spaces of same-sex desire were vitally important to the creation and maintenance of gay male communities. As authors such as Samuel Delany and José Esteban Muñoz have argued, public venues utilized for sexual encounters were vital for gay cultural connections that transcended classed and racialized boundaries.[36] They provided for the production of community that existed outside of heteronormative frameworks. Just as the gay community is seen as a hindrance to Fashanu's career, so too is it the source of Griffith's downfall, as he is the victim of a mugging outside of a gay bar that sends him to the hospital. Despite the fact that Griffith took punches for a living, this attack is positioned as causing him "more pain" than any of his previous fights. It is the gay community, not the boxing ring, where he suffers his most devastating knockout. Though these films do reference spaces of gay community, their engagement with these notions of sex, desire, and urban space positions these enclaves as detrimental, rather than productive, to a gay sporting identity.

While the gay community is imagined in static terms, or erased, in most of these documentaries, it receives a more nuanced and layered representation that ultimately makes a case for LGBT bonds, fostered through a connection to community, as recuperative spaces for Clemens. While the LGBT community initially serves as a safe haven in high school, it is his gay friends to whom he attributes his criminal endeavors. As Clemens states:

> When I got here to Crenshaw, I met some guys and considered them family. And that was more so because they were going through the same situation that I was going through as far as hiding our sexuality. Most of them were out trying to take care of themselves at young ages of sixteen, seventeen. They were stealing, credit card fraud, basically any kind of scam that could keep money in their pockets. I guess the freedom to be able to have your own money and just to hang with those guys, it kinda drew me in. And I got in trouble, got caught.

However, his reconnection to the LGBT community serves as a turning point in his aspiring athletic career. After a season of struggles at NEO, Clemens joins the NGBA and relishes the ability to play freely and without concern: "When I come here, I'm relaxed, I'm free, I meet people that are like me. And to me that's the best thing that I could have." After this experience Clemens reaches out to Jason Collins for guidance, and the two meet in Los Angeles during Clemens's off-season. Collins discusses what Clemens is facing by saying, "You know it's going to be tough going into the realm of sports and try[ing] to change a culture, change a mind-set. But I'm a part of it. You're a part of it. Every person who steps forward and raises their hand is a part of changing that culture." Collins situates Clemens's struggles within a history of struggles for members of the broader LGBT community and the LGBT athletic community specifically. From here we see Clemens becoming more comfortable with, and even invigorated by, his connection to the LGBT community in particular. He then attends the Nike #BeTrue Summit in Portland, Oregon, part of the sports manufacturer's outreach to the LGBT community. Clemens again is energized by this gathering of LGBT athletes and supporters of LGBT sports culture, and he channels this into his training for his second and final year at NEO. As Clemens's coach notices, "What we see in preseason is that Terrence has brought back that same level of intensity to this year, and he's competed for his job." Clemens's renewed fight to compete and succeed in the world of sports is set up, cinematically, as directly related to his ability to find a community of gay athletes. The gay bonds he discovers through the NGBA, his friendship with Collins, and his participation in the Nike #BeTrue Summit are the most rewarding and soul-affirming experiences on his road to self-acceptance. While community and coalition are visualized as detrimental, or absent, to most narratives present within these films, *Game Face* provides for a more holistic and queer approach to LGBT coalition building.

The Openness of Urbanity and the Isolation of Rurality

The city has often served as the assumed and expected backdrop for media narratives about gay individuals. It is imagined and visualized as the ideal environment for the LGBT community and juxtaposed against a backward and less accepting rural setting. This conception of the urban as acceptance and the rural as repression is commonly coined metronormativity.[37] Even the most nuanced histories of homosexual culture have often relied on the city as crucial to identity and community construction. These accounts situate the rural as inherently hostile to LGBT individuals and, conversely, establish the urban as the ideal opposite; however, these binary poles are *not*, in fact, equally oppositional, but rather exist in a relational stance that ideologically naturalizes one position and devalues the other. As Christopher J. Stapel writes, "Rural queernesses are 'rendered invisible' by a singular metropolitan account of rurality" that privileges the metropolitan.[38] This overreliance on a metronormative technique for establishing stories of gay experience is evident in the documentaries examined for this chapter.

For instance, in *Forbidden Games* Fashanu's ability to succeed is hindered by rural settings that are seemingly at odds with his positionality as a gay man. Fashanu joined the Hamilton Steelers of the Canadian Soccer League in 1990, just after his official mediated coming out. Team owner Mario DiBartolomeo stated that after he saw Justin with a young kid, "that's when it was better for Justin to go to a bigger city." While what he means by the term *kid* is never identified, it is clear that the assumption is that a larger, more urban location would be more welcoming of Fashanu's identity and actions.

Michael Sam also positions the rural as antigay. This is shown in both the description of his upbringing and the ways rural locations are juxtaposed with urban locations as less tolerant. The film begins with images of Sam's hometown of Hitchcock, Texas. We see railroad tracks and visuals of isolated figures walking along desolate roads. A voice-over from Sam describes growing up with no father and eight siblings, of whom two are deceased, one has been missing since 1998, and two others are currently incarcerated. As Sam notes, "I didn't grow up in an environment where homosexuality was accepting. You didn't see gays parading down the street during Pride." But the documentary does not solely rely on historical narratives and images of small-town Texas to create this understanding of the rural as intolerant. The film also uses interviews with everyday individuals to further this dichotomy between rural rejection and urban acceptance. When asking everyday individuals what they think about gay NFL players the viewer is shown, in one interview, a black man, with an obvious drawl and in a setting that mirrors Sam's hometown, saying that the National Football League "represents masculinity and manhood. It's an aggressive sport. And with him coming out and saying things like that—I didn't feel like the other players on the NFL team would be comfortable with it."

This is contrasted with a white individual, in an easily identifiable urban environment, stating that "it is ridiculous to think gay players shouldn't be in the NFL because gay people are everywhere." These narrative techniques are also coded with assumptions that black communities are more intolerant and homophobic than white communities, an idea explored more through the analysis of *Game Face* that follows.

This entrenchment of the urban-versus-rural divide is additionally presented during Sam's first visit to New York City for press obligations prior to the NFL draft. As Sam is looking out the car window, experiencing New York's metropolitan qualities for the first time, such as the height of its buildings and the commotion of its traffic, individuals driving in cars nearby recognize him. They shout their support to Sam and ask to take pictures, and since they are all stuck in traffic, Sam obliges. When he returns to the car, in obvious euphoria, Sam exclaims, "Oh my God. I can't believe it, dude. See, this is the place I need to go. . . . They love gay people here." While the viewer is never explicitly told what the "here" of New York might be contrasted with, through the film's earlier usage of rural images and auditory cues, we are left to assume that the approachability of New York contrasts with Sam's previous experiences growing up in Texas and attending college in Missouri.[39]

The rural-versus-urban divide receives the most nuanced treatment in *Game Face*. Both the urban and the rural are imagined as antagonistic to Clemens's positionality. For example, his early career at basketball powerhouse Artesia High School in Southeast Los Angeles County is derailed after his sophomore year by rumors regarding his sexuality. As Clemens notes, his teammates stopped talking to him on a regular basis and no longer invited him places. As he laments, "These were guys that I knew since childhood, guys I called brothers, just disowned me basically. I was supposed to play varsity my junior year. It didn't happen." Additionally, Clemens is imagined as out of place in rural Miami, Oklahoma, while attending NEO. The documentary produces this relationship through visual and auditory cues that situate the town of Miami as antithetical to gay individuals, similar to the destitute and isolated setting of Sam's hometown. In fact, both films rely on images of water towers and railroad tracks. When Clemens's closest administrative contact, Mrs. Lisa, the same individual the athletes at NEO lovingly refer to as "Mom," finds out that Clemens is gay, the film displays religious imagery from the town (churches, signs, and the like) while a voice-over of Mrs. Lisa laments that "Miami, Oklahoma, Ottawa County, is not really known for a real strong gay community. You know, I think there's reasons that it's not, you know what I mean?" Lisa's difficulty articulating why the town is seemingly not gay friendly is aided by the film's use of religious iconography, which further entrenches the stereotype of rural religion as homophobic.

While the city does not escape unscathed, the film's presentation of the city is reliant on racialized understandings of space in urban life. For example, Artesia High School, a predominantly minority-serving institution, functions as the start of Clemens's experience with homophobia. While he finds a more accepting community of LGBT folk in his hometown of Crenshaw, these are also the individuals who introduced Clemens to criminal endeavors that ultimately landed him in federal prison for nine months. After Clemens's release from prison the film shows him trying to return to competitive basketball. The images we see here are decidedly different from those that picture Clemens's early troubled life. Instead of dilapidated streets inhabited by vagrants in Southeast Los Angeles, Clemens is seen running and training in the Hollywood Hills. Furthermore, the meeting Clemens has with Collins later in the film, a pivotal moment that reinvigorates him from an emotional and athletic low while playing in rural Oklahoma, takes place again in the hills of Los Angeles. During their discussion they look out across the Los Angeles cityscape, and we see Clemens gazing off at the parts of the city he grew up in, almost unrecognizable from his elevated vantage point. While the city does not escape from discussions of homophobia and bias, the white economically advantaged areas of the city, just next to the wealthy and predominantly white LGBT enclave of West Hollywood, become the sanctuary space for Clemens. His recovery, both physically and emotionally, is supported by this seemingly all-accepting white-washed urban space. This is perhaps not surprising, since "people of color, people of faith, rural dwellers and those at the intersections are often imagined as intolerant of queer folks" and their intolerance is imagined as more insidious, just like their acceptance less welcoming, than that of white, secular, or urban people.[40]

Despite academic research showing that urban areas are not immune to homophobia, that urban areas index at a similar rate to rural areas with regards to LGBT bias crimes, and that the rural is often oversimplified with regards to its tolerance of nonnormative sexualities, the axiomatic trope of rural as antithetical to the LGBT community still persists through representational practices.[41]

Moving beyond Representation for Representation's Sake

In an analysis of the documentary, Bill Nichols asks, "When documentaries tell a story whose story is it? The filmmaker's or the subject's?"[42] In this chapter I complicate this question by arguing that socially constructed and prescribed frameworks of understanding and binaries, especially as they relate to gay men's experiences and identification practices, must also be interrogated to better understand the limitations and shorthands that guide both the filmmaker's and the subject's potential. I argue that documentaries of gay athletes are as much tales of the modern normative societies that produce and consume them as they are of the athletes and filmmakers themselves.

If past discussions of gay representation have focused on moving story lines from fringe characters to more sustained engagements, then the films outlined in this chapter have accomplished this goal by putting gay men at the core of their focus. However, this centering of gay experiences should not forgo a more detailed investigation into what tropes are concomitant to modern storytelling techniques for gay individuals. While these films attempt to offer up a variety of stories related to professional athletic achievement and the gay community, and contain transgressive potential that gestures toward a more queered documentary technique, they are still reliant on storytelling devices that restrict the possibilities for engaging with queer narratives and they entrench normative representational limits. They represent gay individuals, but they lack the power of resistance and possibility that comes from queerness as a way to "question and exceed binary distinction."[43]

Documentaries of gay men are considered especially important because they "represent active social agency, and to some degree form part of a political and social movement."[44] Therefore better understanding what their limitations and possibilities are helps to acknowledge how they ingrain, or challenge, normative ideologies. If we are to truly engage with gay characters, we must also allow for queer narrative strategies that push us beyond static or heteronormative portrayals of the LGBT community rather than relying on axiomatic binaries that further assumptions about the range of acceptable portrayals available for LGBT sports media narratives.

NOTES

1. Travis Vogan, "ESPN Films and the Construction of Prestige in Contemporary Sports Television," *International Journal of Sport Communication* 5 (2012): 139.
2. Kristen Fuhs, "How Documentary Remade Mike Tyson," *Journal of Sport and Social Issues* 41, no. 6 (2017): 480.
3. Mary Gray, *Out in the Country: Youth, Media, and Queer Visibility in Rural America* (New York: New York University Press, 2012), 12.
4. Joshua Gamson, "Diversity Follies," *American Prospect*, 2000; Herman Gray, "Subject(ed) to Recognition," *American Quarterly* 65, no. 4 (2013): 772.
5. Christopher Pullen, *Documenting Gay Men: Identity and Performance in Reality Television and Documentary Film* (Jefferson NC: McFarland, 2007), 12.
6. Su Friedrich, "Does Radical Content Deserve Radical Form?," *Millennium Film Journal* 22 (1988): 118.
7. Fuhs, "How Documentary Remade Mike Tyson," 480.
8. Travis Vogan, *ESPN: The Making of a Sports Media Empire* (Urbana: University of Illinois Press, 2015), 45.
9. For more examples, see, among others, Judith Butler, *Gender Trouble: Feminism and the Subversion of Identity* (New York: Routledge, 1990); Eve Kosofsky Sedgwick, *Epistemology of the Closet* (Berkeley: University of California Press, 2008); Gayle S. Rubin, "Thinking Sex: Notes for a Radical Theory of the Politics of Sexuality," in *Deviations: A Gayle Rubin Reader*, ed. Gayle S. Rubin (Durham: Duke University Press, 2011); and Patrick S. Chang, "Contributions from Queer Theory," in *The Oxford Handbook of Theology, Sexuality, and Gender*, ed. Adrian Thatcher, 153–69 (Oxford: Oxford University Press, 2014).
10. Cathy J. Cohen, "Punks, Bulldaggers, and Welfare Queens: The Radical Potential of Queer Politics?," *GLQ: A Journal of Gay and Lesbian Studies* 3 (1997): 438.
11. William B. Turner, *A Genealogy of Queer Theory* (Philadelphia: Temple University Press, 2000), 168.
12. Mary G. McDonald, "Beyond the Pale: The Whiteness of Sport Studies and Queer Scholarship," in *Sports, Sexualities, and Queer/Theory*, ed. Jayne Caudwell (New York: Routledge, 2006), 34; Evan Brody, "With the 249th Pick . . . : Michael Sam and Imagining Failure Otherwise," *Journal of Sport and Social Issues* 43, no. 4 (2019): 297.

13. Examples of such analyses include, among others, Katherine L. Lavelle, "As Venus Turns: A Feminist Soap Opera Analysis of *Venus Vs.*," *Journal of Sports Media* 10, no. 2 (2015): 1–16; Samantha N. Sheppard, "Historical Contestants: African American Documentary Traditions in *On The Shoulders of Giants*," *Journal of Sport and Social Issues* 41, no. 6 (2017): 462–77; James L. Cherney and Kurt Lindemann, "Sporting Images of Disability: Murderball and the Rehabilitation of Masculine Identity," in *Examining Identity in Sports Media*, ed. Heather L. Hundley and Andrew C. Billings, 195–215 (Los Angeles: Sage, 2010); Zachary Ingle and David M. Sutera, eds., *Identity and Myths in Sports Documentaries* (Lanham MD: Scarecrow Press, 2013); bell hooks, *Reel to Real: Race, Class and Sex at the Movies* (New York: Routledge, 1996); Lee Jones, "*Hoop Dreams*: Hoop Realities," *Jump Cut: A Review of Contemporary Media*, no. 40 (1996): 8–14; and Katherine Cipriano, "Hoops: Escape or Illusion? A Review Essay," *Film and History: An Interdisciplinary Journal of Film and Television Studies* 35, no. 2 (2005): 78–80.

14. Sarah Boslaugh, "Out and Proud: The Brave New World of Gay, Lesbian, and Transsexual Sports Documentaries," in *Gender and Genre in Sports Documentaries: Critical Essays*, ed. Zachary Ingle and David M. Sutera, 107–18 (Lanham: Scarecrow Press, 2013).

15. Larry Gross, *Up from Invisibility: Lesbians, Gay Men, and the Media in America* (New York: Columbia University Press, 2001), 69.

16. Johanna Schorn, "Coming Out into the 21st Century: Queer on Contemporary TV," in *Narratives at the Beginning of the 3rd Millennium*, ed. Jessica Homberg-Schramm, Anna Rasokat, and Felicitas Schweiker (Newcastle upon Tyne, UK: Cambridge Scholars, 2016), 39.

17. Amy Villarejo, *Ethereal Queer: Television, Historicity, Desire* (Durham NC: Duke University Press, 2014), 56.

18. Michel Foucault, *The History of Sexuality*, vol. 1, *An Introduction*, trans. Robert Hurley (New York: Vintage Books, 1980), 59.

19. It is this distinction that, perhaps, situates this chapter in a decidedly different manner from Christopher Pullen's work. For Pullen, "Confessional performance can be powerful in its property to generate discourse" (*Documenting Gay Men*, 88). While I do not necessarily disagree with this claim, what I am arguing is that the type of forced confession, generated through the "coming-out" narrative, places limitations around the types of discourse that are available. It might provide for a space through which to engage in discussion, but it severely contains the possibility for transformative or transgressive potential.

20. Evan Brody, "Categorizing Coming Out: The Modern Televisual Mediation of Queer Youth Identification," *Spectator* 31, no. 2 (2011): 37.

21. Jeffrey Q. McCune, "'Out' in the Club: The Down Low, Hip-Hop and the Architecture of Black Masculinity," *Text and Performance Quarterly* 28, no. 3 (2008): 298–314.

22. For more, see Gail Bederman, *Manliness and Civilization: A Cultural History of Gender and Race in the US, 1880–1917* (Chicago: University of Chicago Press, 1995); and Roderick A. Ferguson, *Aberrations in Black: Toward a Queer of Color Critique* (Minneapolis: University of Minnesota Press, 2004).

23. For more, see Diana Fuss, *Inside/Out: Lesbian Theories, Gay Theories* (New York: Routledge, 1991); and Sedgwick, *Epistemology of the Closet.*

24. Not all members of the NGBA, or other LGBT-oriented sports leagues, identify as LGBT. Many straight-identified players also participate in these leagues.

25. George Chauncey, *Gay New York: Gender, Urban Culture, and the Making of the Gay Male World, 1890–1940* (New York: Basic Books, 1994); Michael P. Brown, *Closet Space: Geographies of Metaphor from the Body to the Globe* (London: Routledge, 2000), 5.

26. Villarejo, *Ethereal Queer*, 32.

27. Villarejo, *Ethereal Queer*, 63.

28. Ralph Fevre, *Individualism and Inequality: The Future of Work and Politics* (Cheltenham MA: Edward Elgar, 2016).

29. Among others, see Lisa Duggan, *The Twilight of Equality? Neoliberalism, Cultural Politics, and the Attack on Democracy* (Boston: Beacon Press, 2003); David Harvey, *A Brief History of Neoliberalism* (Oxford: Oxford University Press, 2005); and Jack Halberstam, *The Queer Art of Failure* (Durham NC: Duke University Press, 2011).

30. Joshua Malitsky, "Knowing Sports: The Logic of the Contemporary Sports Documentary," *Journal of Sport History* 41, no. 2 (2014): 209.

31. Zora Neale Hurston, "How It Feels to Be Colored Me," *World Tomorrow*, 1928, 215–16.

32. Aaron Baker, *Contesting Identities: Sports in American Film* (Urbana: University of Illinois Press, 2006), 49.

33. Nancy Fraser, *Justice Interruptus: Critical Reflections on the "Postsocialist" Condition* (New York: Routledge, 1997), 23.

34. Baker, *Contesting Identities*, 69.

35. Duggan, *Twilight of Equality?*, 50.

36. See Samuel R. Delany, *Times Square Red, Times Square Blue* (New York: New York University Press, 1999); and José Esteban Muñoz, *Cruising Utopia: The Then and There of Queer Futurity* (New York: New York University Press, 2009).

37. J. Jack Halberstam, *In a Queer Time and Place: Transgender Bodies, Subcultural Lives* (New York: New York University Press, 2005).

38. Christopher J. Stapel, "'Fagging' the Countryside? (De) 'Queering' Rural Queer Studies," in *Studies in Urbanormativity: Rural Community in Urban Society*, ed. Gregory M. Fulkerson and Alexander R. Thomas (Lanham: Lexington Books, 2014), 152.

39. Furthermore, no mention is made of the fact that Sam's college alma mater was based in Columbia, Missouri, a city that not only scores a perfect 100 on the Human Rights Campaign's equality index but is also a rural town that passed laws to protect LGBT individuals despite a lack of statewide protections.

40. Stapel, "'Fagging' the Countryside?," 155.

41. See, respectively, Michele J. Eliason and Tonda Hughes, "Treatment Counselor's Attitudes about Lesbian, Gay, Bisexual, and Transgendered Clients: Urban vs. Rural Settings," *Substance Use & Misuse* 39, no. 4 (2004): 625–44; April Guasp, Anne Gammon, and Gavin Ellison, "Homophobic Hate Crime: The Gay British Crime Survey 2013," *Stonewall*, 2013; and Stapel, "'Fagging' the Countryside?"

42. Bill Nichols, *Introduction to Documentary* (Bloomington: Indiana University Press, 2010), 10.

43. Chris Holmlund and Cynthia Fuchs, introduction to *Between the Sheets, in the Streets: Queer, Lesbian, and Gay Documentary* (Minneapolis: University of Minnesota Press, 1997), 6.

44. Pullen, *Documenting Gay Men*, 22.

5

To the (Black) Athlete Dying Young

Documenting and Mythologizing Len Bias and Ben Wilson

JUSTIN HUDSON

In the mid-1980s Ben Wilson and Len Bias seemed destined to become National Basketball Association (NBA) superstars. Wilson, a student at Simeon High School on Chicago's South Side, had grown from a six-foot-one point guard who barely made his freshman-sophomore team to a six-foot-nine superathlete who became the first Chicago basketball player to be named the top high school player in the country. Bias, a six-foot-eight forward at the University of Maryland, used his mixture of strength and athleticism to become the best player in school history and the second pick in the 1986 NBA draft. However, neither Bias nor Wilson would play a game in the NBA. Wilson, only seventeen years old, was struck down in a shooting outside of his high school in 1984, just one day before the start of his senior season. Two days after being drafted by the Celtics, the twenty-two-year-old Bias died of a cocaine overdose.

Wilson would become a symbol of black-on-black violence in Chicago and spark a local crusade against gangs. Similarly, Bias's death directly led to the creation of the Anti-Drug Abuse Act of 1986, which intensified the War on Drugs and led to heightened incarceration rates for black drug offenders. Both incidents relied on simplified narratives that were part of larger cultural patterns that demonized and criminalized young black men while amplifying right-wing concerns about the inner city, promoting the Reagan administration's War on Drugs, and supporting aggressive policing tactics within black neighborhoods.[1]

In his study of the afterlives of young dead athletes, sports historian Richard Ian Kimball argues that only certain athletes linger in our collective memories. Mythmakers such as corporations, film directors, politicians, and family members shape the legacies of these "immortal" athletes by connecting them to a host of often competing causes such as commercial film productions, crusades over athlete safety, and political campaigns.[2] Over the past three decades mythmakers have retold the stories of Ben Wilson and Len Bias in the chambers of Congress, newspaper columns, shoe commercials, and as a part of ESPN's *30 for 30* documentary series. In keeping with the *30 for 30* series' stated theme of offering alternative readings of the sporting past, both *Benji: The True Story of a Dream Cut Short* (Coodie and Chike, 2012) and *Without Bias* (Kirk Fraser, 2009) question the "official" narratives of Wilson's and Bias's deaths that were sanctioned by both government officials and mainstream media outlets.[3] The films also serve as cautionary tales for younger viewers. *Benji* producers Coodie Simmons and Chike Ozah, the hip-hop video directing duo known as Coodie and Chike, made the film with the ongoing gang violence in Chicago in mind and expressed a desire to "make thugs cry" with their portrayal of Wilson's death.[4] Similarly, *Without Bias* producer Kirk Fraser thought it was necessary to tell Bias's story to a younger generation more familiar with success stories such as LeBron James and Kobe Bryant and sought to avoid another young athlete following Bias's path to destruction.[5]

By giving political meaning to the lives and deaths of Ben Wilson and Len Bias, *Benji* and *Without Bias* both reaffirm and challenge stereotypical depictions of the black male. The films are the latest of an "apparently endless supply of morality and cautionary tales" that have centered on the black "urban basketball player" since the 1980s.[6] They can be read through the sport/gang dyad, which contrasts successful black athletes such as Michael Jordan with the black male criminal. This dyad erases race and economic conditions as reasons for the decline of inner-city communities and instead places the blame on the black gang member and, by extension, the broken black family.[7] Through a series of success stories and cautionary tales, the dyad both affirms the American Dream through figures such as Jordan and teaches young black men that their choices, not their racial and class background, will dictate the course of their futures.[8] Ultimately, these simplified narratives are used by politicians to enact tougher laws, like the legislation implemented after Wilson's and Bias's deaths aimed at young black criminals.[9] However, while *Benji* and *Without Bias* embrace this dyad by focusing on the choices made by Wilson and Bias, the films also challenge the dyad by offering counternarratives to the mediated moral panics created after their deaths. Pushed by government officials and the mainstream media, these narratives were central in building public support for the policy that would target black inner-city neighborhoods, particularly young black men.

Benji and *Without Bias* are two examples of recent black sport documentaries that challenge dominant mediated narratives of the African American athlete.[10] As black sport documentaries *Benji* and *Without Bias* critique the sports/gang dyad and, more specifically, the mediated moral panics of the 1980s that criminalized young black men. However, as black men promoting narratives within the sports/gang dyad, the producers of *Benji* and *Without Bias* are also examples of the "agenda setters and moral entrepreneurs in the black middle class" who have produced media texts that address concerns about inner-city blacks.[11] In their attempt to "make thugs cry" and "prevent the cycle and the production of another Len Bias," the producers have embraced narratives that largely ignore the political and economic issues that created the black inner city and focus instead on the importance of work ethic and choice.[12] These narratives transform both Wilson and Bias into martyrs, symbols meant to represent the potential lost by making the wrong choices.

The Basketball Documentary, Race, and the American Dream

Sport documentaries often embrace the depoliticized conventions of mainstream feature films by pushing narratives that promote sport as a character-building ticket out of poverty and highlight the importance of winning above all else.[13] According to film scholar Aaron Baker, these depoliticized narratives were defining features of basketball films during the NBA's rise in popularity during the 1980s and 1990s. As Baker points out, "The narrative conventions of racial representation that still dominate American popular culture strongly influence films about Black basketball, populating them, like athletic contests, with winners and losers: exceptional individuals and moral misfits." The embrace of the sports/gang dyad in basketball films such as *Above the Rim* (Jeff Pollack, 1994), *He Got Game* (Spike Lee, 1998), and *White Men Can't Jump* (Ron Shelton, 1992) mirrors the conventions of sports documentary and sports narratives in general, as these narratives "obscure the role of structures or institutions, instead highlighting individuals who succeed or fail according to their ability to meet established demands and expectations."[14]

The critically acclaimed 1994 documentary *Hoop Dreams* (Steve James) illustrates how both the mythology of the American Dream and the sports/gang dyad are embedded within the basketball documentary. Film reviewers praised *Hoop Dreams*, which tracks the high school careers of Chicago inner-city residents and college prospects Arthur Agee and William Gates, for providing an authentic picture of urban life for middle-class white audiences and for attacking the exploitative system of amateur athletics.[15] However, academic critiques of *Hoop Dreams* have noted the film's limitations. C. L. Cole and Samantha King argue that instead of examining the racial and economic underpinnings of the American sports system, the film places blame on individuals. According to cultural critic bell hooks, Agee and Gates are driven to succeed in professional basketball because they see no other viable economic option. Yet "this spirit of defeat and hopelessness that informs their options in life and their life choices is not stressed in the film."[16] Instead, the poverty Agee and Gates overcome is connected to their unstable family units. Agee's drug-addicted, unemployed father cannot provide for his family, while Gates's father is absent altogether.[17] William, who eventually earns a degree from Marquette University, is also contrasted with his brother Curtis, a failed basketball player who works a low-wage security job. C. Richard King and Charles Springwood see this dichotomy as typical of the racially coded morality tale, as they argue: "Read against one another, the operations of the American Dream become apparent, as do their consequences for criminal understandings of race and class. Individual character and choices and personal discipline and drive, not social conditions, determine who one becomes—a failure who made a bad choice or a success who pursued his dreams."[18] Basketball films such as *Hoop Dreams* have historically done little to interrogate race and class relations in America and actually help to reinforce dominant stereotypes of

African American men. These films, along with other mediated mortality tales, both push the myth of the American Dream and castigate those who make poor choices that keep them from their dream.

In offering alternative narratives of black athletes *Benji* and *Without Bias* have at least partially embraced the black documentary film tradition, which, according to Phyllis Klotman and Janet Cutler, features black filmmakers whose works "fill gaps, correct errors, and expose distortions in order to provide counter-narratives of African American experience."[19] The black sports documentary challenges the "reductionist narratives and blunted sporting histories" associated with mainstream film treatment of race and sport.[20] Scholars have highlighted that white filmmakers, such as the producers of *Hoop Dreams*, can provide only an outsider's view of black culture.[21] Though black filmmakers have historically defended black subjects, more attention should be paid to black documentaries that deal with issues plaguing working-class black subjects, especially as black middle-class media producers have often expressed concern with the behavior of the black underclass.[22] As Herman Gray argues, scholars should look beyond the accuracy of mediated representations of minority groups and consider how these representations are used to cultivate public opinion around these groups and related social issues.[23] Through this prism *Benji* and *Without Bias* both push narratives that mobilize concern over the actions of modern-day black young men.

30 for 30 and Challenging Narratives

Through promotional strategies that stress the high-profile filmmakers involved with the series, the originality of the films, and other markers of cinematic prestige, ESPN positions the *30 for 30* series as an artistic endeavor that challenges the norms of conventional sports documentaries. ESPN's previous documentary series, *SportsCentury*, relied heavily on "familiar narratives that perpetuate sport's stereotypical reinforcement of dominant power relations" that often left out diverse viewpoints.[24] By contrast, *30 for 30* has been lauded for offering new story lines and a platform for minority filmmakers to tell these "original" stories. The series *30 for 30* was awarded the National Association of Black Journalists Best Practices Award in 2011 for its diverse group of filmmakers and "quality in-depth reporting to give viewers the complete versions of these events that often went untold."[25] However, scholars have painted a more complex view of the series. Even with its willingness to tackle events from alternative angles, some *30 for 30* films offer an incomplete picture of historic events more in line with conventional Hollywood films, ignoring key issues of race and gender and giving scant attention to the political conditions that shaped past events.[26] The political possibilities of *30 for 30* films are often hurt by an embrace of these dramatic conventions, such as the need for failed athletes to redeem themselves. This simplification of sporting success and failure helps to obscure the role of gender and race in determining the fate of athletes.[27]

The Afterlives of Ben Wilson and Len Bias

Analyzing the eulogies of slain hip-hop artists Tupac Shakur and Biggie Smalls, Lindon Barrett suggests that given the black body's historic position as a threat, "the dead black body may be an ultimate figure of regulation, unruly desire and its risks fully mastered." According to Barrett, dead black male bodies, especially those that have met violent ends, are sites of crisis where commentators, including black men, address concerns about inner-city youth as a whole.[28] These concerns often lead to legislation targeted at young African American men. The deaths of Ben Wilson and Len Bias were used to mobilize such policy. In the wake of Wilson's death, Chicago mayor Harold Washington introduced a multiprong attack on gangs, which included increased police patrols in black neighborhoods, the establishment of an antigang task force, and the eviction of gang members from public housing.[29] As journalism theorist James Carey observed, Wilson became the "personification of the problems of growing up black, of the constant threat of gang violence, and of the toll taken by ghetto life."[30] Similarly, Len Bias's death represented the growing threat of drugs (and blackness) on sport and society.[31] In the wake of his death, Congress passed the Anti-Drug Bill of 1986, which contained mandatory minimum sentences for possession of drugs such as crack cocaine, a drug associated with black neighborhoods.[32]

In the three decades since their deaths Wilson and Bias have continually been deployed as politicized symbols of lost potential. Nike used Wilson's story in a 1997 television commercial that addressed the issue of violence in Chicago and other inner cities across America. After briefly highlighting Wilson's career and tragic death, a narrator implores young black men to "shoot over brothers. Not at them." This commercial tied Wilson's death to the ongoing issue of gun violence in urban centers. A producer of expensive athletic shoes and clothing, Nike itself was blamed for fueling part of this growing crisis. Stories of young black men robbing or even killing other young black men over Nike gear appeared in the national media throughout the late 1980s and early 1990s, with the company facing criticism for advertising high-priced products in poor black communities.[33] Nike produced the Wilson commercial and other public service campaigns addressing youth violence during the 1990s to position the company as a solution, not a cause, of the urban crisis.[34] Len Bias's story has been heavily mythologized, with recollections of his death relying on details that have been proven false, such as Bias died from a crack overdose or that he died the first time he ingested cocaine. However, mythmakers still push these narratives, which are vital to the antidrug messaging surrounding Bias's passing.[35] After their deaths both Wilson and Bias were transformed into convenient symbols for journalists, corporations, and politicians who looked to address ongoing concerns about drug abuse and inner-city violence.

On the Road to a Dream

While both *Benji* and *Without Bias* mourn and honor their subjects, the films are also cautionary tales that lament the lost potential and missed opportunities at NBA greatness. Both films emphasize that Wilson and Bias had the work ethic, talent, and maturity to flourish in professional basketball. Narratives about social mobility and basketball construct the NBA as the ultimate goal and frame amateur basketball as "a staging ground to develop and demonstrate one's discipline, talent, and character."[36] The first half of each film focuses on its subject's development into an elite basketball prospect on the cusp of stardom. After portraying their deaths *Benji* and *Without Bias* search for answers to how these young athletes so close to professional stardom (and riches) died in such senseless fashion. Both films blame the deaths of their protagonists on a series of ill-timed mistakes. In doing so they miss opportunities to tackle structural race and class issues plaguing both Chicago and Washington DC.

Benji and *Without Bias* showcase the physical talent of their subjects, but also emphasize that each had the work ethic, leadership skills, and mental fortitude to become NBA stars. Through archival footage viewers see the physical dominance of both Wilson and Bias on the court. *Benji* shows the six-foot-nine Wilson handling the ball like a point guard, blocking shots and rebounding like a post player, and scoring basket upon basket on hapless opponents. *Without Bias* focuses on Bias's slam dunks and ability to play on the perimeter and in the paint. The success of Wilson and Bias on the court is framed as the culmination of hard work and mental toughness off the court. In *Benji* viewers learn that Wilson had an all-consuming passion for basketball since middle school and worked hard emulating players he saw on Chicago's playgrounds. After a growth spurt Wilson made Simeon's varsity team as a sophomore and soon became the leader in coach Bob Hambric's offense. As friend Mario Coleman observes, Wilson grew physically and mentally early in his career: "Before you knew it, he was grown. He did that in more ways than just growing in height. He did that in the mature way, too. His mind-set was different. His focus had become different." *Benji* frames Wilson's leadership ability as vital to Simeon's 1984 Illinois state championship run.

Similarly, *Without Bias* traces Len Bias's transformation into a college All-American. Viewers learn from Bias's childhood friend Reginald Gaskins that the future star was cut from his junior high team, yet vowed to make the NBA. *Without Bias* argues that Bias's strong work ethic and determination almost made this dream a reality. "You can just see his whole demeanor change," said teammate Keith Gatlin of Bias after he led Maryland to the 1984 Atlantic Coast Conference Tournament. "He just worked extremely hard after that and started lifting weights in the summer with the football guys, started dedicating his body to . . . becoming a much better player and a pro." In focusing on Wilson's and Bias's paths to stardom, both *Benji* and *Without Bias* show that each player was achingly close to fulfilling the American Dream through their own hard work and determination. According to the films, Wilson and Bias's individualism and passion for the game help to distinguish them from other young prospects and made professional stardom imminent. These narratives also distinguish Wilson and Bias from other young black men. In an era where black men increasingly fell victim to the ills of the inner city, these two black basketball players were beating the odds and looked to be on the path to fame and stardom. Unlike the deaths of other young black men during the 1980s, the deaths of Wilson and Bias resonated within the general public because they were deemed exceptional by broader society for their play on the court and their good behavior off of it.

The Next Jordan?

To establish further Wilson and Bias as superstars on the cusp of the American Dream, *Benji* and *Without Bias* link their subjects to Michael Jordan, who has often been invoked in black basketball movies and other sports narratives as the embodiment of the American Dream.[37] With the success of his Nike shoe line, Air Jordan, and frequent airtime on highlight-friendly ESPN, Jordan represented the possibilities of a new era in which the commercialized superstar could cultivate a brand off the playing field. Through a mediated persona that de-emphasized race in favor of his work ethic and warm personality, Jordan was able to become popular among white suburban fans.[38] Jordan represented the economic possibilities now available to the young black athletes such as Wilson and Bias. *Benji*'s opening sequence, a montage of Wilson highlights and video of other notable Chicagoans during 1984, shows Jordan attacking the basketball in his signature "Jumpman" form, followed by a clip of Wilson similarly attacking the basket. *Without Bias* shows highlights of Bias battling Jordan during their college careers, with Bias often coming out on top. Discussing the greatness of both Bias and Jordan, ESPN commentator and former *Washington Post* columnist Michael Wilbon relayed a story from Duke basketball coach Mike Krzyzewski, who named the duo the two best players he saw ever saw in the Atlantic Coast Conference. Attesting to Bias's on-the-court prowess, Wilbon argues, "Of course, that sounds like incredible praise, unbelievable praise for them. But for those of us who watched Len Bias play night after night, it wasn't unbelievable. It was very believable." Wilbon further links the pair's approach to the game: "They both played with a rage, controlled rage, almost anger. But it wasn't anger, because if it was anger, then it's sort of destructive. But it wasn't destructive." In other words, Bias possessed Jordan's discipline and self-determination, qualities the film suggests would have served him well in the NBA.

Benji goes deeper into its comparison of Jordan and Wilson and considers Wilson's place as a commodity within the NBA star system. Wilson becomes the number-one high school player in the country after attending the Nike-sponsored Athletes for Better Education basketball camp. The camp's sponsor, Sonny Vaccaro, was the Nike executive who was instrumental in signing Michael Jordan to the brand. Vaccaro saw Wilson as his next potential star: "Ben Wilson was my Kevin Garnett, my Tracy McGrady, my Kobe Bryant, my LeBron James." The Nike executive later appears in *Benji* when the film discusses a lawsuit Wilson's family filed against the hospital where he died. Vaccaro calculated Wilson's potential as an NBA player by invoking Jordan. "I was called by the lawyers for Ben's family to testify in this case, showing that you could predict, to a reasonable degree of certainty, what someone's future earnings would be if you were an athlete. And I told them that, until that time, he was one of the best players I had ever seen. I'm the one who said, 'Sign Michael Jordan,' so it gave me credibility." The film would later note that the family eventually settled out of court with the hospital for an undisclosed sum. Vaccaro's appearance in the film underscores Wilson's lost potential as an athlete, as well as his potential as a Jordanesque commercial icon.

The comparisons to Michael Jordan are part of a larger effort by both films to underscore the potential lost with the early deaths of Wilson and Bias. Though neither played professional basketball, both Wilson and Bias are given a place in professional basketball lore. By labeling Wilson as Magic Johnson with a jump shot and showing that even future NBA all-star players such as Tim Hardaway idolized him, *Benji* hints that Wilson would have been a transformative NBA star. Similarly, *Without Bias* positions Bias as the next major superstar for the Boston Celtics. Yago Colas argues that ESPN's basketball films help to reconstruct basketball history through the profile of individual stars. Along these lines *Benji* and *Without Bias* attempt to demonstrate that both young men were NBA superstars in training who carried the expectations of their communities. *Benji* portrays Wilson as the ticket out of inner-city Chicago for his friends and family. As childhood friend Mario Coleman laments, "This was going to be our 'Little Messiah.'

He's gonna take us to the promised land so that we can make a difference and we can be what we want to be." During a gathering of Wilson's friends Darrin Andrews also bemoans the opportunities lost due to his friend's death. "Had things went differently and had that cat flourished and maximized his potential, a lot of us would have had some experiences that we ain't got right now," Andrews says. "I mean, he would've took us on some of that ride. I know that because he used to tell us that." *Benji* argues that Wilson's professional successes would have enriched his loved ones as well. *Without Bias* shows the devastating impact Bias's death had on the Washington DC area. As local television anchor Jim Vance laments, "This city was rocked when word came out about Len Bias, because . . . you talk about a boy . . . heading for the promised land. Everybody loved them some Len Bias." Richard Ian Kimball notes that young dead athletes often have "fitting, if imaginative futures" imposed on them.[39] The deployment of Wilson and Bias as cautionary tales is dependent on the notion that both young men were tantalizingly close to professional stardom and reaching their American Dreams.

Death of American Dreams

In mourning the deaths of Wilson and Bias, *Benji* and *Without Bias* also mourn the death of their American Dreams and the loss of the "healthy and productive body" of the "urban African American athlete." Both films pin the deaths of Wilson and Bias on poor decision making that the films argue are common in inner-city communities. In focusing on individual behavior the films simplify complex urban issues and de-emphasize the role of race and class barriers in creating those issues. Gangs are depicted in *Benji* as an ever-growing threat to stable middle-class communities such as Chatham, Wilson's neighborhood in Chicago's South Side. File footage throughout the film shows the decayed landscape of Chicago, populated with young black men in gangs. These linkages attribute inner-city decline to gangs, not the postindustrial economy or historic segregation patterns that created inner-city Chicago.[40] This decline is also linked to the black family. According to Wilson's friend Wayne Harris, "If you grew up in Chatham, your parents tried to give you an opportunity to not be around too much chaos. It's a pretty good neighborhood. Mostly two-parent households. You know, not too much drama." This statement implies that other, more chaotic, neighborhoods in the city have deteriorated due to the breakdown of the black family. Here, the sport/gang dyad is tied to the "failed black family," a common scapegoat for the problems plaguing black communities.[41]

Wilson's own family is hit by the growing cocaine epidemic in the city. Wilson's brother Curtis Glenn recalls, "I just took Benji for granted. I never went to any of his games. I probably saw five games in my whole life, because I was going through issues myself. I was hanging out with bad crowds, doing drugs. We were freebasing." *Benji* implies Glenn, who carried a gun for protection and hung out in the streets, also contributed to his brother's death. Based on the narrative provided in *Benji*, Wilson was shot and killed after an argument with two other teenagers spiraled out of control. Glenn acknowledges that his life on the street might have influenced Wilson to make the wrong choices that day. "I just wish he could have looked the other way, but I told him how to be a man," Glenn laments. "He knew I was a man. He wanted to be a lot like me. And I wish he hadn't tried to be like me that day." *Benji* reinforces the sport/gang dyad, suggesting Wilson abandoned the discipline that lead him to success on the court and instead relied on the undisciplined advice taught by his brother.

Without Bias links Bias's overdose to the drug scene of Washington DC and the city's casual acceptance of cocaine usage. Drug abuse is viewed as a plague in the city and is framed as an issue of personal responsibility and willpower. Longtime Washington DC news anchor Jim Vance confesses to his own drug abuse while also highlighting how widespread cocaine use was in the region: "Lord knows I consider myself to have wasted some of the most productive years of my life, because instead of focusing on my craft, I was focusing on where can I score next? And I don't think I was singular or unique in that regard." During this discussion *Without Bias* shows archival footage of idle young black men, implying their involvement in the drug trade. Over this footage Brian Tribble, the man arrested for supplying Len Bias with the fatal dose of cocaine, links the drug trade to greed and the relentless pursuit of monetary gain. As Tribble recalls, "Mid-'80s, '84, '85, drugs just seemed to be everywhere, and it seemed to be something that was tempting for lots of people to do because they would have nice material things." Tribble and another black man, Robert Thompson, also describe the general naïveté about cocaine and the dangers of the drug. The breakdown of inner-city life is again associated with the misplaced values of young, irresponsible black men.[42] Within this segment of *Without Bias* there is no serious discussion of how cocaine got into the District or the economic conditions that led to a surge in drug trafficking in the city; instead, viewers see black men discussing their individual struggles with cocaine. The film further argues that this drug culture in Washington DC seduced Bias. Journalist Michael Wilbon observes, "The money was coming. The fame was coming. The girls were coming. All of it was rushing him, was crowding him in Washington DC.... Things were coming at him in a way that he probably wasn't ready for." Though Bias could make the right decisions on the court, *Without Bias* implies he was naive about the stakes off the court. Coupled with comments from Tribble and other black men who regretted their drug use and confessed their naïveté about cocaine and its dangers, the implication is that Bias, like many other black men in the region, ruined his future through a series of poor choices common on the streets of DC.

The producers of *Benji* and *Without Bias* justify their cautionary tales by underscoring the lives Wilson and Bias have saved through their deaths. *Benji* showed that Wilson's death rattled a city accustomed to large death tolls from black gang violence. The activism of community members, such as Wilson's mother, Mary Wilson, as well as the fact that Wilson's death forced the city of Chicago to change its emergency transportation policy, is credited with saving many lives. Chike sees a higher purpose in Wilson's death: "He becomes a martyr now. Maybe this was suppose to happen. Some people die to save other people's lives. It was like he was that martyr. It cost one life to save who knows how many more lives." In a *Washington Times* interview before the film's release *Without Bias* producer Kirk Fraser revealed that Bias's death had a personal effect on his life and served as a warning for him and other young people of his generation to avoid cocaine.[43] The film argues that the shock of Bias's death was comparable to that of the assassination of John F. Kennedy. As a former classmate of Bias reveals in the film, Bias's passing forced his fellow students to deal with their own mortality: "It was the innocence that was taken from us.

We were not naive anymore. We weren't in that fantasy world anymore where we didn't feel invincible anymore." The film views this generational wake-up call as beneficial. Bias's mother, Lonise, now an antidrug activist, and a number of other interviewees suggest that Bias's death was meant to happen and has helped curb drug abuse. Underscoring the political usage of such martyrdom, Washington DC radio host Donnie Simpson views Bias both as a the embodiment of the American Dream and an example of how that dream can be extinguished by one bad decision: "I think that Len's life serves as an example to our youth of the heights that you can go to, you know, with hard work and determination, and the lows you can go to for making wrong decisions." Both films transform Wilson and Bias into martyrs in an effort to affect present-day discussions about the choices made by young black men. If Wilson and Bias could save lives three decades ago, the producers of *Benji* and *Without Bias* believe they could save the lives of gang members and budding young athletes overwhelmed by their newfound fame.

Pushing Back: A Response to Reagan-Era Politics

While both *Benji* and *Without Bias* affirm the mythology of the American Dream and the sport/gang dyad, they also push back against some of the dominant narratives surrounding Wilson and Bias. These counternarratives displace the sport/gang dyad. C. L. Cole links the growth of the sport/gang dyad to legislation—including the 1986 crime bill constructed in the aftermath of Bias's death—to the large number of black men currently incarcerated in American prisons.[44] Both films show how moral panics surrounding race and sports can be used to enact harmful legislation and demonize young black men. In challenging dominant narratives about the deaths of Wilson and Bias, both films align themselves with other films within ESPN's *30 for 30* series that challenge "official" versions of sports history.

    Benji challenges the mediated narrative that Omar Dixon and Billy Moore, the two teenagers arrested and convicted for Wilson's murder, were hardened, cold-blooded gang members. The film argues local television coverage was especially complicit in promoting a certain narrative surrounding Wilson's death that cast Dixon and Moore as predators. This pushback against local news coverage is particularly significant given the role of television news in constructing black men as a criminal threat during the 1980s, helping to cultivate public support for unusually tough penalties for black offenders.[45] As *Benji* narrator Wood Harris notes, "The news reports were all too clear. After they bumped into Ben Wilson, Omar Dixon rifled through his pockets demanding money. When Wilson resisted, Billy Moore shot him with a .22 revolver. But to those who knew the suspects well, the public image of cold-blooded killers didn't quite fit." Viewers learn that Dixon was "from a quiet South Side neighborhood." His mother was a jazz singer, and his grandfather was blues legend Willie Dixon. Moore was a quiet kid who played youth baseball, but turned to the streets after the death of his father from cancer. In an interview with Moore *Benji* recaps his fateful encounter with Wilson. Contrary to media reports, Moore contends the incident was an argument that spiraled out of control. The sport/gang dyad is reliant on the image of the out-of-control, remorseless black gang member, but Moore's remorseful appearance in the film contradicts this image.[46] In fact, the closing credits of *Benji* inform viewers that Moore has worked for a nonprofit aiding ex-convicts since his release in 2004 and was even honored during a 2009 White House ceremony "as a model of exemplary rehabilitation." The sport/gang dyad is part of a larger cultural project where the two dominant images of black men are innocent victims or violent criminals.[47] These images work in concert to justify punishing black men. Moore's treatment in *Benji* challenges these images and the reductive view of blackness they cultivate.

Without Bias also interrogates the sport/gang dyad through counternarratives that challenge the political usages of the Bias narrative. The Reagan administration's "Just Say No" messaging was reliant on the idea that the clean-cut Bias only took cocaine on the night of his fatal overdose. The film suggests otherwise. Though several friends interviewed in *Without Bias* say they never saw Bias take cocaine, Brian Tribble said he used with Bias regularly. The film goes on to suggest Tribble, who would be tried and acquitted for Bias's death, became an unfair target. Former Georgetown basketball coach John Thompson attacks the morality play surrounding Tribble and Bias and, more broadly, the media's fascination with constructing safe black role models: "The need for Len Bias accentuates who he was hanging with. The need for black kids to have him as role model.

The need for him to be an example. The need for all those other things accentuated what happened to [Bias]." Tribble speaks candidly about the night of June 19, 1986, and expresses regret for his past drug use with Bias. Though Tribble would ultimately spend time in jail for dealing cocaine in another case, the closing credits inform viewers that he is now married, a father of three girls, and both a personal trainer and a real estate agent. As Fraser noted in an interview with *Washingtonian* magazine, Tribble's appearance in the film challenges the notion that he was "the monster" he was portrayed as during the 1980s. In doing so it complicates dominant recollections of the moral crisis surrounding Bias's death.[48]

Without Bias also attacks the Reagan administration's War on Drugs and the use of Bias's death to push antidrug legislation aimed at young black men. The Anti-Drug Abuse Act of 1986, which Bias's death sparked, is linked to the growing number of black men in jail today. Eric Sterling, counsel to the U.S. House Judiciary Committee at the time of the act's passage, acknowledges the mistake was equating five grams of crack cocaine with five grams of powder cocaine, which specifically targeted black low-level offenders. "We screwed up. We totally picked the wrong numbers," Sterling loudly proclaims. Viewers learn that a rogue narcotics detective who lied about his credentials concocted the formula used to construct the antidrug bill. Fraser believes it was critical to discuss the act in his film, especially as the laws have disproportionately affected African American communities. "That was the springboard for the laws we have now, that went after lower-level criminals [and meted out] harsher punishment," says Fraser. "It's a huge story, not just from the standpoint of sports itself, but how his death, still, to this moment, affected a lot of people in the community. That law right now is still being fought to this day."[49] In pushing against the antidrug bill, Fraser highlights how the transformation of Bias into a martyr for tough-on-crime legislators in the months after his death led to devastating consequences for the black community and, more specifically, young black men.

The Cost of Redemption

By complicating the dominant narratives surrounding the deaths of Ben Wilson and Len Bias, *Benji* and *Without Bias* align themselves with the counterhegemonic tradition of the black documentary. The films directly attack both the initial media coverage of these deaths, as well as the legislative fallout that resulted from this coverage. The films bring redemption to Billy Moore and Brian Tribble, who in the 1980s came to represent black criminality and the need for tougher legislation aimed at inner-city residents. Fraser's film also connects Bias's death to the rise of the prison-industrial complex and the growing number of young black men caught up in the judicial system. In this sense *Without Bias* and *Benji* are a part of a larger group of documentaries, such as Ava DuVernay's *13th* (2016), that have attacked the moral panics of the 1980s and early 1990s and the legislative fallout that reverberates to this day. Furthering the *30 for 30* series' push for alternate retellings of the sports past, both films help to tear down some of the mythology surrounding Ben Wilson and Len Bias and their deaths, which was dramatized through the sports/gang dyad.

However, the political promise of *Benji* and *Without Bias* is stymied by their producers' embrace of black middle-class politics and the depoliticized conventions of the sports documentary. With their films Coodie and Chike and Kirk Fraser align themselves with other black men such as sport journalists Scoop Jackson and Michael Wilbon, who have invoked Wilson and Bias to tackle contemporary issues surrounding gang violence and young black male athletes.[50] Even three decades after their deaths Wilson and Bias are made to matter, often in discussions centered on young black men. Media texts such as *Benji* and *Without Bias* have helped to transform Wilson and Bias into martyrs for a community, young black men perpetually framed to be in crisis. This martyrdom fits seamlessly into the narrative conventions of the televised sports documentary. Sports documentary profiles that feature failed athletes often end with a note of redemption, as the individual triumphs over past obstacles.[51] The young deaths of athletes would seem to preclude any redemption. However, both *Benji* and *Without Bias* argue that through the lives they saved and their continued usage as a cautionary tale, Wilson and Bias have indeed been redeemed. The arc toward redemption allows the films to end on a positive note and is crucial in establishing both the films' educational mission and their entertainment value. However, the arc ultimately prevents *Benji* and *Without Bias* from deeply interrogating the economic and social conditions that created the black urban core that the films link to the deaths of Wilson and Bias.

NOTES

1. Steve Macek, *Urban Nightmares: The Media, the Right, and the Moral Panic over the City* (Minneapolis: University of Minnesota Press, 2006); Jimmie L. Reeves and Richard Campbell, *Cracked Coverage: Television News, the Anti-cocaine Crusade, and the Reagan Legacy* (Durham NC: Duke University Press, 1994); and David Wilson, *Inventing Black on Black Violence: Discourse, Space, and Representation* (Syracuse NY: Syracuse University Press, 2005) all focus on the media's depiction of the black inner city during the 1980s and the promotion of heightened police and government surveillance.

2. Richard Ian Kimball, *Legends Never Die: Athletes and Their Afterlives in Modern America* (Syracuse NY: Syracuse University Press, 2017), 4–7.

3. Travis Vogan, *ESPN: The Making of a Sports Media Empire* (Urbana: University of Illinois Press, 2015), 45.

4. Jon Greenberg, "Chicago's Transcendent Tragedy," ESPN.com, August 23, 2012, www.espn.com.

5. Rick Snider, "*Without Bias* Tells an Untold Story," *Washington Examiner*, November 2, 2009, www.washingtonexaminer.com; Sam Alipour, "Keeping Up with Reggie and Kim at Sundance," ESPN.com, January 29, 2008, www.espn.com.

6. Cheryl L. Cole and Samantha King, "Representing Black Masculinity and Urban Possibilities: Racism, Realism, and *Hoop Dreams*," in *Sport and Postmodern Times*, ed. Genevieve Rail (Albany: State University of New York Press, 1998), 52.

7. C. L. Cole, "Nike's America/America's Michael Jordan," in *Michael Jordan, Inc.: Corporate Sport, Media Culture, and Late Modern America*, ed. David L. Andrews (Albany: State University of New York Press, 2001), 69–70.

8. Cole and King, "Representing Black Masculinity and Urban Possibilities," 52.

9. Cole, "Nike's America/America's Michael Jordan," 68.

10. Samantha Sheppard, "Historical Contestants: African American Documentary Traditions in *On the Shoulders of Giants*," *Journal of Sport and Social Issues* 41, no. 6 (2017): 467, doi: 10.1177/0193723517719667.

11. Herman Gray, "Culture, Masculinity, and the Time after Race," in *Culture, Masculinity, and the Time after Race*, ed. Herman Gray and Macarena Gomez-Barris (Minneapolis: University of Minnesota Press, 2010), 87.

12. Greenberg, "Chicago's Transcendent Tragedy"; Alipour, "Keeping Up with Reggie and Kim at Sundance."

13. Ian McDonald, "Situating the Sports Documentary," *Journal of Sport and Social Issues* 31, no. 3 (2007): 221; Sean Crosson, *Sport and Film* (London: Routledge,

2013), 57–58; Thomas Patrick Oates, "Failure Is Not an Option: Sport Documentary and the Politics of Redemption," *Journal of Sport History* 41, no. 2 (2014): 216.

14. Aaron Baker, "*Hoop Dreams* in Black and White: Race and Basketball Movies," in *Basketball Jones: America above the Rim*, ed. Toddy Boyd and Kenneth L. Shropshire (New York: New York University Press, 2000), 216, 234–35; Oates, "Failure Is Not an Option," 222.

15. Cole and King, "Representing Black Masculinity and Urban Possibilities," 65; bell hooks, "Neo-colonial Fantasies of Conquest: *Hoop Dreams*," in *Reel to Real: Race, Sex, and Class at the Movies*, ed. bell hooks (London: Routledge, 1996), 78; Jillian Sandell, "Out of the Ghetto and into the Marketplace: Hoop Dreams and the Commodification of Marginality," *Socialist Review* 25, no. 2 (1995): 60.

16. Cole and King, "Representing Black Masculinity and Urban Possibilities," 71; hooks, "Neo-colonial Fantasies of Conquest," 79.

17. Cole and King, "Representing Black Masculinity and Urban Possibilities," 79.

18. C. Richard King and Charles Fruehling Springwood, *Beyond the Cheers: Race as Spectacle in College Sport* (Albany: State University of New York Press, 2001), 37.

19. Phyllis R. Klotman and Janet K. Cutler, introduction to *Struggles for Representation: African American Documentary Film and Video*, ed. Phyllis R. Klotman and Janet K. Cutler (Bloomington and Indianapolis: Indiana University Press, 1999), xvi.

20. Sheppard, "Historical Contestants," 6.

21. Thomas Mc Laughlin, *Give and Go: Basketball as a Cultural Practice* (Albany: State University of New York Press, 2008), 231.

22. Gray, "Culture, Masculinity, and the Time after Race," 87; David Wellman, "Reconfiguring the Color Line: Racializing Inner-City Youth and Rearticulating Class Hierarchy in Black America," *Transforming Anthropology* 17, no. 2 (2009): 131.

23. Herman Gray, "Race, Media, and the Cultivation of Concern," *Communication and Critical/Cultural Studies* 10, nos. 2–3 (2013): 255.

24. Vogan, *ESPN*, 129–36; Andrew C. Billings and Kevin B. Blackistone, "Sprawling Hagiography: ESPN's *30 for 30* Series and the Untangling of Sports Memories," in *The ESPN Effect: Exploring the Worldwide Leader in Sports*, ed. John McGuire, Greg G. Armfield, and Adam Earnheardt (New York: Peter Lang, 2015), 159; Joshua Malitsky, "Knowing Sports: The Logic of the Contemporary Sports Documentary," *Journal of Sport History* 41, no. 2 (2014): 206.

25. April Turner, "NABJ News: NABJ Honors ESPN's *30 for 30* series with Annual Best Practices Award," NABJ.org, July 13, 2011, www.nabj.org.

26. Oates, "Failure Is Not an Option," 222; Billings and Blackistone, "Sprawling Hagiography," 161; Lindsay J. Mean, "Celebrating the Mythological," *Journal of Sports Media* 10, no. 2 (2015): 41; Yago Colas, "Visualizing Basketball's Past:

The Historical Imagination of ESPN's Basketball Documentaries," *Journal of Sport and Social Issues* 41, no. 6 (2017): 453, doi: 10.1177/0193723517719666.

27. Oates, "Failure Is Not an Option," 222.

28. Lindon Barrett, "Dead Men Printed: Tupac Shakur, Biggie Smalls, and Hip-Hop Eulogy," *Callaloo* 22, no. 2 (1999): 306, 307.

29. Thom Shanker, "Mayor Rewrites Budget to Fund War on Gangs," *Chicago Tribune*, December 4, 1984.

30. James Carey, "The Dark Continent of American Journalism," in *Reading the News: A Pantheon Guide to Popular Culture*, ed. Robert Karl Manoff and Michael Schudson (New York: Pantheon Books, 1987), 193.

31. Dan Baum, *Smoke and Mirrors: The War on Drugs and the Politics of Failure* (New York: Little, Brown, 1996), 223, 225; Reeves and Campbell, *Cracked Coverage*, 139.

32. Baum, *Smoke and Mirrors*, 219–20, 228.

33. Robert Goldman and Stephen Papson, *Nike Culture: The Sign of the Swoosh* (London, Thousand Oaks CA, and New Delhi: Sage, 1998), 103, 102; Catherine A. Coleman, "Classic Campaigns—'It's Gotta Be the Shoes': Nike, Mike and Mars and the 'Sneaker Killings,'" *Advertising & Society Review* 14, no. 2 (2013): 1.

34. Coleman, "Classic Campaigns," 11; Goldman and Papson, *Nike Culture*, 112.

35. Michael Weinreb, "The Day Innocence Died," ESPN.com, June 24, 2008, www.espn.com.

36. Baker, "*Hoop Dreams* in Black and White," 216; King and Springwood, *Beyond the Cheers*, 32.

37. Baker, "*Hoop Dreams* in Black and White," 222–23.

38. Michael Weinreb, *Bigger than the Game: Bo, Boz, the Punky QB, and How the '80s Created the Modern Athlete* (New York: Gotham Books, 2010), 37–42.

39. Colas, "Visualizing Basketball's Past," 7; Kimball, *Legends Never Die*, 4.

40. Cole, "Nike's America/America's Michael Jordan," 70.

41. Cole and King, "Representing Black Masculinity and Urban Possibilities," 55.

42. Cole, "Nike's America/America's Michael Jordan," 70.

43. Will Eidam, "*Benji* Directors Coodie and Chike: Change, for Better and for Worse," *Austin Chronicle*, October 23, 2012, www.austinchronicle.com; Snider, "*Without Bias* Tells an Untold Story."

44. Cole, "Nike's America/America's Michael Jordan," 68.

45. Herman Gray, *Watching Race: Television and the Struggle for Blackness* (Minneapolis: University of Minnesota Press, 2004), 14, 34.

46. Cole, "Nike's America/America's Michael Jordan," 67.

47. Gray, *Watching Race*, 156.

48. Drew Bratcher, "A Death of a Legend," *Washingtonian*, June 1, 2009, www.washingtonian.com.

49. Mike Miliard, "Hoop Nightmare," *Boston Phoenix*, October 28, 2009, http:// thephoenix.com.

50. See Michael Wilbon, "The Story of Bias's Death Should Always Have Life," *Washington Post*, June 19, 2006, www.washingtonpost.com; and Scoop Jackson, "Benji Wilson's Ongoing Journey," ESPN.com, October 23, 2012, www.espn.com.

51. Oates, "Failure Is Not an Option," 220.

6

Protest and Public Memory

Documenting the 1968 Summer Olympic Games

EMILY PLEC AND SHAUN M. ANDERSON

How do sport documentaries figure in the formation of the public imagination? How does their accounting of the past offer lessons for the present? Ian McDonald explains that sport documentaries have the propensity to critique the intersections of sport and society. There has been, however, a dearth of work dedicated to understanding these intersections. McDonald surmises that the reason is largely because of the documentary form's alignment with what Bill Nichols calls "discourses of sobriety," which include law, science, and policy.[1] McDonald explains that sport diverges from this sobriety by expounding upon aspects of entertainment that often promise an escape from real-life issues.[2] Still, history has shown that sport often transcends the realm of entertainment.

Many prominent sports figures have addressed a plethora of civil rights issues. To cite just a few notorious examples, the 1947 Major League Baseball season introduced the reintegration of baseball when Jackie Robinson became the first African American to play in the MLB. Two decades later, heavyweight boxing champion Muhammad Ali refused induction into the U.S. Army for religious reasons. Remaining steadfast to his beliefs, Ali ultimately was banned from boxing for three years, fined $10,000, and sentenced to five years in prison (reversed upon appeal) for draft evasion. A short time later, baseball player Curt Flood sacrificed his own career to challenge the MLB's reserve clause and establish free agency. Almost a half century later, professional basketball players Jason Collins, John Amaechi, and Brittney Griner came out publicly and have used their celebrity status to advocate for greater acceptance of LGBTQ+ people. And in a manner reminiscent of the demonstrations of earlier black athletes, some professional football and basketball teams and players have protested racism and used their platforms to advance the Black Lives Matter movement.

As these examples illustrate, sport provides a platform for discussion and dialogue into the realm of political, economic, and social injustices. The stories of some of these athletes' struggles (and triumphs) have been circulated and have gained cultural currency, in part, due to sports documentaries. Yet, as Travis Vogan points out, the sport documentary has yet to receive the level of scholarly inquiry deserving of such a robust genre.[3] Sports documentaries that feature brave athletes standing up against injustice provide powerful narratives that shape public memory in important ways. Perhaps no moment in sports history better exemplifies the ideological capacity of athletes to shape public consciousness than the raised fist salute by African American medalists Tommie Smith and John Carlos at the 1968 Summer Olympics in Mexico City, an image so widely circulated and reproduced as to have become iconic.

This chapter analyzes two sport documentaries released almost a decade apart, *Fists of Freedom: The Story of the '68 Olympic Games* (George Roy, 1999) and *Salute* (Matt Norman, 2008), which tell the story behind that famous moment with the three men on the victory dais during the 200-meter medal ceremony.[4] The films provide avenues for examining the power of sports documentaries to perpetuate hegemonic ideologies and problematic stereotypes as well as promote narratives supportive of societal transformation and change.

Fists of Freedom is an award-winning documentary film that aired as part of the HBO series *Sports of the 20th Century*. It chronicles the issues and events surrounding the notorious demonstration by gold and bronze medalists Tommie Smith and John Carlos. *Salute* premiered at the Sydney Film Festival almost a decade later and focuses on Peter Norman, the Australian silver medalist who became lifelong friends with Smith and Carlos after sharing the famed Olympic podium with them and showing his support. Norman was criticized and ostracized for the support he showed for the cause of human equality at home as well as abroad. His decision to wear an Olympic Project for Human Rights (OPHR) button during the medals ceremony and his public opposition to racist governmental policies and practices in Australia following the Games cost him immense professional opportunities.

Written, directed, and produced by Peter Norman's nephew Matt Norman, *Salute* tells more of the story of what happened to the three Olympians after the Games and emphasizes the enduring friendship they built upon the foundation of their shared experience and values. In contrast, *Fists of Freedom* focuses on the events leading up to the Games, including the politicization of Tommie Smith, John Carlos, and other members of the U.S. Olympic Team via the OPHR and black boycott movement. Both documentaries stress the theme of individualism and individual decision making and downplay the role of organized, collective action in the '68 Olympic protest.

Likewise, both documentaries employ what Bill Nichols describes as the participatory mode of filmmaking, which "stresses images of testimony or verbal exchange," shifts textual authority toward social actors, and features "various forms of monologue and dialogue." Such films rely, for their rhetorical effect, upon an assumed correspondence between representation and reality. Sports documentaries achieve this illusion by indexing the past with historical footage, while also framing the images with contemporary interview segments. Nichols describes how a documentary film can construct what seems to be authentic "history" for viewers: "The indexical image authenticates testimony now about what happened then. With historical footage from the time recounted appended to it, indexicality may guarantee an apparent congruity between what happened then and what is said now. The historic footage enjoys the legitimating power of indexicality while the spoken testimony determines its meaning."[5]

It is through the spoken testimony of principal characters that we come to see these narratives as *the story* of the 1968 Olympic demonstration. Sport documentaries often reproduce a familiar narrative of achievement against great odds and the inspirational defiance of physical or social barriers. *Salute* and *Fists of Freedom* are no exception. As we would expect, they enable the social actors of sport to transcend the entertainment realm yet again, through the construction of public memory of their significant political statements. To varying degrees, these documentaries engage the critical possibilities that occur when athletes use their platforms to address social issues.

Neither film purports to tell Tommie Smith's and John Carlos's stories (which both men have done in autobiographies), but they do tell a story of the Olympic protest that helps audience members in the present moment make cultural and historical sense of the past. In doing so, they activate narrative structures that have the ability to frame viewers' interpretations of subsequent, and similar, antiracist protest by athletes today. In *Fists of Freedom*, Smith describes his actions on "the victory stand" as "a cry for freedom" in contrast to public perceptions of it as "a hate message." In addition to considering the raised fists of Smith and Carlos as "signifying," or rhetorically "embodying the ambiguities of language," we argue that these documentaries signify civil rights and Black Power in ways that obscure the complexities of both movements, emphasize individualism as a hegemonic ideology, subtly perpetuate racist stereotypes, and hinder the ability of athletes to advance movements such as Black Lives Matter.[6]

After briefly discussing how Smith and Carlos signified on racist oppression in the United States by raising their fists, we examine *Fists of Freedom* as a text that contrasts the hero, Smith, and antihero, Carlos, by troping racist stereotypes of the Uncle Tom and Bad Buck. We then discuss the film's characterization of Carlos and sociologist Harry Edwards, the architect behind the call to boycott the 1968 Olympic Games, to illustrate how *Fists of Freedom* frames public memory of the civil rights and Black Power movements. We also explore the depiction of antiracist white allies in both films and critique the way *Salute* renders Black Power absent by positioning a sympathetic white bystander as a civil rights hero and advancing a discourse of humanitarian color blindness. Finally, we consider the contemporary ideological implications of *Salute, Fists of Freedom*, and other memorializing discourses focused on sport history for public memory of racial protest.

Signifying Black Power

Signifying is a rhetorical practice that engages the past, dialogically, in the present. As Henry Louis Gates points out in *The Signifying Monkey*, "Writers signify upon each other's texts by rewriting the received textual tradition. This can be accomplished by the revision of tropes." In a similar vein, Kim Euell argues, "Through the ritual of remembering and revising we can be made whole."[7] Euell's discussion highlights signifying as a critical praxis for the reconstitution of social narratives. Signifying depends upon culturally specific references to generate the revisionary power of the trope. Within this framework, the Olympic demonstration by Carlos and Smith can be understood as a practice of signifying that addresses multiple audiences in culturally specific ways.

The African American rhetorical practice of signifying differs somewhat from the semiotic concept of signification in that tropes are often inseparable from the concepts to which they are attached; they are, in fact, partially constitutive of those concepts.[8] In the case of the victory stand, the fists build on and multiply the meanings of a symbol conceptually linked to the radical politics of the Black Power movement. As a result, the image becomes inseparable from the meaning it references. As a polysemic rhetorical gesture, the victory-stand demonstration by Tommie Smith and John Carlos on the Olympic platform invites multiple, often conflicting, interpretations—as a threat to the white establishment, an expression of cultural pride, a gesture of race and class solidarity. The black fist can, for example, signify "the material irreducibility of space and agency in civic practice" for a contemporary urban audience, as the Monument to Joe Louis does for some Detroiters.[9] As bell hooks argues, aesthetics "is more than a philosophy or theory of art and beauty; it is a way of inhabiting space, a particular location, a way of looking and becoming."[10] The Olympic demonstration signifies a complex and nonreductive black cultural identity grounded in particular performances of masculinity, political opposition, and symbolic liberation.

In *Fists of Freedom*, Steven Millner claims the raised black fist was symbolic of "Black men who would stand up in a racist society." On the Olympic podium, Smith and Carlos signify upon the visual imagery of the black fist, turning received meanings back upon the Olympic organizers and spectators. They also signify on the ritual space and meaning of the medal platform. Criticized by Olympic officials for failing to observe due order and decorum, the two athletes in fact signify on the very logic that permits them to represent their nation at its best while, at home, they experience it at its worst. Their signifying challenges implicit assumptions that the Olympics is not, and should not be, politicized. Perhaps due to the gravity of what they are signifying, the death threats they received, or jeers from the crowd, Smith and Carlos do not demonstrate the playful disregard often associated with the Signifying Monkey. They do, however, much like the folkloric Monkey, "start some shit."[11]

Brent Musburger, a columnist for the *Chicago American* at the time, described Smith and Carlos as "a couple of dark-skinned storm troopers" and their demonstration as "no more than a juvenile gesture by a couple of athletes who should have known better."[12] Musburger's interpretation was popular among many whites and conservative Americans in 1968. Olympic documentarian Bud Greenspan, interviewed in *Fists of Freedom*, admits that he was "one of those who said . . . 'Who do these guys think they are?'" In retrospect, Greenspan acknowledges, "these guys proved to be correct. They opened our eyes, like anybody who starts a revolution." Greenspan's observation both summarizes and stands in for the focus of the documentaries upon the eradication of racial inequality. In essence, these are stories of individual men who risked their futures to inspire social change. Greenspan's account also indicates a shift from the perception of the victory stand as a radical gesture by black militants to an updated and revised understanding of it as a watershed moment in the history of both sports and civil rights.

As suggested previously, *Fists of Freedom* and *Salute* (re)present the victory stand as a courageous act of self-sacrifice. In this way, the documentaries redeem Smith, Carlos, and, in the case of *Salute*, Norman as heroes rather than the International Olympic Committee–painted villains of the 1968 Summer Olympic story. Tommie Smith emerges as the primary hero in *Fists of Freedom*'s representation of the 1968 Summer Games. Carlos, who did not agree to the terms of the contract offered by the film's producers, appears as the antihero.[13] The juxtaposition of Smith and Carlos as hero and antihero is one of the primary ways the film perpetuates racist stereotypes and characterizations. *Salute* contests the negative representation of Carlos in interesting ways, but also succumbs to problematic depictions of him as a hypersexual, aggressive black male. Both films set Carlos apart as different from his more reserved and principled competitors, especially Smith.

The Troping of (Uncle) Tommie Smith

The opening scenes of *Fists of Freedom* and *Salute* set the stage for the Mexico City Olympics against the backdrop of the political conflicts of the late 1960s. Flames at the edges of the screen and dramatic music frame a montage of images that open *Fists of Freedom*. Among these images are photographs of pilots in Vietnam, a white medic tending a black soldier, Robert F. Kennedy, and Martin Luther King Jr. Black-and-white photographs of several of the athletes featured in the documentary follow. The bordering flames then consume, from within, a picture of a Ku Klux Klan cross. The camera focuses on the image of the clenched, gloved fist and then moves down the arm of Tommie Smith and pans out to reveal the victory stand and Olympic spectators. These introductory images connect the victory stand with the politics and protest of the late 1960s. In a voice-over, Michael Eric Dyson describes 1968 as a "smoldering summer of discontent" in which "cities burned, night in, night out." References to the assassinations of Kennedy and King reinforce the connection to the civil rights movement by calling upon public memory of the slain American civil rights champions. Their deaths are positioned rhetorically as the measure of human life in a racist society. *Salute* references King's and Kennedy's deaths as well. Unlike *Fists of Freedom*, it also emphasizes the racist white Australian policies and the Aboriginal justice movements that shaped Peter Norman's worldview.

Significantly, the image of the Klan cross in *Fists of Freedom* immediately precedes the image of the clenched black fists and the victory stand. The burning Klan cross signifies white racism in its most obvious and overt form, defining it as a deviant and marginal ideology expressed in acts of material and physical aggression. Likewise, the images of police using fire hoses against demonstrators in *Salute* draw attention away from the subtle discursive racisms still lingering in the body of these stories of the '68 Summer Games. In short, *Fists of Freedom* deploys a variation on the Uncle Tom stereotype—a term "generally applied to blacks who are subservient toward whites"—to frame the civil rights movement and Tommie Smith.[14] The film articulates the Bad Buck stereotype—often used to describe an ill-tempered, violent black man who is aroused by white women—to the

Black Power movement and John Carlos.[15] These articulations contribute to the shaping of public memory of both movements and constrain narratives of black achievement by falsely dichotomizing black male identity and downplaying radical collective action.

Mirroring much of the popular media discourse of the late 1960s and '70s, *Fists of Freedom* depicts Smith as obedient and reluctant in his activism and Carlos as brash and verbally aggressive. Both documentaries introduce Smith as a young man and devout Christian who had humble beginnings picking cotton and supporting his family while dreaming of being a track star. Liev Schreiber, the narrator of *Fists of Freedom* states, "Tommie arrived at San Jose State in the fall of '63. Afraid of having to go back and work the fields, he was determined not to fail academically." Smith himself recounts his father's statement that if he came in second at his track meet, he would be "out in the field next Saturday with the rest of your brothers and sisters. And I didn't lose too many races after that!"

Like the image of the Klan cross, experiences of overt racism are featured prominently as discursive reference points for audience understandings of discrimination. Smith's friend and teammate Lee Evans describes his childhood experiences picking cotton from sunup to sundown, only to be cheated at the scales by the racist white buyer. Smith describes going to town for ice cream as a child and being told, "Get out of the road little n——. Go on back to the jungle." Again, the presence of overt racism in Evans's and Smith's childhoods overshadows the presence of subtle racism in their contemporary depiction. It also reinforces an underlying premise linked to the theme of progressive individualism in which the ability to overcome great hardship is attributed to hard work and personal sacrifice.

In addition to being a hard worker, Smith is represented in *Fists of Freedom* as studious: "I had my horn-rimmed glasses, I had my big old bag of books, I had my trail to go to the library." He is also depicted as someone primarily concerned for others, an altruism characteristic of the classic literary figure of Uncle Tom. For example, Lee Evans recalls his first few days at San Jose State and his early encounters with Smith, who counseled him, saying "Evans . . . here are all of the classes you have to take to graduate. Make sure you take them all." Although these depictions help to deconstruct and counter some negative stereotypes, such as that of student athletes as poor scholars, they also signify on historical characterizations, such as the Uncle Tom, that can be articulated to public memory and contemporary racial politics in troubling ways, such as the assumptions made about African Americans who excel academically.

The stereotype of the Uncle Tom draws more upon received wisdom than its namesake, the patriarch in Harriet Beecher Stowe's 1851 abolitionist novel. The distinction between the Uncle Tom of *Uncle Tom's Cabin* and the popular stereotype of the Uncle Tom is important here because *Fists of Freedom* describes African American boxer George Foreman as an "Uncle Tom" in the eyes of other blacks. In the documentary Foreman recounts the criticism he received from peers who were disappointed when he celebrated in the boxing ring by waving a small American flag and bowing to the audience. Following Smith and Carlos's ejection from the Olympic Village, Foreman was criticized by many blacks and praised by many whites for his unbridled patriotism. Because of this characterization, Muhammad Ali's 1974 victory over Foreman in Zaire was seen by many blacks as symbolic of the defeat of the "old-style Negro." In *Fists of Freedom* Olympic champion Jesse Owens—who was recruited by the U.S. Olympic Committee to dissuade other athletes from demonstrating—is also characterized as an Uncle Tom. For instance, outspoken OPHR advocate and organizer Harry Edwards refers to Owens as an "Uncle Tom" in a manner that signifies on the popular understanding of a Tom as a man who is elderly, servile, and, as Patricia Turner describes, "always willing to 'sell out' blacks to placate whites and improve his personal well-being."[16] Through such signifying practices, "Uncle Tom" has evolved into a label for blacks who capitulate to white interests due to their desire to achieve personal success.

As Turner points out, the stereotype of the Uncle Tom differs in many ways from the character developed in Harriet Beecher Stowe's original narrative. The original Uncle Tom is depicted as humble, heroic, healthy, and altruistic, a "proactive Christian warrior." He is a worthy hero because he is "wise, venerable, and kind" and can "work long days in the field," proving his physical stamina.[17] Both films depict Smith as a patriotic, blue-collar young man who joined the Reserve Officers' Training Corps, which *Salute* calls "very right wing" and *Fists of Freedom* describes as "his nation's most conservative symbol." Audience members are reminded of Smith's hardships as a youth, working the fields alongside his siblings. His church affiliation is described in *Fists of Freedom* in conjunction with a clip of Smith as a young man, singing "Nobody Knows the Trouble I've Seen." This "troping of Uncle Tom" also emphasizes Tommie Smith's personal sacrifices. After returning from the Games, his offer of a professional football contract was withdrawn. He had difficulty finding a job and ended up washing cars to support his family, a fact both documentaries point out.

Like Uncle Tom of *Uncle Tom's Cabin*, the depiction of Smith counters dominant stereotypes about African Americans in general. Also like Stowe's Uncle Tom, however, the characterization can be articulated to rhetorical history and cultural memory of black struggle in a manner that undermines the aims and strategies of radical movements such as Black Power. Simultaneously redeeming Smith and Stowe's Uncle Tom as true heroes, *Fists of Freedom* perpetuates an association between the two that has consequences for public memory of the 1968 Summer Olympic Games and the civil rights movement. As Turner notes, "Each new depiction of Uncle Tom reveals much about the racial politics of a given era or group within American history."[18] The characterization of (Uncle) Tommie Smith redeems the real Tommie Smith from (official) historical vilification and positions him as both a role model and a cultural hero. Understanding how and why these characterizations emerge helps us to better understand the racial politics and ideological underpinnings of a film such as *Fists of Freedom*.

The redemptive portrayal of (Uncle) Tommie Smith in *Fists of Freedom* works in several ways. It plays upon and against some of the racist reiterations of the Uncle Tom stereotype, but most assuredly revives the original Uncle Tom as an ideal type of black masculinity. By portraying Smith as the hero of the narrative, and situating the victory stand in the context of the civil rights movement, *Fists of Freedom* celebrates the studious, religious, and conservative qualities embodied by Smith and downplays his involvement in racial protest more broadly. Smith is shown (with Lee Evans) dancing and studying, and the narrator mentions that he had no trouble fitting in at San Jose State University.[19] Smith's assimilation into college life is disrupted, however, by his inability to find housing near campus. In fact, *Fists of Freedom* and *Salute* attribute the athletes' burgeoning activism primarily to their experiences of formal racial discrimination in housing. This interpretation, and the articulation to the civil rights movement, is further reinforced by Dyson's assertion in *Fists of Freedom* that the athletes "began to be persuaded by the logic of Tommie Smith [because] they saw he wasn't a fire breathing radical, he wasn't some behemoth of ideology against white people. He was simply saying, 'Look, I want to be treated like a man.'"

The films also position Smith as the reluctant hero of the narrative due to his early conservatism and conformism. Consistent with the characterizations offered by the mainstream press, *Fists of Freedom* suggests that Smith was goaded into activism by external forces—namely, overt racism and the influential rhetoric of Harry Edwards. Most important, the troping of Uncle Tom signifies an ideology of progressive individualism. Smith eventually succeeds because of his strength, perseverance, and independence. In the end, his heroic sacrifice, like that of Stowe's Tom, is made for the benefit of others. Smith's portrayal is relatively consistent across both documentaries, but John Carlos is depicted quite differently.

Bad Bucks and Black Power

John Carlos is noticeably absent in the contemporary interview footage that constitutes a large part of the narrative in *Fists of Freedom*, and Peter Norman is shown primarily in his role as ally and supporter of the principles of the Olympic Project for Human Rights, like most of the other white Olympians featured in the films. Carlos's presence in the documentary is marked only by secondhand accounts and historical footage. *Fists of Freedom* depicts John Carlos as a Bad Buck and positions him alongside the Black Power movement as it is rendered within racist white historical imagination. *Salute* presents a different image of Carlos by emphasizing his spiritual beliefs and activism while still sharing some of the same general characterizations. *Salute* also shows Carlos speaking publicly about the Mexican government's massacre of student protesters prior to the Games and describing the harm his family members experienced after his expulsion from the Olympic Village. Carlos states that his brothers were immediately discharged from the military and his wife committed suicide, yet he repeatedly asserts that "God orchestrated it" and that "God chose the three of us" to be on the victory stand together. *Fists of Freedom* denies him this voice and perspective, and the result is a caricature of the Black Power radicalism and collectivist values he represents.

Carlos is introduced in both *Fists of Freedom* and *Salute* through a geographical metaphor. He is depicted as a product of the mean streets of Harlem, where he learned to "fight his battles and handle his hustles." In *Salute* Carlos describes his adolescence spent "breaking into freight yards and stealing to give to people who didn't have," later admitting he spent a lot of time "talking smack" as a young man. In *Fists of Freedom* teammate Ralph Boston recounts an instance in which "this guy was giving his little daughter some grief," and Carlos responded aggressively toward the father. Summarizing the stereotype of the Bad Buck, Boston says, "You wanted him to be your friend because you didn't want John Carlos as your enemy." The stereotypically outspoken and unreserved Bad Buck is also characterized by his sexual potency and the threat he poses to women, especially white women.[20] *Fists of Freedom* alludes to this aspect of the stereotype in a clip of Steven Millner describing Carlos: "He was boisterous on the track, he was boisterous in the classroom, he was boisterous with women." Indeed, Carlos jokes in *Salute* about his interest in women and old track and field footage shows him kissing a young woman on the sidelines, further reinforcing the suggestion of his sexual prowess.

Similar to the trope that was displayed in *Salute*, *Fist of Freedom* reinforces the outspoken brashness that is also stereotypically associated with the Bad Buck when fellow runner Larry Livers describes meeting a "high-school kid named Carlos" who was "talking all this smack, making noise." In a sequence that constitutes the primary introduction and characterization of John Carlos in the documentary, Livers also points out that Carlos "could eat a hot dog, drink a soda and come out and beat most guys" on the track. Writer Jack Scott recalls, "They're announcing 'last call for the hundred meters.' All the other guys are there at the starting line. John is sitting up in the stands joking with his friends." Millner adds, "Drinking wine, smoking dope, after being challenged by three sprinters, he walked down underneath the stands, got in a track uniform." Jack Scott then describes the way Carlos would "get down at the starting block and be talking to the sprinters." The sequence of edited clips ends with teammate Ralph

Boston's account. "Carlos says in his heavy New York accent, 'Come on sucker, I want to see what you got.'" In short, *Fists of Freedom* signifies on the Bad Buck trope by characterizing Carlos as the aggressive, undisciplined, rebellious, competitive black male. Casual references to confrontation, drinking, illegal drug use, and macho language on the track all reinforce Carlos's image as the Bad Buck. These decontextualized characterizations also position Carlos as an antihero who lacks the Christian morality and personal discipline of Smith and Norman.[21]

The characterization of Carlos is discursively tied to the Black Power movement in two major ways. First, as Michael Omi and Howard Winant point out, "Black Power was a flexible, even amorphous concept, but it was frequently interpreted to mean separatism."[22] Black Power is also often equated erroneously with racism against whites. In *Salute* Carlos was shown leaving the Olympic Village, threatening a journalist, and stating his feelings of anger toward "a bunch of white people." Second, the Black Power Movement is characterized in terms of violent appropriation of power in response to institutionally racist rhetorical situations. Carlos's hostile responses to whites and to the abusive father mentioned previously exemplify his aggressive responses to oppressive rhetorical situations.

Since both John Carlos and the Black Power movement are, for the most part, absent from *Fists of Freedom* (and the Black Power movement is largely absent in *Salute*), their limited presence is even more significant. The subtle association between John Carlos and Black Power reinforces public memory of the movement as an aggressively antiwhite rebellion. *Fists of Freedom* also signifies on Black Power by signifying upon the black glasses, attire, and berets associated with the Black Panthers. For example, in one scene Harry Edwards describes his strategic use of Black Power rhetoric while the accompanying images show him in sunglasses, a black beret, and black jacket and, in one shot, blowing cigar smoke at the camera: "If you go back and look at the earliest pictures, I was wearing a suit and a tie anytime I went before the media. As it became crystal clear that the name of the game was keeping the media attention on the movement, one had to go right up to the edge of civility . . . because the white media fed on that."

Charles Korr summarizes the rhetorical effect produced by Edwards's transformation. He argues that Edwards was able to "cut through the hypocrisy that was both organized sport and the Olympics," because "they saw somebody like Edwards standing up there as a visible sign of something that was dangerous." The linkages among Black Power as an image, as something that signifies a lack (or the edge) of "civility," and as a "sign of something that was dangerous" shore up the superficial representation of Black Power as an aggressively antiwhite movement.

Lee Evans also associates the black berets that he and his 100-meter teammates wore on the victory stand with the Black Panther Party in the contemporary footage, yet he is silenced in the accompanying historical footage. In the historical footage an interviewer asks Evans about the boycott movement: "Was it an individual thing or could you get complete unity? And do you feel that there is complete unity now or do you think that it is still pretty much an individual thing amongst the Black athletes?" Before Evans can reply the film cuts to an interview with Jack Scott, who argues, "'Black athletes' is the term we use but they were all individuals with individual opinions." Evans is not given the chance to contest the individualistic frame, further downplaying the collectivist dimensions of the OPHR, in which he played a prominent part. Significantly, edited clips of Edwards, Evans, Scott, and others show them espousing liberal, progressive, and individualistic solutions to racism throughout *Fists of Freedom*. Also, the criticism Evans and other Olympic medalists received from some athletes and OPHR supporters for not explicitly protesting like Smith and Carlos is briefly mentioned, further underscoring the individual nature of the demonstration.

In contrast, *Salute* barely mentions the organized protest movement and influence of figures such as Harry Edwards and Lee Evans. In contrast to *Fists of Freedom*'s depiction of John Carlos as the Bad Buck, *Salute* shows Carlos as a man broken by racial oppression after participating in the raised-fist demonstration. Although he is still juxtaposed to Smith, Carlos's suffering is highlighted, including how he dealt with the suicide of his wife after being expelled from the Olympics and his disappointment with individuals such as Harry Edwards, who he felt monetarily benefited from his and Smith's sacrifice.

White Allies and the Rhetoric of Individual Achievement

Peter Norman, who became a sprinter "by accident," is introduced in *Salute* as the son of a working-class laborer. "Dad wasn't wealthy by any means," Norman recalls, as the narrator describes him as a "poor white boy from the working-class suburbs of Melbourne." The theme of Christian compassion underscores Norman's heroic, if ordinary, humanitarianism. The narrator says, "Norman was brought up with the staunchly religious teachings of the Salvation Army, which preached God, compassion, and the equality of his fellow man." Norman describes the humanitarian ideology of his religious upbringing at several points in the documentary: "There was no such thing as discrimination. . . . [P]eople were treated because they were a person not because they were any particular type of person. . . . [T]hat didn't come into it. . . . It wasn't a matter of color. You like some-one because you like them, not because of their color, or their non-color, or anything else," and, later, "I believe in human rights. The fact that we were in different teams, our skins were different colors, didn't make any difference." Norman's rhetoric of color blindness differs from that of white U.S. men's track and field teammate Larry Questad, who admits to being insulated from the racism his black teammates experienced. "I didn't see those things," Questad says, "And I never treated anybody like that. I'm kind of a White guy living in a Black world anyway, as being a sprinter. So, you know I had lots of friends and I trained with Black men. Until these games . . . oh, I suppose I made some, told jokes some time in my life I shouldn't have told. But I told jokes about Norwegians and Swedes, too, you know? It's all kind of the same thing." Questad's defensiveness and, later, accusations of reverse racism provide a critical counterpoint to Norman's racial sensitivity and interest in allyship.[23]

After describing some of the backlash following the Olympic demonstra-tion, Carlos says of Norman, "Though he did not raise a fist, he did lend a hand," while the narrator explains how the Australian establishment turned on Norman, including not fielding a team of sprinters at the subsequent Munich Games to keep Norman from competing in another Olympics (at the time he was ranked fifth in the world and had qualified numerous times for two events). In a clip from a speech Carlos astutely notes that he and Smith were able to shield each other, whereas "Norman had no one." The theme of progressive individualism is reasserted here by Olympian Cleve Livingston from the Harvard rowing team, who argues that 1968 was pivotal because of "the kind of leadership that Peter and Tommie and John showed. In 1968, I think you had a coming together of . . . an unusual collection of people who were willing to step up and show the kind of leadership it takes to move societies from one level to the next." What can safely be assumed from this depiction is that the Olympic demonstration would not have happened in the way it did were it not for the individual efforts of Smith, Carlos, and Norman.

Despite the fact that the demonstration and OPHR were led by black athletes, white allies and supporters are prominently featured in the documentaries. Media critics, particularly those interested in the ways white supremacy is reproduced in popular film, have shown how narrative structures privilege white experiences and characterize whites as heroes.[24] Even documentaries about a demonstration by black athletes give such sustained attention to white allies. In addition to the examples cited above, *Salute* is largely dedicated to the story of "antiracist-white-hero" Peter Norman and represents him as an equal partner in the event made memorable by Smith and Carlos's gesture (Norman did suggest the two Americans share the single pair of black gloves and asked them for an OPHR button to wear to the medal ceremony).

Fists of Freedom devotes substantial attention to the all-white Harvard rowing team's role in the Olympic Project for Human Rights, especially coxswain Paul Hoffman, who is interviewed in the film. *Salute* also mentions two members of the rowing team, Hoffman and Livingston, and reiterates the team's statement that "whatever the black athletes choose to do, we will support them, we'll be with them." This privileging of white experiences and allies relies upon some problematic signifying practices. In her analysis of how Orientalist tropes of "civilization" and "progress" are advanced discursively from a ubiquitous white Western standpoint in film, media scholar Raka Shome argues: "We now urgently need a critical vocabulary that can enable both White and non-White people to 'see' the operations of whiteness better—especially the hidden rhetorics through which it secures its everyday dominance in the cultural landscape. This is important because whiteness dominates all other racial configurations in this society. . . . Thus, unless we can build a vocabulary that can map the specificities through which whiteness enacts its dominance, we will not be able to devise adequate anti-racist strategies or rewrite the racial matrix in productive ways."[25]

Like Shome and others, we are concerned with the ways whiteness (as both a discourse and a racial identity) is "recentering, reasserting, and resecuring its power and privilege through various aspects of public life," including sport.[26] In the case of the aforementioned documentaries, whiteness has been shown to shape a "shut up and play" mentality that has been prominent in official responses to athletes' activism and protest. In particular, we are interested in exposing the ways in which sports culture, sports media, and documentaries reproduce hegemonic ideologies by signifying on racist stereotypes, promoting narratives of racial progress through individual achievement and gradual social change, and suppressing the collectivist dimensions and critical revolutionary potential of sports protest.

Throughout *Fists of Freedom* the demonstration is described as an "individual thing" and the athletes as "individuals with their own individual opinions" about racial politics. In *Fists of Freedom* Ralph Boston suggests the boycott failed because "everybody had their own purpose, their own reasons, their own ideas, and their own identity." Boston acknowledges that, being twenty-eight years old, having a family, and "having to go back to work when the Olympics were over," he did not want to boycott. In much the same way Bob Beamon argues that participation in the Olympic Games was "too much for me to sacrifice. I want a gold medal." Harry Edwards says, "Everybody is supposed to be piloting their own ship." Statements such as these reinforce an individualist narrative that conceals the substantial organizing and collective action that constituted the OPHR and that continues to influence sport protest to his day.

Even in *Salute*, in which collective action and shared burden are slightly more pronounced as themes than in *Fists of Freedom*, Carlos says of Norman, "I wish he was an American because we need someone like that around right now," suggesting that movements for racial equality require special (white) individuals with the heroic will to sacrifice. Carlos's statement echoes the concern among contemporary critics of racism that the impediments to justice are as much psychological as rhetorical challenges. As such they require white people to be willing to put their security on the line in the interests of freedom. In this regard Norman's lifelong commitment and friendship with Carlos and Smith (who served as pallbearers at Norman's funeral) exemplify solidarity in the struggle for racial equality. Norman's example again stands in stark contrast to the perspective shared by Larry Questad, who describes his reaction to the demonstration in *Salute*:

> I again was with some other people who were sitting up in the stands directly in front of the victory stand and I was just [exhales] sick. . . . I just think that what people should think about that 200-meter race in Mexico City is that Tommie broke the world record by three tenths of a second . . . and when I talk to people and when we talk about track and field and the 200 meters in Mexico City . . . I have yet in all these years, have someone tell me what they thought about the tremendous performance that he put on. . . . All they talk about is the black fist. That's a crime to me. . . . It's wrong. And if they hadn't done that, they would probably be happier, healthier, wealthier, and been more influential in their own community then they have been with what they're doing now.

Questad's stunning lack of understanding of his teammates' motives and the racism and discrimination they faced in their home country is countered by coach Payton Jordan, who says, "I thought it was a social statement that addressed some problems that had to be addressed. It had nothing to do with the Olympic Games, it had nothing to do with me as a coach. It had everything to do with society. . . . It came from their heart." Norman summarizes: "I say that they are heroes. They sacrificed what could have and should have been for them, a moment of personal glory that they worked very hard to attain."

Tommie Smith's implicated, communal reading of the demonstration stands within *Fists of Freedom* as a critique of the ideology of individual achievement, an ideology that is too often maintained at the expense of our memories of collective struggle: "As soon as the national anthem starts playing, my glove is going toward God. The black fist in the air was only in recognition of those who had gone. It was a prayer of solidarity. It was a cry for help by my fellow brothers and sisters in this country who had been lynched, who had been shot, who water hoses had been turned on. A cry for freedom." Smith's use of religious language and the rhetoric of commemoration situates the victory stand as critical resistance to active oppression. Yet the representations of John Carlos, especially in *Fists of Freedom*, reinvigorate Bad Buck stereotypes and tie them to the openly rebellious black athlete. As a result the rhetorical strategies of the Black Power movement are marginalized alongside the voice and perspective of John Carlos.

Reflections on Race and Representation

In the late 1960s many interpreted the victory stand as a Black Power statement. *Fists of Freedom* replaces this with a narrative in which Black Power is little more than a superficial marker of radical black identity. The new narrative, echoed in *Salute*, asserts that the progressive politics of a sanitized civil rights movement provided the impetus for the individual athletes' courageous action. Organizational efforts undertaken by the athletes, Harry Edwards, and other members of the Olympic Project for Human Rights are pushed aside in favor of Smith's and Norman's admittedly admirable stories of heroic individual achievement against adversity.

Moreover, by emptying Black Power of its radical social and political ideology and associating it with the violent actions of the Bad Buck–antihero, *Fists of Freedom* effectively constrains public memory of the Black Power movement. It glorifies the humble, nonviolent, and self-sacrificial strategies of the civil rights movement by positioning Smith as the hero of the 1968 Summer Olympics, but it does so at the expense of a more thoughtful depiction of the wider range of Black liberation politics. It denies the rhetorical complexity of both the civil rights and the Black Power movements by articulating the victory stand to the rhetorical strategies of the civil rights movement and to an ideology of progressive individualism. Likewise, *Salute* tempers its otherwise radical, collectivist message of interracial, international alliances among Olympic competitors with a combination of humanitarian rhetoric and antiracist white apologia.

Fists of Freedom and *Salute* both liberate and constrain public memory of the 1968 Olympic Games and the social movements that surrounded them. Relying upon subtle Uncle Tom and Bad Buck stereotypes, the films place Smith and Carlos in opposition to each other as a classic, but troubling, "odd couple." On the surface, both men are portrayed as heroes for their "courageous stand." The differences call attention to the ideologies embedded in the HBO documentary and can be articulated to public memory of the civil rights and Black Power movements. Peter Norman's story is told in detail in *Salute*, and the result is a more humanizing and complex portrayal of the lifelong relationship of the three Olympians who stood together as they received their medals on that fateful October day. Yet it is one that nonetheless downplays the influence of radical social movements and their members. Both films, albeit hinting at the plight of African Americans during that time, never fully focus on the issues that led to the creation of the Olympic Project for Human Rights or the larger movements to which it was articulated. As Phillips, O'Neill, and Osmond point out in their essay on sports history, although some documentaries delve into important issues such as race relations and other social issues, they often lack a clear and factual description of contexts and events.[27]

The implications of these articulations extend well beyond public memory of the 1968 Olympic Games, the civil rights movement, or the Black Power movement. Contemporary ideological orientations toward symbolic and institutional racism are shaped, in part, by our understandings of, and relationships to, the past. In fact, for many audience members documentaries such as *Fists of Freedom* and *Salute* communicate a progressive ideology of race relations on the mend. Such an ideology can both perpetuate and conceal contemporary iterations of racism that are often the premise of sport documentaries. Through this lens sport documentaries can be valued as resources with the potential to accurately depict historical events by challenging caricatures of sport heroes, antiheroes, and villains, providing a richer context and understanding of sport as a site of social meaning.

Representations of historical figures, the events with which they are associated, and their relationship to the past constitute discursive formations that shape understandings of the present and future. The signifying practices by which racist stereotypes and tropes persist in popular representations of black male athletes, for example, must be interrogated if we are to broaden and deepen the discursive reserve of representation, "devise adequate anti-racist strategies," and "rewrite the racial matrix in productive ways."[28] *Fists of Freedom* and *Salute* stand as important rhetorical and cultural artifacts, not just because of the significance of the story they tell about the Olympic protest, but also because of the how that story is told and the implications it has for a host of other athletic protests, from the 2014 "Hands Up, Don't Shoot" demonstration by St. Louis Rams players to NFL quarterback Colin Kaepernick's refusal to stand for the national anthem. As Herman Gray notes, "Representations of blackness that are produced and circulate within commercial media and popular culture constitute strategic cultural resources and social spaces where the traces, memories, textures, definitions, and, above all, struggles for and over social and cultural life are lived and waged."[29] By focusing on individuals, and framing them within a narrative of moderate, progressive social change due to heroic self-sacrifice and suffering, sports documentaries like these celebrate and promote significant moments in sports at the same time as they diminish the importance of collective struggle and movement politics in achieving that change. Shaping the meaning of already widely mediated events in these ways, sports documentaries become social issue anchors, challenging us to unmoor their representations so that we may chart a new course.

NOTES

1. Ian McDonald, "Situating the Sport Documentary," *Journal of Sport and Social Issues* 31, no. 3 (2007): 208–25; Bill Nichols, *Representing Reality: Issues and Concepts in Documentary* (Bloomington: Indiana University Press, 1991), 3–4.

2. McDonald, "Situating the Sport Documentary," 208–9.

3. Travis Vogan, "Institutionalizing Sport History in the Contemporary Sports Television Documentary," *Journal of Sport History* 41, no. 2 (2014): 195–204.

4. Ross Greenburg, *Fists of Freedom: The Story of the '68 Summer Games* (Home Box Office Productions, 1999); Matt Norman, *Salute* (Wingman Pictures International, 2008). These two documentaries can be considered as catalysts to more contemporary documentaries that focused on athlete activism such as *Shut Up and Dribble* and *More than an Athlete*.

5. Bill Nichols, *Blurred Boundaries: Questions of Meaning in Contemporary Culture* (Bloomington: Indiana University Press, 1994), 44, 4.

6. Henry Louis Gates, *The Signifying Monkey: A Theory of African-American Literary Criticism* (New York: Oxford University Press, 1988), 236.

7. Gates, *Signifying Monkey*, 124; Kim Euell, "Signifyin(g) Ritual: Subverting Stereotypes, Salvaging Icons," *African American Review* 31, no. 4 (1997): 667–75.

8. Elizabeth Birmingham, "Reframing the Ruins: Pruitt-Igoe, Structural Racism, and African American Rhetoric as a Space for Cultural Critique," *Western Journal of Communication* 63, no. 3 (1999): 291–309.

9. Richard Marback, "Detroit and the Closed Fist: Toward a Theory of Materialist Rhetoric," *Rhetoric Review* 17, no. 1 (1998): 74–76.

10. bell hooks, *Yearning: Race, Gender, and Cultural Politics* (Boston: South End Press, 1994), 104.

11. Gates, *Signifying Monkey*, 239. Citing Roger D. Abraham's *Deep Down in the Jungle: Negro Narrative Folklore from the Streets of Philadelphia*, Gates recounts one of "thousands of 'toasts' of the Signifying Monkey." It ends with this line: "Deep down in the jungle so they say / There's a signifying monkey down the way / There hadn't been no disturbin' in the jungle for quite a bit, / For up jumped the monkey in the tree one day and laughed, / 'I guess I'll start some shit.'"

12. Brent Musburger, "U.S. Olympic Chiefs Suspend 2 Black Medalists," *Chicago American*, October 18, 1968, C1.

13. John Carlos in discussion with the first author, February 23, 2001.

14. Clifford V. Thompson, "Dear White People: Stop Using the Term 'Uncle Tom,'" *Washington Post*, November 15, 2018, www.washingtonpost.com.

15. Clifford V. Thompson, *The Tragic Black Buck: Racial Masquerading in the American Literary Imagination* (New York: Peter Lang, 2004).

16. Patricia A. Turner, *Ceramic Uncles & Celluloid Mammies: Black Images and Their Influence on Culture* (New York: Anchor, 1994), 69.

17. Turner, *Ceramic Uncles & Celluloid Mammies*, 73.

18. Turner, *Ceramic Uncles & Celluloid Mammies*, 71.

19. At least three separate scenes in *Fists of Freedom* show black athletes dancing. We attend to this feature because of the prevalence in much popular culture, especially network television commercials, of images of young black people dancing despite their relative dearth of representation in most other recreational or professional settings. See Ellen Seiter, "Different Children, Different Dreams," in *Readings in Intercultural Communication: Experiences and Contexts*, ed. Judith Martin, Thomas Nakayama, and Lisa Flores, 212–19 (Boston: McGraw-Hill, 2002).

20. Don Bogle, *Toms, Coons, Mulattoes, Mammies, & Bucks: An Interpretive History of Blacks in American Film* (New York: Viking Press, 1973).

21. *Salute* includes several examples of Norman's humorous chiding of his competition, particularly Carlos, including verbal behaviors that could easily be described as "trash talking." In one heat, as he and John cross the finish line with Norman just a half step behind, he says, "You have this one, Carlos. I'll take the next!" and,

in the starting blocks of the 200-meter final, when a phone rang on the side of the track, Norman said, "You better get that, John. It's probably for you." Notably, Norman's behavior is treated in the film as a humorous means of relieving stress, whereas Carlos's antics are attributed to his boisterous personality and contentious character.

22. Michael Omi and Howard Winant, *Racial Formation in the United States from the 1960s to the 1990s* (New York: Routledge, 1994), 102.

23. *Salute* delves more deeply into the perspective of white 200-meter finalist Larry Questad and, through him, offers up a narrative of reverse discrimination for consideration by audience members. Questad, shot close-up in a white shirt and hat, describes a team meeting in the middle of the track when teammate Charlie Green got hurt and Questad was the first alternate: "That's five blacks and one white. In that meeting, they voted to run all black or not at all. So I know what prejudice is about. And I can tell you it was not fun being on that end of discrimination 'cause it cost me a gold medal. Five guys looked at me and said, 'Sorry. You're the wrong color; you're out.'"

24. Richard Dyer, "White," *Screen* 29, no. 4 (1988): 44–64; Kelly J. Madison, "Legitimation Crisis and Containment: The 'Anti-racist-White-Hero' Film," *Critical Studies in Mass Communication* 16, no. 4 (1999): 399–416.

25. Raka Shome, "Race and Popular Cinema: The Rhetorical Strategies of Whiteness in *City of Joy*," *Communication Quarterly* 44, no. 4 (1996): 515.

26. Shome, "Race and Popular Cinema," 515.

27. Murray G. Phillips, Mark E. O'Neill, and Gary Osmond, "Broadening Horizons in Sport History: Films, Photographs, and Monuments," *Journal of Sport History* 34, no. 2 (2007): 271–93.

28. Shome, "Race and Popular Cinema," 515.

29. Herman Gray, *Watching Race: Television and the Struggle for "Blackness"* (Minneapolis: University of Minnesota Press, 1995), 55.

7

Of Friends and Foes

Remembering Yugoslavia in Sport Documentaries

DARIO BRENTIN AND DAVID BROWN

There is a widespread tale in post-Yugoslav societies that closely ties the overall destiny of the former socialist federation to its sporting history. Often told as a somewhat joking conspiracy theory, the mystifying story claims that socialist Yugoslavia had to be broken apart from outside forces. Not because of political, military, or economic reasons, but because the West was scared of the ostensibly inevitable Yugoslav dominance in numerous global team sports that was to come in the 1990s.[1] While this popular tale blatantly simplifies the complexity of the Yugoslav dissolution and the myriad scholarly explanations as to why and how the federation fell apart, it nonetheless illustrates the centrality of sport to the ways that Yugoslavness and the breakup of the socialist federation was and still is understood.[2] To this day sport, among other fields of popular culture, remains one of the few social fields of late-socialist Yugoslavia that is remembered nostalgically across post-Yugoslav societies.[3] Documentary films have been of the most significant multipliers of narratives and debates through which Yugoslav sport history is remembered.[4]

Through five documentary films, *Once Brothers* (Michael Tolajian, 2010), *The Last Yugoslav Football Team* (Vuk Janic, 2000), *Znam Sta Je Ofsajd* (I know what offside means) (Arijana Saracevic Helac and Darko Sper, 2015), *Nedelja 13* (Sunday the 13th) (Mario Kovac and Igor Grahovec, 2015), and *Dinamo–Crvena zvezda / Domovinski rat je počeo na Maksimiru* (Dinamo–Red Star / The homeland war started on Maksimir) (Miljenko Manjkas, 2014), we take stock of how Yugoslav sports are represented and remembered in documentary films. Our analysis illustrates that more than just re-presenting historical facts and narratives, these films reflect social tensions. The sport documentaries in question encompass the tensions of narratives largely identifying Yugoslavia as a negative historical legacy, on the one hand, and popular sentiments toward its sporting history and achievements, on the other. This echoes Travis Vogan's assertion that "documentaries do not simply display reality but build histories that arrange indexical images into ideologically loaded narratives with the potential to resist and perpetuate the conditions they showcase."[5] By exploring how these films engage with, perpetuate, or challenge popular notions of Yugoslav history, we offer insight into the conflicted nature of memory in post-Yugoslav societies and explain how sport documentaries function in that context. In that sense we identify a number of recurring tropes in the mentioned documentaries: the memories of socialist Yugoslavia; "the day the war started" and the Maksimir riots on May 13, 1990; the Yugoslav wars of dissolution; and postwar reconciliation. As the representation of interaction between sport, the collapse of Yugoslavia, and the successes and failures of reconciliation have not been widely explored in film, this chapter makes both an empirical contribution to scholarship as well as an analysis of underrepresented thematics in sport documentaries.

Approaching Representation

The post-Yugoslav sport documentary remains marginal among the region's overall documentary output. However, in this genre the collapse of Yugoslavia is an omnipresent theme portrayed as a defining moment of the region's sporting history. Bernd Buder described the social roles of post-Yugoslav documentary production as caught between "national conscience-building and political enlightenment" and thus oscillating between "myth-making" and "analysis." Post-Yugoslav sports documentaries function similarly. Also, as pointed out by Margit Rohringer in her comprehensive study of Balkan documentary film, "In the Balkan case, the most dominant discourses of the new documentary films focus exactly on historical representations, particularly in correspondence with memory and identity discourses."[6]

Documentaries focusing on Yugoslav sport narrate the country's dissolution in particular ways, thereby shaping not just regional perception(s) but also the perception(s) of the region from the outside. The global commodity of sport and the established international interest in the peculiar role of sport during the Yugoslav dissolution make documentaries covering the topic marketable and translatable to a variety of audiences and contexts. Thus, some of the films we analyze use sport to teach global audiences about the country's descent into the wars of the 1990s. These films often prioritize commercial success over objectivity by catering to lucrative international audiences with marketable stories that simplify the political complexities they ostensibly illumine. Many of these documentaries prioritize "watchability" over critical substance, as Rob Stones argues in reference to post-Yugoslav war documentaries. Ian McDonald writes, "Sport documentaries have tended to capitalize on the market that has opened up for documentaries by emphasizing the human drama decontextualized from issues of power, and therefore are complicit in reinforcing dominant ideologies: here, the ideology of sport as the route to success and the exemplar of character."[7] The Yugoslav war and dissolution are precisely such situations in which sport documentary narratives tend to emphasize the personal and reproduce prevailing ideologies by avoiding contextualized reflection.

In this chapter, we look at how the discourse around the Yugoslav war and the postwar reconciliations function via documentary film. Following Stuart Hall we examine how the discourse "produces and connects with power, regulates conduct, makes up or constructs identities and subjectivities, and defines the way certain things are represented, thought about, practiced and studied." We identify the documentaries chosen for this study as spaces for reproducing memory narratives for local as well as international audiences. Similar to Richard Mills, who examined how football-related monuments in Southeast Europe produce memory narratives, we argue that sport documentaries function as popular *lieux de memoire*.[8] In addition to Mills, other recent scholarship has illustrated the salient ways in which the Yugoslav dissolution is remembered in and through post-Yugoslav sport.[9] The scholarship has yet to address how this remembering is addressed in sports documentaries, a gap our chapter addresses. We, however, do not differentiate analytically between documentaries produced for an international audience and those targeting local audiences, as both are significant transmitters of historical narratives that Dagmar Brunow calls "transcultural memory."[10]

Yugoslav Sporting Success

Yugoslavia's development into a global sports power during the 1980s stood out as a positive and integrative experience amid its economic hardship and political disintegration. As the historian Vjekoslav Perica put it, "While the country was falling apart, its athletes kept on winning together." After hosting the 1984 Winter Olympic Games in Sarajevo, Yugoslavia's athletes experienced a period of unprecedented international success. In basketball the Yugoslav national team was among the three best teams in the world, together with those of the United States and the Soviet Union; in 1987 the national football team won the U-20 FIFA World Cup; and in club competitions Jugoplastika Split dominated European basketball, while Red Star Belgrade won the European Champions Cup in 1990–91. The *Guardian*'s Jonathan Wilson argued that this "Golden Generation" of Yugoslav sport was destined for greatness throughout the 1990s, a narrative widely spread among international journalists and the broader public.[11]

Their "destiny" was, however, never fulfilled, as the country for which these athletes were competing dissolved. The "anachronistic" development of Yugoslav sport was accompanied by several other paradoxes. Simultaneous with the rising level of international success, the politicization of everyday life in late-socialist Yugoslavia was strongly mirrored in the social field of sport. Articulated predominantly within the community of "football fan tribes," sporting arenas increasingly witnessed recurring scenes of physical violence throughout the late 1980s and early 1990s.[12] This politicization of organized football fandom, particularly in combination with the fact that a significant number of organized football fans actively participated in the Yugoslav dissolution wars, resulted in an ever-growing, mostly journalistic, and particularly international fascination with the role of sport (athletes, fans, officials, and others) during this period. Perhaps the most outstanding incident illustrating how closely sport was intertwined with the country's overall fragility and dissolution into bloody conflict were the Maksimir riots on May 13, 1990. That day the "never-played game" between the football clubs Dinamo Zagreb and Red

Star Belgrade descended into violence among fans—and between fans and the police—is often marked as the symbolic date "when the war began."[13]

Yugoslav sport's ascribed significance during the Yugoslav dissolution underlines arguments in social sciences that identify sport as not merely a "reflection" of society but an "integral part of society . . . which may be used as a means of *reflecting on* society."[14] Documentaries are instrumental in this process of reflection. Sport's salient roles during the Yugoslav dissolution and subsequently in the formation and reproduction of collective identities in post-Yugoslav societies have been a field of intense scholarly research ever since.[15] While scholars recognized the peculiarity of sport during the Yugoslav dissolution and beyond, documentary filmmakers "discovered" this social field only recently. All the more impressive is that over the past several years a number of high-profile and popular documentaries have taken up Yugoslav sport as a central point of reference through which to narrate the late stages of Yugoslav history.

Yugoslav Sport Documentaries

To analyze the narratives of Yugoslav legacies in post-Yugoslav sport, the question of Yugoslav dissolution and subsequent wars, and the process of tentative reconciliation in the region, we selected documentaries we felt were most pertinent to our objectives rather than attempt an all-encompassing overview. We excluded the numerous documentaries dealing with contemporary football hooliganism in the region because of their lack of in-depth debate about the issues central to our research questions and their often uncritical attention to violence, which Emma Poulton describes as "hooliporn."[16]

Once Brothers and *The Last Yugoslav Football Team* are international productions broadcast on ESPN, though only *Once Brothers* was produced by the network. *Znam Sta Je Ofsajd* and *Nedelja 13* were both produced by regional teams of journalists, the first by Radio Television Vojvodina and the second by Al Jazeera Balkans. The final documentary was also produced in the region, albeit told from a "Croatian" perspective that uncritically reproduced nationalist and mythologized narratives about the Yugoslav dissolution in the context of football: *Dinamo–Crvena zvezda / Domovinski rat je počeo na Maksimiru*. Albeit from different national and international contexts, the chosen documentaries had very similar analytical deficiencies perpetuating similar "mythologized" and simplified narratives. As a result we elected not to distinguish between the different national settings of the productions.

Once Brothers, part of ESPN's *30 for 30* series, follows former National Basketball Association player Vlade Divac through contemporary ex-Yugoslavia while narrating the history of Yugoslavia's national basketball team. It focuses on Divac's relationship with another former NBA player, Drazen Petrovic, in the buildup to and during the wars. In a similar vein *The Last Yugoslav Football Team* looks back at the generation of football players from Yugoslavia who won the 1987 U-20 FIFA World Cup. Through a series of interviews with players and officials, the film reflects on the experience of playing together and then against each other. *Znam Sta Je Ofsajd* opens and closes in a cultural center in Belgrade, Serbia, where a group of young men and women from across the region watch Bosnia-Herzegovina and Croatia play their matches in the 2014 FIFA World Cup, while the rest of the film deals with the interaction of the Yugoslav wars and sports. *Dinamo–Crvena zvezda / Domovinski rat je počeo na Maksimiru* and *Nedelja 13* focus solely on the events at Maksimir. They reflect the happenings around May 13, 1990, and the "symbolic initiation" of the Yugoslav dissolution at Maksimir stadium.

Memories of Yugoslavia

All of our selected documentaries address, directly or indirectly, causes behind the collapse of Yugoslavia. While the manner, level of sophistication, and time devoted to explaining the conflict varies significantly, they all recycle a limited number of reasons for this collapse. More complex, though, is how the interviewees, in this case mostly athletes, look back on the Yugoslav period of their career and the conflicting memories of Yugoslavia they present.

Once Brothers provides a sophisticated look at Yugoslavia and the interaction of sport with the Yugoslav state, as well as the collapse, war and postwar transition. On the surface the film is about friendship as reflected through a civil war that cut along the same lines of the national origins of friends and teammates Divac, from the Serbian Republic, and Petrovic, from the Croatian Republic. Their friendship ultimately follows the same fate as that of the Yugoslav state, from unity to conflict to uneasy reconciliation. Through archival footage of various interviews with Petrovic (who died in a 1993 car accident) as well as original footage with Petrovic's family, Divac, and fellow basketball players Dino Radja and Toni Kukoč, *Once Brothers* presents the Yugoslavian years as the best of their lives and the state collapse and war as a deep, but ultimately inevitable, tragedy. At the center of the film is Divac's relationship with Petrovic and his other Croatian teammates, which followed the fate of the state. As the war intensifies the friendships fall apart, as the Croatian players were unable to resist calls to sever contact with Divac.

This is the only film from our selection that engages an academic figure to explain the Yugoslav context, particularly the war. The insertion of an academic perspective gives credibility to the film's explanation of complex historical context. It is also useful as a narrative tool to give a fast and easily understandable explanation of the conflict for an audience that may be otherwise uninformed. Gordon Baros, a well-known historian on the Balkan region, effectively presents what is widely known as the "ancient hatreds" narrative. This narrative posits that conflict between Croats and Serbs is the resurgence of lingering resentments from pre-Yugoslav times. As the state receded in the 1980s these conflicts were again able to be openly expressed. Baros's explanation, however, is at odds with how the players themselves remember the Yugoslav period, something that is never addressed in the film. They emphasize unity and claim that national origins played little to no role. They also indicate that these national differences were essentialized by the war and did not play much of a role in daily life before it.[17]

The Last Yugoslav Football Team follows a similar format, narrating the collapse in the team and the state through interviews with the last coach of a unified Yugoslav football team, Ivica Osim, and various players. The film presents a "Golden Generation" of Yugoslav football through the Yugoslav team that was supposed to achieve great success in the 1990s, but was ripped apart like the state. The players of this generation won the FIFA U-20 World Cup in Chile in 1987 as Yugoslavia. Many of the same players then qualified for FIFA World Cup in Italy in 1990 and reached the quarterfinals. They also qualified for the UEFA 1992 European Championships, but were removed ten days before the start of the tournament due to war. Shortly before that Ivica Osim left his position due to the start of the siege of Sarajevo.

As with *Once Brothers* the interviewed players present differing views, from nationalistic (former AC Milan player Zvonimir Boban and former Real Madrid player Predrag Mijatovic) to ambivalent (former AC Milan player Dejan Savićević) and regretful (former Lazio player Sinisa Mihajlovic as well as coach Ivica Osim). Yet the memories of Yugoslavia are always positive. Mijatovic and Robert Prosinecki discuss their happy childhood of playing football with other local boys in dirt lots and fields.[18] They also reflect on the unity of the youth team that won the FIFA U-20 World Cup, which Savićević calls the peak of his career. On a superficial level the film explains how these friendships fared with the war and its aftermath. The players, interviewed after the war, all reflect and negotiate this change from a unified Yugoslavia with successful sports teams, to a divided peninsula with poor teams.

Znam Sta Je Ofsajd reflects on how people responded to the war, how they acted in the wartime, and how they negotiated, also in the postwar generation, the reality of having been at war and experiencing such a radical shift in identity. In the film a young, and presumably Bosniak, man born in 1993 points out that his parents had told him how beautiful the "Brotherhood and Unity" feeling was during Yugoslavia. In *The Last Yugoslav Football Team* Ivica Osim reflects upon how the places like Sarajevo, and particularly the Bosniak population within those places, had the most to lose from the collapse of the state.

"The Day the War Started"

All the films locate the Maksimir riots of May 13, 1990, as the symbolic start to the Yugoslav wars. Even when the riots are not directly addressed, such as in *Once Brothers*, images from the stadium are central to representing the Yugoslav collapse.

The two documentaries that exclusively focus on the Maksimir riots are *Nedelja 13* and *Dinamo–Crvena zvezda / Domovinski rat je počeo na Maksimiru*. *Nedelja 13* adopts a deliberately post-Yugoslav orientation that gives voice to players, fans, officials, and security personnel from all over former Yugoslavia to offer a comprehensive representation of "what really happened that day." Underlining the singularity of the incident, the documentary meticulously reconstructs the event by focusing on the failed securitization of the high-risk game. It reiterates how despite "everyone feeling that something might happen," the outburst of violence came as a surprise. Throughout the documentary members of the organized fan groups utilized the opportunity to perpetuate a glorified image as "defenders of the nation [they represented]" during the riots. In contrast to *Nedelja 13*, *Dinamo–Crvena zvezda / Domovinski rat je počeo na Maksimiru* portrays an unequivocally "Croatian" perspective. Albeit similar in style, it roots the riots in a popular Croatian political myth that understands them as a constitutive part in the formation of Croatian independent statehood.[19]

The Wars That Followed

Nedelja 13 and *Dinamo–Crvena zvezda / Domovinski rat je počeo na Maksimiru* connect the Yugoslav wars of dissolution to the ritualized violence of organized football fans.[20] It emphasizes rivalries around Yugoslavia, the manipulation of fans at Maksimir, and the recruitment of the Red Star Belgrade–organized fan group Delije by Zeljko Ražnatović-Arkan.[21] War is thus thematically interwoven with football fan culture. The fans continued their rivalry as soldiers. The documentaries suggest that the fans were largely manipulated into the conflict, yet were the standard-bearers for nationalism. Giving virtually no other context or information for the conflict, the films suggest the war was inevitable and happened suddenly. The narrative never gets much more complex than that: there was nationalism, the fans were agents of nationalism, the fans were manipulated into fighting each other and going into the war, and not much has changed except there are separate states.

Traveling to Croatia and Serbia is then the perfect occasion for documentaries to connect the fan cultures to actual war. In both films the fans are presented as the source and epitome of nationalist ideology. The documentaries continually return to the narrative and mythology of the football fans that started the war in the stadium riot in Zagreb and then went to the front lines of the Yugoslav wars to continue their fight. The short explanatory sequences give the impression that the fans literally ran out of the stadium and into the trenches. But this was not the case. Before any of the fighting started Red Star Belgrade won the European Cup, and the Yugoslav football team reached the quarterfinal of the 1990 FIFA World Cup.

With these examples the films gloss over important and complex events that are vital to the context of the events the purport to document. They select particular narratives, images, and events to provide the bare minimum context that makes the "real story" understandable and, more important, entertaining and marketable. This is precisely where inaccurate discourses are perpetuated, such as a particular side being the aggressor or the "ancient hatreds" narrative.

But the broader social relationships changed with the onset of the war, and the films show this change. *Once Brothers* offers two factors that explain this transformation in the relationships between the players. First, Divac gets wrapped up in an altercation with a fan as the Yugoslavian basketball team is celebrating its victory at the 1990 World Championships. The fan had run to the players after the final buzzer brandishing the Croatian flag. Divac pushed him away and threw the flag to the floor. Media in Croatia and Serbia jumped on this, with the Croatians labeling him a traitor and the Serbians proclaiming him a hero. Divac himself claims he saw the tournament, taking place in Zagreb, as a chance to present a unified Yugoslavia and that he simply did not want nationalist symbols to usurp the Yugoslav ones. But Petrovic took it as a slight. The other factor in dividing the team and the relationships among its players that *Once Brothers* cites is the fact that the Croatian players were pressured by friends and family to avoid Divac during the war years. While he was already problematic for the flag incident, he was now also seen as a Serb and, consequently, a political enemy. The documentary includes Divac discussing the sadness of losing this Yugoslav community within the NBA and in the national team.

At the same time *Once Brothers* presents Divac and Petrovic as taking very different views toward the war and the collapse of Yugoslavia. Petrovic turns more toward nationalism and identifies squarely with Croatia. Divac remains a Yugoslav and claims Serbs and Croats are the same people. This documentary shows this tension reflected in their personalities. Divac is warm, happy-go-lucky, and funny; Petrovic is serious, cold, and intense. *Once Brothers* suggests the national struggle was reproduced between the players and symbolically by the teams as a whole. The Croatian national team, for example, refused to remain on the podium for the Yugoslav anthem at the European Championships award ceremony in 1995. *Once Brothers* combines with *The Last Yugoslav Football Team* to suggest that the symbolic struggle was carried by the fans in football and by the players in basketball.

Unlike Divac and Petrovic, the football players *The Last Yugoslav Football Team* presents did not reproduce the political conflict within their personal relationships. Rather, they retained their friendships above it all. This becomes paradoxical at times in the film. Zvonimir Boban talks about his love for Croatia, how the Yugoslav anthem was never his own, and how he even felt some guilt over not being in the war. Later he talks about how much he misses Savićević and how they remain in touch and good friends. But Savićević does not share Boban's clear nationalist sentiment. Feeling that something was lost, even if he does not lament the failure of the state as such, he says that the obsession with defining each other as "Serb, Montenegrian, or Croat" was "our tragedy." Reinforcing the existence of an enduring bond, the filmmakers show images such as the one where Mihajlovic and former Real Madrid player Davor Šuker, playing on opposite teams in the Croatia-Yugoslavia qualification match, exchange friendly words and a high-five while play is going on. This is clearly meant to illustrate the symbolism of the match. It indicated that while fans booed the opponent's national anthem—and respectively chanted either "Kill the Serbs" or "Kill the Croats"—this sentiment was not necessarily felt on the pitch.

The documentaries simplify the war by representing it through personal relationships. They suggest that war destroys the sense of unity that had been the norm, which manifests through teams and friendships dissolving. In a similar vein *Znam Sta Je Ofsajd* portrays the Yugoslav wars through gruesome individual stories happening during the siege of Sarajevo. In particular, the story of the handball player Goran Čengić, who was murdered in 1992 while trying to defend a neighbor, occupies a central narrative in the documentary.

Forms of Reconciliation (or Not)

In general, each documentary identifies sport as a potential social field of reconciliation for the post-Yugoslav space. The narratives and messages they portray, however, are often ambivalent. While *Once Brothers* is about two estranged former teammates who parted ways due to the breakup of Yugoslavia and were incapable of reconciling, the public discourse about the documentary was filled with contestation and disagreement—particularly in Croatia.[22] But apart from the contentious public discourse about *Once Brothers*, the film itself also exhibits a number of scenes that contradict its overall reconciliatory nature. It counterposes a scene of Divac meeting the family of Petrovic and visiting his grave with footage of the fan in Zagreb calling him a "Četnik," the name for Serbia's nationalist paramilitary, again adopted during the Yugoslav war.[23] A very similar, and also unscripted, incident occurs in *The Last Yugoslav Football Team* when Dejan Savićević is confronted during an interview in front of the hotel before the Croatia-Yugoslavia football match and called a "piece of shit" at almost the precise moment he was talking about feeling comfortable in Zagreb.

The films suggest that if everything would have been left to the athletes, there would not have been such a bloody dissolution in the first place and there would be no need for such nationalist animosity between the former Yugoslav republics. In general, the athletes remained adamant that (organized) fans, the political class, and everyday people experienced and reproduced the conflict in the sport arena more than the players, with some notable exceptions, of course. Furthermore, the documentaries often distinguish between the national team and the state/political system. Athletes highlight the camaraderie and feelings of togetherness among them independent of a patriotism toward Yugoslavia.

The question of reconciliation through sport is most tangibly addressed through the regional leagues that have established in several sports since the early 2000s in the former Yugoslavia, though they are not covered in great detail in our selected films.[24] While almost all interviewees express strong support for the idea of a regional football league's potentially integrative and reconciliatory roles, they more or less agree that "it is too early" and that "the wounds of the wars still need to heal."

Znam Sta Je Ofsajd most directly addresses the question of reconciliation through sport. Presenting a counternarrative to the nationalist and sectarian discourses coming out of stadia throughout the region, the film portrays a screening of the 2014 Bosnian-Herzegovinian and Croatian World Cup matches in Belgrade. Contrasting themselves to the "hooligans in the stadia," the people in the opening scene highlight that they want to initiate regional understanding and friendship through sport. The interviewees express numerous "Yugo-nostalgic" views such as a young participant who states: "My parents and elders have told me how there was a really beautiful brotherhood, and unity and I am really happy that this is slowly and gradually coming back . . . and I am happy that we are finally coming together in the capital of former Yugoslavia. I am really happy because of that." Neither this nor further such statements is critically questioned in the film.[25]

Nationalistic Yugo-Nostalgics

We set out to consider how Yugoslavia, the wars that dismantled the country in the 1990s, and the postwar reconciliation have been represented in sport documentaries. While there are fewer sport documentaries dealing with Yugoslavia and its disintegration than social or political ones, the popularity and visibility of these films have nonetheless been significant. The common features across all films revolve around largely nostalgic memories of Yugoslav times, a sense that the war was something tragic but unavoidable, and the belief that the separation was ultimately the logical path. The documentaries use sport to depict Yugoslavia as a doomed project that inevitably and necessarily collapsed. But there is a certain nostalgia for togetherness that remains in reference to the "Golden Generation." Athletes kept friendships alive across the lines of conflict or reconstituted them since. There is some regret over the emphasis on what differentiates people in the region, but also a sense that there is no going back and that the war and separation created the correct path for the states.

Nationalism is part of many of the featured athletes' perspectives, but often in a soft form that suggests there can be a friendly, civil rivalry between the ex-Yugoslav states. The juxtaposition of the devastating war with players in their villas, who have little to say about the total devastation of some parts of their state and the economy (along with the contin-ued suffering of people through the economic transition of the 1990s), is striking. In the films we studied the violent form of nationalism is largely attributed to fans.

Some of these films end up reproducing notions of Balkanism, where the Balkans is depicted as the internal other compared to (western) Euro-pean stability, high living standards, and so forth.[26] They reinforce this with a lack of any reference to (western) European involvement in the Yugoslav conflict. Even when there are images of the 1999 NATO bomb-ing of Belgrade—as in *The Last Yugoslav Football Team*—they are left unexplained and function as a temporal reference and justification for the delay of the Serbia-Croatia 2000 European football championship qualification game. Absent from the films' narratives of the state's col-lapse and subsequent disintegration are the role played by political elites in Yugoslavia and western Europe, and the economy. As a result we are given the impression of relations between the successor states defined by Balkanism, forming a crude, reductive view of the conflict that is interested in selling us on the worst stereotypes of football fans but also of the Balkans/Yugoslavia, as an inherently violent and "different" peo-ple. Such oversimplified representation relates back to our point about the tension that exists between making an accurate documentary and a documentary that is marketable.

These documentaries, like many mainstream and commercial produc-tions, perpetuate rather than question dominant national narratives. This echoes Margit Rohringer's assessment of post-Yugoslav documentaries as spaces that rarely question historical representations. International pro-ductions usually tend to focus on more than "just one side" of the story by offering conflicting views of the Yugoslav dissolution. At the same time, however, these productions struggle to go beyond dominant, simplistic international narratives of the collapse of Yugoslavia and the subsequent wars. This is certainly a problem of setting a sport documentary in a context that includes war and state collapse. Rather than explore the nuances of the collapse, the documentaries only superficially address it through focusing on people and teams in the interest of the commercially driven efforts to foster watchability. In short, we argue the films stay within confines of the most popular and problematic narratives and chose to tell the stories through themes that have dominated the Yugoslav documentary genre in general.

NOTES

1. See Sanjin Pejkovic, "Dražen, Divac i mi-zauvijek," November 18, 2010, www.e -novine.com.

2. For a scholarly overview about the Yugoslav dissolution and the Yugoslav wars, see Catherine Baker, *The Yugoslav Wars of the 1990s* (London: Palgrave Macmillan, 2015).

3. See Mitja Velikonja, "Lost in Transition: Nostalgia for Socialism in Post-socialist Countries," *East European Politics and Societies* 23, no. 4 (2009): 535–51; and Breda Luthar and Maruša Pušnik, "The Lure of Utopia: Socialist Everyday Spaces," in *Remembering Utopia: The Culture of Everyday Life in Socialist Yugoslavia*, ed. Bread Luthar and Maruša Pušnik, 1–37 (Washington DC: New Academia, 2010).

4. See Margit Rohringer, *Documents on the Balkans: History, Memory, Identity— Representations of Historical Discourses in the Balkan Documentary Film* (Newcastle upon Tyne: Cambridge Scholars, 2009), 45–46.

5. Travis Vogan, "Institutionalizing and Industrializing Sport History in the Contemporary Sports Television Documentary," *Journal of Sport History* 41, no. 2 (2014): 196.

6. Bernd Buder, "Nationale Fragen und Kriegsverbrechen im Post-Jugoslawischen Film," *Südosteuropa* 56, no. 4 (2008): 556–71; Rohringer, *Documents on the Balkans*, 5.

7. Rob Stones, "Social Theory, the Civic Imagination and Documentary Film: A Postmodern Critique of the 'Bloody Bosnia' Season's *The Roots of War*," *Sociology* 36, no. 2 (2002): 356; Ian McDonald, "Situating the Sport Documentary," *Journal of Sport & Social Issues* 31, no. 3 (2007): 221. See also Vogan, "Institutionalizing and Industrializing Sport History," 196.

8. Stuart Hall, "The Work of Representation," in *Representation: Cultural Representations and Signifying Practices*, ed. Stuart Hall (London: SAGE, 1997), 6; Richard Mills, "Commemorating a Disputed Past: Football Club and Supporters' Group War Memorials in the Former Yugoslavia," *History: The Journal of the Historical Association* 97 (2012): 540–77; Pierre Nora, "Between Memory and History: Les Lieux de Mémoire," *Representations* 26 (1989): 7–25.

9. Benjamin Perasović and Marko Mustapić, "Football, Politics and Cultural Memory: The Case of HNK Hajduk Split," *Culture/Културa* 6 (2014): 51–61; Dario Brentin, "Ready for the Homeland? Ritual, Remembrance and Political Extremism in Croatian Football," *Nationalities Papers* 44, no. 6 (2016).

10. Dagmar Brunow, *Remediating Transcultural Memory: Documentary Filmmaking as Archival Intervention* (Berlin: De Gruyter, 2015).

11. Vjekoslav Perica, "United They Stood, Divided They Fell: Nationalism and the Yugoslav School of Basketball, 1968–2000," *Nationalities Papers* 29, no. 2 (2001): 269. See Jonathan Wilson, *Behind the Curtain: Travels in Eastern European Football* (London: Orion, 2006); and Tom Hawking, "Why the Most Important Olympic Basketball Team Wasn't the Dream Team," *Rolling Stone*, August 2, 2016, www.rollingstone.com.

12. Srđan Vrcan, *Nogomet—politika—nasilje: Ogledi iz sociologije nogometa* (Zagreb: Jesenski i Turk, 2003), 21.

13. See Diego Pacheco, "Heroes and Bad Blue Boys," *In Bed with Maradona*, July 19, 2011; Olivia Goldhill, "Why Football Can Change the World," *Telegraph*, July 9, 2014; Matt Gault, "Zvonimir Boban and the Kick That Started a War," *These Football Times*, September 28, 2015. As a critique to these interpretations, see Dario Brentin, "The 'Maksimir Myth': 25 Years since the 'Symbolic Dissolution' of Socialist Yugoslavia," *Balkanist Magazine*, May 13, 2015.

14. Jeremy MacClancy, ed., *Sport, Identity and Ethnicity* (Oxford: Berg, 1996), 4.

15. Neven Andjelić, "The Rise and Fall of Yugoslavia: Politics and Football in the Service of the Nation(s)," *Südosteuropa* 62, no. 2 (2014): 99–125; Dario Brentin, "'A Lofty Battle for the Nation': The Social Roles of Sport in Tuđman's Croatia," *Sport in Society* 16, no. 8 (2013): 993–1008; Ivan Đorđević, "Twenty Years Later: The War Did (Not) Begin at Maksimir; An Anthropological Analysis of the Media Narratives about a Never Ended Football Game," *Glasnik Etnografskog Instituta SANU* 60, no. 2 (2012): 201–16.

16. Emma Poulton, "'I Predict a Riot': Forecasts, Facts and Fiction in 'Football Hooligan' Documentaries," *Sport in Society* 11, no. 2–3 (2008): 334.

17. Another problem with this interpretation is that that it has been largely discredited in academia. Although popularized by journalistic accounts of the war, and thus very present in popular accounts of the war, it doesn't hold up under scrutiny. See, for example, Robert Kaplan, *Balkan Ghosts: A Journey through History* (New York: St. Martin's Press, 1993). For critical discussion on the theory, see Dejan Jović, "The Disintegration of Yugoslavia: A Critical Review of Explanatory Approaches," *European Journal of Social Theory* 4, no. 1 (2001): 101–20; Jasna Dragović-Soso, "Why Did Yugoslavia Collapse? An Overview of Contending Explanations," in *State Collapse in South-Eastern Europe: New Perspectives on Yugoslavia's Disintegration*, ed. Jasna Dragović-Soso and Lenard J. Cohen (Lafayette IN: Purdue University Press, 2008).

18. Only featured in an extended version of the film released in 2011.

19. Mills, *Commemorating a Disputed Past*, 575; Brentin, *A Lofty Battle for the Nation*, 1002–3.

20. See Srđan Vrcan and Dražen Lalić, "From Ends to Trenches, and Back: Football in the Former Yugoslavia," in *Football Cultures and Identities*, ed. Gary Armstrong and Richard Giulianotti, 176–85 (London: Macmillan, 1999).

21. Zeljko Ražnatović-Arkan made a name for himself through numerous criminal offenses across Western Europe during the 1980s. In collaboration with the Yugoslav State Security Service he rose to become the leader of the Red Star fans, uniting them into a single fan group, the Delije. His illustrious career furthermore saw him become the head of the Serbian Volunteers Guard. He was indicted by the International Criminal Tribunal for the former Yugoslavia for war crimes committed in Croatia and Bosnia-Herzegovina but did not live to see his trial, as he was killed in a shoot-out in a Belgrade hotel in 2000. See Christian Axboe Nielsen, "The Goalposts of Transition: Football as a Metaphor for Serbia's Long Journey to the Rule of Law," *Nationalities Papers* 38, no. 1 (2010): 87–103.

22. Vjekoslav Perica, "Heroes of a New Kind: Commemorations and Appropriations of Yugoslavia's Sporting and Pop-Cultural Heritage," in *Post-Yugoslavia: New Cultural and Political Perspectives*, ed. Dino Abazović and Mitja Velikonja (Basingstoke: Palgrave Macmillan, 2014), 113. For a debate in Croatian media, see Tomislav Pakrac and Vlado Radičević, "Pet velikih propusta u filmu o Draženu i Divcu," Gol.hr, November 3, 2011, http://gol.dnevnik.hr; and Ojdana Koharevic, "Dražena i Divca nije posvadila zastava već nešto drugo," *Slobodna Dalmacija*, October 22, 2016.

23. The Četnik movement was a Serbian nationalist and monarchist paramilitary organization existing from the first half of the twentieth century. Loyal to the monarchy, it was formally headed by Dragoljub "Draža" Mihailovic during World War II. Although initially formed as a resistance group opposing Germany, it was responsible for massive atrocities against Croats and Muslims in Croatia and Bosnia-Herzegovina while openly cooperating with the Italian and German forces during World War II.

24. See Shay Wood, "Football after Yugoslavia: Conflict, Reconciliation and the Regional Football League Debate," *Sport in Society* 16, no. 8 (2013): 1077–90.

25. See Zala Volcic, "Yugo-Nostalgia: Cultural Memory and Media in the Former Yugoslavia," *Critical Studies in Media Communication* 24, no. 1 (2007): 21–38.

26. See Maria Todorova, *Imagining the Balkans* (Oxford: Oxford University Press, 1997); and Vesna Goldsworthy, "Invention and In(ter)vention: The Rhetoric of Balkanization," in *Balkan as Metaphor: Between Globalization and Fragmentation*, ed. Dušan Bjelić and Obrad Savić, 25–38 (Cambridge MA: MIT Press, 2002).

8

"Measuring Up"

Fathers, Sons, and the Economy of Death in Mountain Film Documentaries

RAY GAMACHE

This chapter analyzes cinematic practices and tropes in William A. Kerig's *The Edge of Never* (2009) and Stephen Judson's *The Alps* (2007) that utilize an economy of death to satisfy audience expectations for what has been called "ecstatic transcendence." Bringing the specter of death to the foreground, the discourse around ecstatic transcendence emphasizes the performative aspect of the participants as well as offering viewers a possibility of resistance to the existential angst of modern life in which the contemplation of one's own mortality has been all but suppressed. Both of these mountain film documentaries offer a ritualized connection between those who died while participating in a sport and the heirs who follow in their footsteps. This ritualized connection is conceptualized through a discourse of practical nostalgia, symbolic imagery, and the creation of martyrs. The dead men, Trevor Petersen and John Harlin II, are portrayed as fallen heroes worthy of emulation by their sons, Kye Petersen and John Harlin III, who claim vindication over the mountain by skiing or climbing the same route on which each man's father was killed. This project argues that while risk and death are an intrinsic part of adventure sports, they are discursively even more fundamental to providing film viewers with a mediated postadventure experience whose narrative representations suggest redemption is achieved by facing death with courage.[1]

Both *The Edge of Never* and *The Alps* exemplify the mountain film documentary, an important subgenre of the sport documentary, which consists of films with defining features, ideologies, and modes of production, as

153

well as specific systems of expectations and repertoires that viewers bring to the cinema. The repetitive nature of genre production and consumption produces "generic verisimilitude," the idea that works within a (sub)genre are so defined as they conform to the rules of the genre.[2] As more films are produced within a (sub)genre, audience expectations evolve, "continually hybridizing and adding characteristics with time—all of which add to the historical identity of the genre." In the mountain film documentary, historical identity is rooted within an incredibly large body of alpinism literature as well as travelogue lectures and slide shows that predate film. Additionally, mountain film documentaries, slotted into events like the Banff Centre Mountain Film and Book Festival and an accompanying World Tour—one of more than seventy such festivals—have created a nomenclature of adventure that engenders genre-based viewing expectations, as well as a commercial infrastructure with exhibition and distribution networks that market to a wider audience than aficionados of sport.[3] Mountain film documentaries such as *Into Thin Air* (Robert Maskowitz, 1997), *Touching the Void* (Kevin Macdonald, 2004), *Skiing Everest* (Les Guthman, 2009), *The Wildest Dream* (Anthony Geffen, 2011), and *Meru* (Jimmy Chin and Elizabeth Chai Vasarhelyi, 2015) enjoyed considerable popular and critical attention. The fascination for high-intensity adventure culminated in the recent release of *Free Solo* (Chin and Vasarhelyi, 2018), documenting Alex Honnold's free climb up El Capitan, where certain death hung to his every move. Satisfying interests requires a constant stream of content, along with extratextual materials like advertising posters, stills, reviews, interviews, websites, and social media, to which digital portals allow easy access.

Death is positioned as the central discursive motif in both *The Edge of Never* and *The Alps*. Kerig and Judson have invested representations of mountaineering expeditions with religious, mystical overtones around the two dead men as a means to organize audience involvement and response.[4] By providing a glimpse into the reality, immediacy, and humanness of death, the films offer narratives in which the fallen are commemorated as heroes. The viewer identifies with the dead and the bereaved. This economy of death is constructed around discourse elevating the dead mountaineers into martyrs, satisfying a cultural need for symbolic heroes. Linking present practitioners to fallen heroes reminds viewers the endeavor is larger than any individual.[5] In this sense the past presents a sense of tradition, "a sense of value and significance that connects contemporary performances and conditions of the past."[6]

Awareness of death anchors viewers in particular experiences, identities, and pleasures that invariably legitimate a filmmaker's view of reality. Death becomes a powerful means to capture the real, similar to narrative movement in fictional films. As Vivian Sobchack observes, "While death is generally experienced in fiction films as representable and often excessively visible, in documentary films it is experienced as confounding representation, as exceeding visibility." The documentary camera's ability to capture a death on screen allows viewers access to endangerment without real risk, calling to mind Edmund Burke's idea that the passions associated with pain, risk, and endangerment activate deeply rooted feelings related to self-survival but only when we can experience them without encountering actual danger. Viewers become willfully immersed in cinematic terror because they are protected against actual injury or death by the medium. For viewers the specter of death constantly hovers around the protagonists, as though mountaineers live every moment as if it were their last, enraptured by what Peter Berger called the experience of ecstasy, "standing, or stepping *outside* reality as commonly defined."[7] However, this is clearly the result of deleting the mundane—shots of preparation, training, reconnaissance, packing, traveling, and the oftentimes endless waiting for the right conditions.

Kerig and Judson instead offer a distillation of the spectacular, an accommodation of the hyperreal in which risk and ecstatic transcendence are translated into discursive narratives.[8] Overcoming death by facing fear, arguably a foundational trope of alpinism literature and mountain films, is presented as a possibility for resistance to the safe and secure mundane life. The importance of the individual, shown on an intimate level combating extraordinary real-life situations, lends a universality to the story. Production techniques must span the gap between viewer and adventurer since many mountain film documentaries involve expeditions far removed from the realm of the viewing audience. Those techniques involve creating empathy for the protagonist, oftentimes by zooming in on the individual within a panoramic view of the particular environment, which in turn conveys the immensity of the landscape, as well as its threatening and challenging nature. In shaping their narratives around death, Kerig and Judson invariably promote and legitimate a particular way of remembering events of the past. How "facts" of the past are produced and mobilized in discourse is an appropriate focus for analysis. As Susan Birrell notes, "If one conceptualizes the events of the past as texts, a focus on intertextuality—on the interconnections among texts and narratives as they stretch from the past to the present and back again—provides a strategy for analysis that promises to reveal the complicated nature of the past and our knowledge of it."[9] Discourse analysis provides a broad cultural context from which to unpack meanings and significances within constituted relations of power.

Last, because these documentaries revolve around sons following in the tracks and trails of their fathers, it is important to contextualize the ways in which these narratives participate in the fluid and situational conversations about the meanings, practices, and contravening discourses of masculinity and the various ways people understand masculinity within adventure sports. Rather than impose a rigid conceptualization of masculinity to these documentaries, this chapter interrogates the complex power relations in being father, son, husband, and friend as well as the conflicting interpretations of masculinity and enactments of manhood that constitute and are constituted by discursive practices within social life. Within the context of the mountain film subgenre, there is no singular way to be a man, for, as Susan Frohlick notes, "The outcome of the highly regulated gender practices of high-altitude mountaineering and its cultural productions and representations is neither straightforward nor predictable. It cannot be read simply as an instance of hypermasculinity."[10] Rather than conceptualize the internalized cultural standards and beliefs that guide men's behaviors, this analysis considers the impact of discourse in articulating masculine norms in the relationships boys have with fathers and father figures.

Trevor in a Can

The first sequence of Kerig's *The Edge of Never: A True Story of Skiing's Big Mountain Tribe* (Eon Productions, 2009) establishes the inherent danger of skiing the mountains in Chamonix, France. Over a series of black-and-white aerial shots of mountains and glaciers, we hear the voice of skier Glen Plake explaining the film's main story line, which centered on the fifteen-year-old son of Trevor Petersen. "Kye wasn't just a little kid anymore. The possibility of him skiing down the run his father died on was a very real possibility." In the next shots a skier checks the snow conditions, and Kerig calls for quiet as the cameras roll. The skier is instructed, "Drop in," and Kerig uses very tight shots of an alpine skier executing a series of turns before suddenly disappearing into a crevasse. Kerig is then shown talking on a device communicating what happened—the skier has a collapsed lung, broken leg, and perhaps a broken back. As a mountain rescue helicopter hoists a stretcher with the injured skier up to transport him to the hospital, Kerig tells the person on the other end of the line, "Say a prayer." The next shot is of Kerig speaking directly to the camera, telling the audience, "That's me . . . trying not to hyperventilate or throw up. I'm living the nightmare I've had since this whole thing began. A friend, a skier, is badly hurt, and it's all my fault. If I hadn't cooked up this whole film, he wouldn't be in a stretcher right now hovering between life and death."

Through dramatic juxtaposition, one of many fiction film techniques employed, the audience is led to believe that the film's protagonist, Kye Petersen, the son of Trevor Petersen and Tanya Reck Petersen and the only person identified by name in this sequence, could be the person badly injured in the accident, precipitating Kerig's nightmare. This opening sequence raises ethical questions related to the "responsibilities of the filmmaker and audience when through their desire to vicariously experience extreme sport, participants experience the very real consequences of injury and death."[11]

That Kerig accepts his responsibilities of filming in an environment of high risk is readily apparent. Kerig flashes back to the film's germination, explaining that he is willing to accept the acute emotional and ethical strain of that responsibility because making the documentary is his vehicle for financial and spiritual redemption. Kerig has carved out a life in the mountains "as a second-rate professional skier and middling ski journalist." However, he now finds himself in a deep hole, living across the street from a methamphetamine dealer, and not knowing how he can provide financial security for his wife, daughter, and a son on the way. Rather than accept a job with benefits and a retirement plan, he wants to find answers as to what "made this mountain life worth living in the first place." By positioning his own story within the quest to have Kye ski down the run that killed Trevor, Kerig follows a trend in filmmaking that incorporates "the self-reflexive, self-promoting, omnipresent filmmaker," who throughout the filming process has an awareness of his own performance, his own rite of passage into a stable career, but one that would not be considered mainstream.[12]

The Edge of Never dramatizes what it means to become a member of the big-mountain skiing tribe by having Kye learn from those entrusted with the roots and core values that define the culture. As such the film uses "practical nostalgia," which Debbora Battaglia defines as a means to provide an enduring sense of continuity while providing the necessary distance for the development of a cultural critique of the contemporary scene.[13] Thus, extreme skiing's heroes, including Glen Plake, Eric Pehota, Anselme Baud, Mike Hattrup, and Doug Coombs, serve as mentors for Kye. Kerig blends the old and the new through a montage of vintage footage of Trevor and Pehota in Alaska, as well as Kye performing tricks in a terrain park at Whistler-Blackcomb in British Columbia, Canada. Establishing Trevor as one of the heroes of the tribe is conveyed by showing his intense love of the sport, unbounded enthusiasm, and ability to balance the demands of skiing and family. Pehota and Trevor are identified as the Butch Cassidy and Sundance Kid of extreme skiing, with Pehota describing those early days in Alaska as "a cowboy show for sure . . . the wild Wild West, with guns, helicopters, and first descents." By providing highlights of their skiing exploits Kerig stimulates emotional responses within affective economies. In this sense the repurposing of "first descents" creates renewable texts about athletic endeavors and human aspiration. This man-against-nature theme facilitates the filmmaker's tendency to veil ideological assumptions about white male privilege with which they are inextricably bound. Those assumptions are constituted around transcendent narratives about democratic freedoms couched in America's manifest destiny that colonized and conquered indigenous peoples, about market capitalism that exploited natural resources regardless of sovereignty, and about an unbridled rugged individualism that reinforces American exceptionalism.

This frontier mythology also allows Kerig to connect the antimainstream image of extreme sports with a nostalgic historical revision of what constituted the good old days—the cowboy's freedom to go anywhere and do anything as long as suffrage was limited to white males. In this rendition elite athletes are associated with celebrated personas—Butch Cassidy and the Sundance Kid—who "embody the competitiveness, determination, responsibility, and rationality underpinning neoliberalism's base individualism, and they are lauded for reaping their just rewards in the form of success on the playing field and (oftentimes) bounteous wealth."[14] As an ultimate entrepreneur of the self, Trevor followed his dream, which ultimately brought him to skiing the exit couloir on the Glacier Rond, where he was swept down the mountain in an avalanche that killed him. At his funeral service his mother, Beth Stewart, offered a eulogy in which Trevor's exploits serve to inspire others: "Whatever you dream to do, begin it. Boldness has power, magic, and genius in it. And I urge all of you to follow Trevor's dream." Trevor is thus elevated to the status of fallen hero, a martyr of the sport. This commemoration, also used in Warren Miller's *Freeriders* (1998), presents images of family and friends gathered at a stone plaque bearing Trevor's name and a mass-produced bumper sticker—*Trevor Would Do It*—to remind viewers his death was not in vain. Joanne Kay and Suzanne Laberge posit that there is "mordant humor" in the idea that facing the same risks will redeem the dead: "Death, as in war, pioneering or religion, is seen here—not as tragic—but as the paradigm of public virtue, as dutiful self-sacrifice for country, mankind and comrades. . . . [F]allen skiers who pushed the limits of danger, leaving children fatherless and spouses widowed, are hailed as freedom fighters who died for a worthy cause. It apparently gives solace to those left alive that death is noble in the name of freedom . . . or a steeper descent."[15]

Satirizing extreme skiers by comparing them to freedom fighters debunks the hagiography that often accompanies these commemorations, but Kerig shows there is little mirth and less humor for those dealing with the deaths of loved ones. Kerig must also confront the obvious conflict of allowing Kye to be placed in a dangerous situation. Having lost her son, Beth Stewart is at first wary. "What right do you have to do this? What do you really know about any of us? About Trevor's skiing? About Kye's skiing? Who are you anyways?" Ultimately, Tanya slowly accepts the idea that it's an opportunity with which she could never provide Kye, an opportunity "to close the circle."

Kye's pilgrimage to Chamonix to spread Trevor's ashes at the top of the Glacier Rond and to avenge his death by skiing it successfully is fraught with symbolic imagery. Chamonix, as Plake explains, is the heart and soul of skiing as well as the Death Sport Capital of the World. "It puts you in your place," he says. "You think you're somebody here; you're wrong, cuz you're not. You're just another one on the lift." Shown a shot of a Chamonix cemetery, the viewer hears that the mountains have taken and continue to take many lives, on average one per week. Another skier turned guide, Kasha Rigby, describes Chamonix as the motherland of all skiing because of its history, the place where "a lot of our heroes started. . . . And there's generation upon generation that have been coming here." That these skiers speak of Chamonix with reverence is not surprising. Philip Stone argues that a faction within the tourism industry caters to places associated with death, which he terms *dark tourism*. "It could be argued that we have always held a fascination with death, whether our own or others, through a combination of respect and reverence or morbid curiosity and superstition. However, it is (western) society's apparent contemporary fascination with death, real or fictional, media inspired or otherwise, that is seemingly driving the dark tourism phenomenon."[16] This is not to say that all so-called dark tourists share a similar fascination about death or that film viewers react to death in a monolithic manner, especially in response to the many films featured in mountain film festivals that celebrate those who face the challenges.

Kerig creates a sense of reverence by seeking the "blessing of the godfather of big mountain skiing," Anselme Baud, who authored the most widely used guidebook for skiing in the Mont Blanc and the Aiguilles Rouges region and who made numerous first descents. Led by guide Stephane "Fanfan" Dan, who accepts the job of guiding Kye so the young man can "understand why his father did what he did because I think I'm close to his father. . . . I mean, we have the same life," Kye is led onto the slopes of the Argentière Basin. From one particular vantage point on the saddle of Le Grands Motets, Baud points out to Kye the Gervasutti Couloir, a seven-hundred-meter vertical face on which he skied the first descent with Patrick Vallencant in 1976, but in May 2004, intending to ski it with his son Edouard and a friend, Baud broke a binding and had to go down and watch the descent, only to see a large serac break off above Edouard, plunging him down the face to his death. He then points to the Aiguille du Midi, behind which is the Glacier Rond. Baud says, "So, my son gets killed in the Gervasutti Couloir, right there, and your father on the Glacier Rond, right there. They die very close. It is difficult to observe that." Connected by the deaths of those closest to them, Baud and Kye are shown sharing a special bond, one that is based on respect for the mountains and on knowing the techniques that will allow him to ski safely and courageously. "We have to take the best of the mountains and follow life," Baud instructs Kye.

Kerig heightens the tension by having Fanfan and Plake warn Kye about the dangers of skiing backward, punctuated by showing him a rescue training session. Plake comments, "Hopefully, we don't have to call these guys," foreshadowing exactly what will happen, as reenacted in the opening sequence. The sequence ends with the three of them standing at the top of the Poubelles Couloir, where they see an eagle, not common in Chamonix, soaring above them. The symbolism becomes obvious when Plake comments that he and Trevor often skied this couloir, and Kye, when asked what he thinks, adds, "Yeah, I'm stoked. I think my dad is stoked, too. I think he was just flying over us." Kerig ends the sequence with shots of himself sitting in a bar looking at pictures of his children on a computer. "Kye's feeling completely at home, and who wouldn't be with guys like Anselme, Fanfan, and Plake. But I've got to remind myself that in the big mountains when you get complacent, bad things can happen."

Through self-reflexivity in which the shot lingers on a photograph of his young child, Kerig reminds of his role in effecting change within the private lives of the participants. As Jerry Rothwell notes, "Where film travels deeply into the private realm, this is particularly acute—it can and often does change the subject's world. . . . This begs the question as to whether this kind of relationship with subjects compromises the documentary filmmaker's other responsibilities, to their audience and to the truth of the story they are telling."[17] The way audiences balance truth and reality with its representational aspects is not as problematic as critics believe, however. Not all viewers want or need reminders to understand that a documentary film stands between reality and representation, interpretation and bias.[18]

Kye's rite of passage continues with his descent of the Poubelles Couloir, in which Kerig connects contemporary performances and conditions to past exploits. Kye relates, "They skied it back in the day in *Blizzard of Ahhs*, and we're going to film it with the crew for *The Edge of Never.*" To ensure safety Kye is clipped to a rope as he sideslips down the rocky, narrow chute at the very top before he is literally and symbolically set free. Baud provides the emotional text. "I wanted to help him, protect him, as if he were my own son. I don't want to let anything happen to him, but if we look at the positive side, it's extraordinary. It moved me a lot." The rest of the descent is rendered as M TV video, guitar riffs accompanying long shots of this imposing couloir intercut with close-ups of the skiers and a shot of the eagle soaring. "The eagle was my dad's favorite animal," Kye says, repeating what he tried to tell them before. "My mom believes that if he were to be reincarnated, he'd come back as that." Fanfan tells him that there is a superstition from the old days—all the birds you see in the mountains are the spirits of dead mountaineers coming back.

Exactly how dangerous the route can be is conveyed when Kerig counterpoints Kye's descent with that of two women skiers, Meg Oster and her guide, Kasha Rigby, a former student of Baud's. After completing the same run, Rigby admits to having taken unnecessary risks by skiing the couloir very late in the day without proper equipment, namely, helmets, when unstable soft conditions often send snow and rocks cascading down. Rigby says, "I don't want to die in an avalanche. I don't want to die in the mountains. It's funny that I feel so strong about not dying in the mountains, and I hear people say, 'They died doing what they loved,' but I don't want to die in the mountains." Even though Kerig has a woman articulate this key idea, it would be an oversimplification to suggest that her discourse is essentially gendered, for while the film does call up cultural idioms and stereotypes about manhood, Kerig has produced a landscape in which discourses are not necessarily gender based. As Sara Mills explains, "Individual subjects should not be seen simply to adopt roles which are mapped out for them by discourses; rather, they experience discomfort with certain elements implicit in discourses, they find pleasure in some elements, and they are openly critical about others."[19] Later in the film Kerig has Plake and Kye reiterate Rigby's point about not wanting to die.

The climax of Kye's rite of passage arrives sooner than expected after Fanfan, hearing bad weather is approaching, informs Kerig that if they want to ski the Glacier Rond, they have to go the next day. That evening Kerig uses shots of Plake telling Kye to prepare what he wants to do for "a memorial or dedication. . . . If you believe in God, say a prayer, or if you want us all to be quiet for a minute, tells us, you know? But, you know, everybody who'll be up there has lost people. . . . It's just one of those emotional roller coasters we get to go on every now and then, for better or for worse." The next morning as the skiers and film crew prepare to board the tram that will take them to the top of the Aiguille du Midi, Mike Hattrup, another member of the tribe, joins the team. When they arrive at the top, the presence of another skiing legend, Doug Coombs, lends the sequence its mordant mystique. Not only had Coombs skied Glacier Rond with Trevor on several occasions, but they also made dozens of first descents together in the early 1990s. "When I could find him. He got lost, like all of us," Coombs tells Kye. While it's not clear what Coombs means by getting lost, Kerig seizes the moment to inform viewers that ten months later Coombs died while skiing in Le Grave, France. As Thomas Austin notes, "The active visual and aural presence of someone who appears in a documentary who we know is going to die is overlaid with the knowledge that he is (will soon be) dead, recalling Roland Barthes' celebrated phrase, 'He is dead and he is going to die.'"[20] The image of Coombs serves as a stark reminder of how momentary and fleeting life can be.

Additional symbolism is lent in a Tibetan scarf that Fanfan has tied to his pack, given to him by a Buddhist monk "to keep him safe." As they prepare to scatter the ashes, Plake says, "We can't deny the memory of the friends who are no longer with us. Lots of people are still up here. That's the reality of the mountains. A lot of our friends go and don't come back." Midway through this scene Kerig uses another shot of the soaring eagle. Hattrup then says, "And I know that nothing would make Trevor more proud than to know that you're skiing Glacier Rond. He's beaming with pride right now." Kye calls the can containing the ashes, which has a *Trevor Would Do It* sticker wrapped around it, "Trevor in a can." Unable to articulate exactly what the brief commemorations means, Kye fumbles for words. Fanfan, Plake, and Hattrup give meaning to the moment. Fanfan says, "This is our life and this is the choice, our choice. It is not depending about the generation; it's depending about what we're doing . . . together. And we know exactly what we are doing. So we are like family, like brothers. We have the same eyes, the same regard. And it's a big family." This statement clearly outlines the boundaries of kinship, norms, values, and sense of identity. In this instance a young man learns to evaluate his own identity against those around them, particularly other men who are very much like his father.

Because it was late afternoon on the Glacier Rond, conditions, which were already thin and unstable, became even riskier. After negotiating the steep top section with Kye roped up, they have to make a long traverse to get to the side with better snow before Fanfan allows Kye to ski untethered. Footage of Kye skiing is narrated by Kerig. "Fanfan takes Kye off the rope for the final time. Now on this run where his father died, Kye is off the tether, on his own, closing the circle." The scene dissolves from a shot of Kye on the Glacier Rond to a shot of a soaring raptor and then to black. Kerig explained that Kye's entire run down the Exit Couloir was not filmed because of safety concerns. "Our trusted guide Fanfan asked me to stop filming immediately so that we could move faster and get everyone off the Glacier Rond safely. I will always err on the side of keeping my friends and associates safe. So, we stopped filming. You saw every frame of footage we had."[21]

Without footage of skiing the exit couloir, Kerig cuts to the phone conversation Kye had with his mother after returning to the hotel. In the final sequence, which provides updates on the film's participants, Plake states, "We're not trying to defy death; we're just trying to have nice ski runs." Clearly, the discourse avers that courage and comradeship redeem the past by having "nice ski runs." The pursuit of transcendence passes to the next generation who learn to measure themselves against those who came before them. The ideology echoes Leonard Kriegel: "To be a man is to carry a tape measure by which you measure yourself in relation to the world."[22]

Mordwand

In MacGillivray Freeman's production *The Alps: Climb of Your Life* (Image Entertainment, 2007), director Stephen Judson helped to establish a trend within the mountain film subgenre to use the audience's attraction to adventure, danger, and death to communicate wider scientific themes, particularly those related to environmental issues.[23] Sponsored by Holcim, "the world leader in building materials," and by Switzerland Tourism, it is not surprising that the film's promotional material highlights the story's two-prong approach. "Featuring some of the most spectacular giant screen imagery yet seen, the film celebrates the unsurpassed beauty of the Alps and the indomitable spirit of the people who live there." Originally created for exhibition in IMAX theaters, *The Alps* documents John Harlin III's attempt to scale the North Face of the Eiger, where his father, John Harlin II, fell to his death in 1966 while attempting the first *direttissima*—or direct route. While Judson's footage and techniques are firmly established in the mountain film subgenre, his accompanying motivation lies in environmental stewardship, evidenced by the fact that the documentary was produced in association with the Alps Film Network Theatres, a consortium of IMAX theaters, science centers, and natural history museums.[24] Throughout the film, climbing footage, captured by a ground crew, a crew on the mountain, and an aerial crew, is intercut with interviews and animation that highlight scientific issues related to erosion, avalanche protection, and responsible development. Not surprisingly, the film originated with Holcim's desire to show the beauty and values of Switzerland and eventually became the vehicle for John Harlin III to climb the Eiger's North Face. As well-known IMAX producer Greg MacGillivray explained in "The Making of *The Alps*" (Image Entertainment, 2007), "I was attracted to the story because it's a story of family, adventure, dedication to sport and the beauty of the world. We wanted to take John's story from the private to the public, share the story, share the celebration." Because viewers of documentaries largely make their choices on the basis of subject, the producers of *The Alps* strategically broadened audience appeal by interweaving general scientific information about the Swiss Alps with the more specific mountain-climbing story of the Harlins.

As the editor of the *American Alpine Journal* and contributing editor for *Backpacker* magazine, John Harlin III is an established figure within the climbing community. As he states early in the film, the main goal for his trip is to pass on to his daughter, Siena, the same respect and love for the natural world that are "still a way of life here. I love the Alps. It speaks to my soul to be in this environment." Harlin embarks on this quest to climb the Eiger and move beyond an obsession that has dominated his life since he was nine years old. To convey the story line and scientific information, Judson blends dual voices—Michael Gambon, a "voice-of-God" narrator who conveys information about the Alps and its people, and Harlin, who narrates the climbing adventure.[25] Judson blends black-and-white archival footage from newsreels along with reenactments to explicate the mountain culture. In many ways that culture survives by learning to cope with the harshness and beauty of the mountains. Harlin wants to confront his "unfinished business with the Eiger," which begins in Leysin, where he grew up and where his father was buried days after becoming the twenty-eighth person to die while climbing the North Face, or Nordwand, and its derivative Mordwand (Death Face). Now, forty years later, Harlin wants to "confront my fears and honor my father," even though that means subjecting his daughter to the possibility of experiencing the same loss that he experienced at the same age. That tension lies at the heart of the Harlin narrative. In his book published in conjunction with the movie's release, Harlin articulates the dilemma, on the one hand criticizing his father for being selfish not to realize how much he and his eight-year-old sister, Andréa, needed him, and on the other realizing that he is following his father.

> My own nine-year-old daughter is watching me through the telescope as I climb past where Dad came down. I didn't want her to be watching; that's just how it worked out. . . . This morning, when I tied into the rope, I was in the grips of destiny. I knew I'd be here someday. I could have changed my fate, except that is the fate I chose. My only fear was whether I would measure up to the challenge. . . . We come because they died, and by dying they created this legend, and we want to be a part of the legend, without dying.[26]

Being a part of the legend by measuring up to the challenge lends a universality of the hero quest that spans the gap between viewer and alpinist.

To become fully immersed in the hero's quest, the viewer must understand the personal values of the private person as well as the history behind the quest. Judson accomplishes this by having Adele tells us, "I knew when I married John that he wasn't afraid of living life on the edge. That's who he is," and by reenacting aspects of two different climbs—Edward Whymper's first successful ascent of the Matterhorn in 1865 and John Harlin II's 1966 unsuccessful climb of the Eiger. Reenactment becomes an important technique to link past exploits with the present. As director John Smithson notes, re-creation is a way to enhance audience appreciation for the narrative. "I have no problem with re-enactment in documentary. Some of the purest school of documentary believe there's no room for re-enactment. I believe when you're telling a story, you should use whatever means at your disposal to best involve your audience in that story, and if that's re-enactment, then use it."[27] After using computer animation to show how successions of glacier recessions, erosion, and weather tore away the base of the Matterhorn, Judson shows actual descendants of the original climbing party donned in 1860s gear, re-creating Whymper's ascent of the Matterhorn "as a way of honoring their ancestors."[28] Viewers also see the Harlins in the village of Zermatt, looking at a plaque dedicated to Whymper and his team, several members of whom died on the descent. Growth in the popularity of mountain film documentaries stems in part from the convergence of fiction and nonfiction forms in which real-life situations are told with a compelling narrative so as to both engage and entertain. As audiences have become more adept at parsing out the real from the representational, concerns about authenticity have ebbed.

Re-creating parts of Harlin II's fall off the Eiger's North Face was one of the most ambitious undertakings of this documentary. Judson utilizes shots of present-day climbers working their way up the face and being slowed by falling snow, which was actually set loose by the crew. He also built a snow cave to show how Harlin II and his team were forced to endure brutally cold conditions for almost two weeks in an area called the Death Bivouac. In the climactic scene Harlin III narrates as a climber, dressed as Harlin II in a red parka with a blue pack, is shown jumaring up fixed ropes that were only seven millimeters thick and frayed from having rubbed against the rock wall. The climber is shown spinning in space under overhangs until the rope snaps and the fall down the face commences. To show this a dummy was dropped from a helicopter to capture it falling against the backdrop of the North Face as well as filming a dummy dropped off the mountain to show the four-thousand-foot vertical fall. These two shots of the falling climber/dummy create an eerie verisimilitude that is enhanced by filming techniques. Such staging techniques are not unprecedented, as British filmmaker Leo Dickinson in his 1982 film *Eiger Solo* staged an elaborate reenactment of Harlin II's fall "using a flailing person dropped out of a helicopter to simulate" the fall.[29] In the moments before the fall, Judson shows a pair of soaring raptors, obvious symbols of dead climbers. Harlin III narrates that other members of the two 1966 climbing teams that had merged into one completed the route and named it the John Harlin Route in honor of their fallen comrade, who was buried on the same day the summit was reached.

Having conveyed the death of a hero through reenactment and archival material, Judson transitions from the historicity of Harlin II's death to his son's finding redemption by climbing "the same route," though in reality Harlin III and his team, which included Daniela and Robert Jasper, climbed the 1938 route. Exactly what aspects of history are shown in documentary is an important consideration, for, as Michael Chanan notes, "History is the referent of documentary which always stands outside the filmic text, 'always referred to but never captured.' The film as such is always made up of images that are never more than fragments, in which history itself is invisible, an absent cause accessible only through textual reconstruction."[30] Unlike the film's producers, Harlin III conveys in his book the negative consequences of his father's death, including the considerable public criticism of the climbers' finishing the climb, as well as his sister's and mother's long-held grief, and the latter's difficult relations with Dougal Haston, who claimed that he knew Harlin II better and was entitled to remove the fallen hero's climbing and ski gear, write the account of the climb, and take over the International School of Modern Mountaineering, the plans for which Harlin II and Marilyn Harlin had worked out together.[31]

Overcoming his fears of the past drives the footage of Harlin III's ascent, beginning with his tearful departure from Siena and Adele, who says, "John is very tense about this climb. It's a dangerous face. Is it worth the risk?" Harlin III answers that question by explaining that he feels completely safe with Robert Jasper because he was "the first person to tell me the Eiger was his favorite mountain, a place that was part of his heart and soul, and the only other person I knew who felt that way was my father." In this way Robert serves as a surrogate for the fatherless son, helping him to conquer obstacles, another significant aspect of embodied masculinity.[32] Judson offers reminders to the audience that the specter of death is never totally absent during the climb. As the team sets off in darkness on the second day of the climb, Daniela has difficulty getting a foothold off the bivouac ledge, which serves as an "ominous start" to the day, prompting her to say: "When you climb the Eiger, I think you cannot avoid thinking about the people who died, especially when you come to places where there were big tragedies and you have to think about it. This also makes the face very special. It's very alive."

Judson serves up another reminder when he shows Harlin III losing grip with his ice picks and dropping about five feet to the steep snow below; as he loses his grip the shot briefly morphs into his father falling. Then the viewer sees Adele, following his progress through a telescope. "I followed John through all the difficult sections, and I just happened to be looking through the scope at the moment when he slipped. Naturally, my heart stopped." Filmed after the climb had been completed and not from the deck of the Kleine Scheidegg resort from where viewing is traditionally done, this re-creation allows Judson to manufacture a dramatic moment in which Adele serves as a stand-in for the audience, who are provided voyeuristic insight into a moment of private despair. It also harks back to the 1966 climb when reporter Peter Gillman "put his eye to the telescope [at Kleine Scheidegg resort] and was following the ropes from the Death Bivouac upward when a red figure fell through his field of vision."[33] J. A. Walter argues that watching unfolding horrors of the Eiger from a safe distance is a blending of admiration and condemnation. It is also little different from other media accounts of them, what he calls armchair mountaineering. "It seems that people enjoy looking at what repels them. No longer allowed to enjoy public executions, perhaps we have found an alternative? . . . Some tourists may actually be able to identify with the ardent adventurers and experience, to a minor degree and with no danger, what they imagine the ardent experience to be like."[34] By sharing Adele's private moment of terror, the film works as cathartic ritual, conjoining viewers and participants through vicarious experience.

To begin the film's climactic sequence, Judson fuses the experiences of father and son by showing Harlin III as he settles down on the second night's bivouac. A black-and-white photograph of the father is superimposed into a panoramic shot of the Eiger face, and above the photo is another frame with a hand scribbling "a final note to us." Only Harlin II's last line of the note is read in the film. "We are hoping to make the top in a few days but we are being very safe so don't worry. Love you all very, very much. Dad." This unfulfilled promise of safety serves as the fulcrum on which Harlin III's own promise to Adele and Siena is balanced. They had stashed a written note in his pack, which he read after being prompted, during the first night's bivouac. These subtle distinctions mark the transformation that Harlin III ultimately experiences the next day. The shot starts in darkness as Harlin III narrates: "After we passed the spot where Dad's rope had broken, I glanced back. I'd been trying to get past that place for forty years. I flung my grief and fear off the mountain and kept going." The shot actually stops as Harlin III momentarily looks back down the face before dissolving into a shot of the three climbers as they ascend to a place "beyond the point of no return. It's terrifying in a way because you know you can't go back down, only up." The symbolic import of this is clear: in order to cast off the past and heal the wound of his father's death, Harlin III must reach the summit. Only then can he feel closer to his wife and daughter and connect Siena with "this love for the mountains that I felt as a boy." Reconnecting with the children signifies the quest's culmination, for in the children lies the future's promise of happiness and prosperity, rather than grief. To show that there are no residual ghosts, Harlin III and family return to Leysin to visit his father's grave site and plant flowers, a final act of redemption and liberation. Judson then connects the personal story with the larger environment, as Gambon narrates. "These mountains attract strong people. They always have. The Alps embrace us just as they welcomed the first settlers who looked up at these peaks many centuries ago and said to themselves, 'We belong here.'" In the final aerial shots of the Matterhorn, an observatory, and a cross atop one peak, Judson delivers an implicit message of environmental stewardship and ecumenism.

If people are to enjoy the sporting adventures offered here, they must be responsible for living in harmony with the natural world.

Final Embraces

The directors and producers of the mountain film documentaries *The Edge of Never* and *The Alps: Climb of Your Life* allow viewers a semiological embrace of risk, danger, and death. Because adventure experiences in which one can confront one's own mortality are beyond the physical or financial means (or both) of most people, these two films allow access through a mediated distillation of the spectacular. Viewers become willfully immersed in terror because they are protected against actual injury or death. Transcendence is achieved through the simulacrum of "postadventure," shaped by production techniques and reception protocols subsumed within postmodern aesthetics.[35] Virtually all aspects of documentary film infrastructure are driven by the interrelated processes of commercialization, commoditization, and spectacularization, subject to the logics of a highly technologized capitalist economy and propelled by the mediated spectacles and circuitry. The commoditized postadventure economy of death creates a myth couched in the mordant cliché about those who have been killed "doing what they loved doing." Elevating the deaths of Trevor Petersen and John Harlin II to the level of martyrdom fits squarely into affective economics that anchor people in particular experiences, identities, and pleasures that invariably promote and legitimate the neoliberal ideology's view of reality through its continuing manipulation of symbolic figures. Such power is seductive in motivating viewers not only to consume the images but also to manifest their emotional needs through consumption. As Roland Barthes suggests, it is not when ideology hovers close to the surface and is easily recognizable that it is most powerful, but when it is strongly present but apparently absent, allowing myths to do their work on the emotions.[36]

Growth in the mountain film subgenre can be attributed to the convergence of fiction and nonfiction forms in which real-life situations are told with a compelling narrative so as to both engage and entertain. Sophisticated filming techniques, vivid re-creations, soaring soundtracks, and archival materials are blended to create hybrid productions that provide viewers with a vicarious experience in which death is made manifest. In these films death is vanquished through a discourse in which courage and companionship redeem the past and advance an understanding about the need for environmental stewardship. What is particularly noteworthy about these two documentaries is their engagement with the past, particularly since they deal specifically with death and aspects of embodied masculinity in father-son relationships. As Susan Birrell notes, narratives constructed to capture the past are always vested with special interests, blending meanings that can be produced and mobilized into the events of a different era.[37] Rather than allowing death to cast a shadow over the lives of the friends and families who have experienced loss, these documentaries serve, in a figurative sense, as memento mori, relics to satisfy audience interests. Removed from its original context, the economy of death becomes the means to cinematic gratification, transferring the thrill of athletic achievement into a concentrated sense of exhilaration meant to maintain that which is of commercial value.

NOTES

1. Peter Varley, "Confecting Adventure and Playing with Meaning: The Adventure Commodification Continuum," *Journal of Sport & Tourism* 11, no. 2 (2006): 182–83, 188–91.
2. Steve Neale, "Questions of Genre," *Screen* 31, no. 1 (1990): 46, 51.
3. Hugh Barnard, "Mountain Film: An Analysis of the History and Characteristics of a Documentary Genre" (master's thesis, University of Otago, Dunedin, New Zealand, 2011), 6, 2.
4. J. A. Walter, "Death as Recreation: Armchair Mountaineering," *Leisure Studies* 3 (1984): 68.
5. For a definition of the economy of death, see Jay W. Baird, *To Die for Germany: Heroes in the Nazi Pantheon* (Bloomington: Indiana University Press, 1990). On the connection between sport and heroism, see the anthology Richard Holt, J. A. Mangan, and Pierre Lanfranchi, eds., *European Heroes: Myth, Identity, Sport* (London: Frank Cass, 1996).
6. Philip Moore, "Practical Nostalgia and the Critique of Commodification: On the 'Death of Hockey' and the National Hockey League," *Australian Journal of Anthropology* 13, no. 3, (2002): 310–11.
7. Vivian Sobchack, *The Address of the Eye: A Phenomenology of Film Experience* (Princeton NJ: Princeton University Press, 1992), 48; Burke cited in J. A. Walter,

"Death as Recreation: Armchair Mountaineering," *Leisure Studies* 3 (1984): 70; Peter Berger, *The Sacred Canopy* (New York: Anchor Books, 1967), 43.

8. See Jean Baudrillard, *The Ecstasy of Communication*, trans. Bernard Schutze and Caroline Schutze (New York: Columbia University, 1988).

9. Susan Birrell, "Approaching Mt. Everest: On Intertextuality and the Past as Narrative," *Journal of Sport History* 34, no. 1 (2007): 17.

10. Susan Frohlick, "The 'Hypermasculine' Landscape of High-Altitude Mountaineering," *Michigan Feminist Studies* 14 (1999–2000): 89.

11. Barnard, "Mountain Film," 55.

12. Joanne Kay and Suzanne Laberge, "Oh Say Can You Ski? Imperialistic Construction of Freedom in Warren Miller's *Freeriders*," in *To the Extreme: Alternative Sports, Inside and Out*, ed. Robert E. Rinehart and Synthia Sydnor (Albany: State University of New York Press, 2003), 393.

13. Debbora Battaglia, "On Practical Nostalgia: Self-Prospecting among Urban Trobrianders," in *Rhetorics of Self-Making*, ed. D. Battaglia, 77–96 (Berkeley: University of California Press, 1995).

14. David L. Andrews and Michael L. Silk, "Sport and Neoliberalism: An Affective-Ideological Articulation," *Journal of Popular Culture* 51, no. 2 (2018): 524.

15. Kay and Laberge, "Oh Say Can You Ski?," 392.

16. Philip R. Stone, "A Dark Tourism Spectrum: Towards a Typology of Death and Macabre Related Tourist Sites, Attractions and Exhibitions," *Tourism* 54, no. 2 (2006): 147.

17. Jerry Rothwell, "Filmmakers and Their Subjects," in *Rethinking Documentary: New Perspectives, New Practices*, ed. Thomas Austin and Wilma de Jong (New York: Open University Press, 2008), 155.

18. Stella Bruzzi, *New Documentary: A Critical Introduction* (London: Routledge, 2000), 4.

19. Sara Mills, *Discourse* (London: Routledge, 1997), 97.

20. Thomas Austin, "'. . . To Leave the Confinements of His Humanness': Authorial Voice, Death and Constructions of Nature in Werner Herzog's *Grizzly Man*," in *Rethinking Documentary: New Perspectives, New Practices*, ed. Thomas Austin and Wilma de Jong (New York: Open University Press, 2008), 56–57.

21. William A. Kerig, email to the author, April 5, 2016.

22. Leonard Kriegel, *On Men and Manhood* (New York: Hawthorn Books, 1979), 34; Kriegel quoted in Leigh Andrea Adams and Kaymarlin Govender, "'Making a Perfect Man': Traditional Masculine Ideology and Perfectionism among Adolescent Boys," *South African Journal of Psychology* 38, no. 3 (2008): 551–62.

23. See Barnard, "Mountain Film," 64–66.

24. In the film's final credits more than thirty sites are listed as part of the IMAX consortium.

25. Bill Nichols, *Introduction to Documentary* (Bloomington: Indiana University Press, 2001), 107.

26. John Harlin III, *The Eiger Obsession: Facing the Mountain That Killed My Father* (New York: Simon & Schuster, 2007), 1–3.

27. Wilma de Jong and Thomas Austin, "'You Want to Know That, This Is Real, This Is What Happened': An Interview with John Smithson," in *Rethinking Documentary: New Perspectives, New Practices*, ed. Thomas Austin and Wilma de Jong (New York: Open University Press, 2008), 164.

28. For another example of climbers donning vintage gear to re-create a climb, see Mark MacKenzie, *The Wildest Dream: Conquest of Everest* (2009) and the National Geographic film of the same title.

29. Harlin, *Eiger Obsession*, 207.

30. Michael Chanan, "Filming *The Invisible*," in *Rethinking Documentary: New Perspectives, New Practices*, ed. Thomas Austin and Wilma de Jong (New York: Open University Press, 2008), 128.

31. Harlin, *Eiger Obsession*, 155.

32. See Michael J. Diamond, "Fathers with Sons: Psychoanalytic Perspectives on 'Good Enough' Fathering throughout the Cycle," *Gender and Psychoanalysis* 3 (1998): 243–99.

33. Harlin, *Eiger Obsession*, 138.

34. Walter, "Death as Recreation," 69.

35. Varley, "Confecting Adventure and Playing with Meaning," 188.

36. Roland Barthes, *Mythologies*, trans. Annette Lavers (New York: Hill and Wang, 1984).

37. Birrell, "Approaching Mt. Everest," 4.

9

Sports Album's Replay

Newsreel Compilations, Early Television, and the Recirculation of Sport History

ALEX KUPFER

Over the past decade scholars, bloggers, and producers have proclaimed that sport documentaries have never been better, more culturally relevant, or more central to the film and television industries. This veneration was most evident after ESPN's *O.J.: Made in America* (Ezra Edelman, 2016) miniseries won a host of prestigious awards, including the Academy Award for Best Documentary Feature. Such accolades illuminate a key tension marking the discourses around sport documentaries: What preceded this golden age? What were the aesthetic, narrative, and institutional contexts that led to the genre's lack of respectability and cultural cachet in the first place? As a historically "lowbrow" form, what industrial and institutional purposes did sport documentaries serve such that they proliferated in film, and especially television?

This chapter uses the early television documentary series *Sports Album* as a case study to explore these questions. Although largely forgotten today, the show exemplifies many of the aesthetic and cultural "shortcomings" that subsequent sport documentaries challenged and positioned themselves against. It can help us understand the current cultural status of the sport documentary since "the cultural legitimization of television," argue Michael Z. Newman and Elana Levine, "is premised upon a rejection and a denigration of 'television' as it has long existed."[1] *Sports Album* reveals how early sports documentary series emphasized celebrity and spectacle in order to prioritize economic efficiency above other institutional and industrial factors. The show suggests that the more recent cultural legitimation of the sport documentary genre has been predicated on the engagement of many of the aesthetic and cultural characteristics that syndicated sports documentary series avoided including complex narratives, nuanced characterizations, and engagement with social issues. Therefore, implicit within the discourse of sport documentary's current "golden age" is a kind of erasure of series like *Sports Album* from the genre's development. A deeper understanding of those shows is necessary to understand the genre's development as well as the sports documentary's current industrial significance and cultural status.

The dominant aesthetic characteristic of *Sports Album* was its reappropriation of archival newsreel footage originally shot in the 1920s and early 1930s, which came from the Kinograms newsreel library acquired by Frederic W. Ziv Productions when the company expanded from radio to television production. A total of 144 episodes of *Sports Album* were produced in 1948–49 by Ziv Productions and distributed via syndication until 1956.[2] Each short episode, between three to five minutes in length, consisted of archival newsreel segments covering historic sporting events, renowned athletes, successful franchises, or prominent rivalries. Different spectator sports were featured in the individual episodes, led by baseball, college football, and wrestling. The use of previously filmed and edited newsreel footage lowered the cost of production, and thus the company's investment in television at a time when independent producers were concerned about the medium's long-term economic viability. Ziv decontextualized this archival material for *Sports Album* by reediting the footage by topic. The original footage underwent significant aesthetic changes, as the images were shown significantly accelerated from their original projection speed, and soundtracks were mostly replaced with Bill Slater's voice-over narration.[3] The audio from post-1927 newsreels was typically used only when famous athletes spoke to players or directly to the cameras.

Ziv's brand shaped the structure of the individual episodes of *Sports Album*, particularly through the company's emphasis on economic efficiency over historical accuracy. The newsreels employed in the show were compiled through figurative relationships, where approximate newsreel images were often used to represent the topic, to the extent that the same shots or scenes were repurposed in multiple episodes. The show developed a nostalgic conception of sports history by mythologizing already famous athletes and teams instead of exploring new areas of sport history or any of the contexts that examined the significance of sport off the field. This figurative and nostalgic approach to sports history was reinforced by Bill Slater's narration, which explicitly minimized viewers' experience of temporal disparity, or what Jaimie Baron describes as the perception by the viewer of a "then" and "now" generated within a single work.[4] By avoiding the social issues surrounding sports and mythologizing individual athletes and teams, *Sports Album* could be easily scheduled and not risk offending local audiences or sponsors.

The approach to history in *Sports Album* was a necessary precondition to the proliferation of subsequent syndicated sport documentary series like *Greatest Sport Legends* (1972–93), *Bob Uecker's Wacky World of Sports* (1985–96), and numerous series produced by NFL Films, such as *NFL Game of the Week* (1965–2007) and *Lost Treasures* (1999–2003). Heavily reliant on archival footage, these syndicated shows helped local television programmers fill dozens of hours of airtime each week in a cost-effective and adaptable way. Live programming was prohibitively expensive for local stations to produce, and Hollywood studios would not sell their feature-film libraries to television until 1956.[5] Live sports were further limited on early television, since leagues and collegiate conferences had a decidedly mixed reaction to television. Some owners and executives were optimistic about the medium's potential to promote fandom, whereas others were concerned that televised broadcasts of games could hurt live attendance.[6] Syndicated first-run shows from telefilm producers were an affordable alternative to live programming and, in the case of *Sports Album*, a flexible complement to televised sporting events. Perhaps just as important, they were also popular with sponsors trying to appeal to the audiences drawn to sports. The program did not need a set airtime, and episodes could be run before live baseball or football games to help local stations fill their broadcast schedules.

This flexibility, combined with low production costs, was essential to *Sports Album*'s proliferation on local stations. Ziv used sport documentaries to further develop his company's distinctive identity, although instead of drawing on documentary's refined social meaning, he foregrounded economic efficiency and adaptable scheduling practices for local stations. By contemporary standards, *Sports Album* lacks many of the qualities of more highly regarded sport documentaries. It foregrounded sports media's association with commercialism and what Derek Kompare characterizes as television's "regime of repetition."[7] Yet these practices enabled the show to be widely scheduled and helped Ziv acquaint new generations to sport history. In introducing the sports documentary series to television, *Sports Album* introduced many of the elements that subsequent television sport documentaries have avoided in order to combat sport documentary's traditional connotations.

Building the Ziv Brand on Radio

When *Sports Album* debuted in 1948, Ziv had established himself as one of the most successful syndicators in the country. He took an indirect path to entering broadcasting and sports media production. After graduating from the University of Michigan Law School, he returned to his hometown of Cincinnati, Ohio, where an interest in writing led him to a job at a local advertising agency as a copywriter. He quickly learned all aspects of the industry and in September 1930 established his own firm, the Frederic W. Ziv Advertising Agency. Using a strategy that he would employ throughout his career, Ziv focused on areas that others in the field had yet to fully explore. He initially concentrated on radio advertising, since, as he recalled, "I realized that there were dozens of agency men who knew ten times what I did about magazine and newspaper advertising. But nobody knew anything about radio in those days."[8]

Ziv began to develop entire radio program concepts for his advertising clients. His first programs were *Oklahoma Bob Albright and His Mountain Music* and *Fashion Parade*. These were soon followed by Ziv's first sports show, *Sports of the Week*, featuring Cincinnati Reds broadcaster Red Barber. Building on this success, Ziv quickly introduced two more sports shows: *Fans in the Stands* and *One for the Books*. *Fans in the Stands* was a long-running fifteen-minute live program produced for the Rubel Baking Company of Cincinnati that enabled local stations to cheaply expand their baseball programming. Prior to every Reds game host Dick Bray, who also was a Cincinnati Reds broadcaster on WCPO, would interview fans either at Crosley Field (while lugging around a thirty-two-pound portable transmitter) or at the 3,500-seat RKO Albee Theater when the team was away. The show reminded listeners of the sponsor at every opportunity, including giving each guest a coupon for a free loaf of Rubel bread. As he would do later with *Sports Album*, Ziv emphasized the broad circulation of his programming over signing exclusive deals with individual stations. He sold *Fans in the Stands* to all of the stations in Cincinnati that aired Reds games to ensure the program's position as the regular lead-in to all of the team's games.[9]

To bolster the repeatability of his programs, and thus increase sponsorship opportunities, Ziv switched to syndication for his next program, the sports radio show *One for the Books*, which was first broadcast in 1939. Each five-minute episode featured a single sports history anecdote told by host Sam Balter, a former basketball player best known for playing on the gold-medal-winning team at the 1936 Berlin Olympics.[10] Over the series' 192 episodes, the anecdotes covered both famous and obscure athletes, teams, and unusual feats from a range of sports. While Ziv claimed that he personally supervised the writing, production, and promotion of the program, Balter researched many of the anecdotes discussed in the show. Balter took special pride in highlighting stories that had been overlooked in other sports media outlets. He later recalled that his two favorite episodes both involved Minor League Baseball oddities. One focused on Ox Eckhardt, a Fort Worth Minor Leaguer who reached second base eight times during a double-header but was never able to advance to third. The other discussed a player in the Three-I League who hit six consecutive home runs in two days, although not a single one counted because he batted out of order on one, missed a base on another, passed a runner, and so on.[11]

The Ziv Company used arcane sports trivia as a way to develop its brand as a producer of popular yet low-cost radio programming. *One for the Books* was a popular and financial success and demonstrated there was a sizable audience for syndicated sports history shows. Thanks in part to the success of these two programs, between 1937 and 1947 Ziv became the largest and most successful radio syndicator in the United States. The company temporarily moved away from sports and expanded its syndicated offerings with new series across a range of popular genres, including the hit western series *The Cisco Kid* (1950–56) and the detective series *Boston Blackie* (1951–53). But the sports documentary's combination of broad appeal and lower production costs drew Ziv back to the genre for his initial forays into television.

Kinograms Newsreel and Ziv's Film Library

Along with his success in the radio industry, Ziv had another asset that led to the success of *Sports Album*: a large archive of sports footage. Although archival sports footage continues to be a central component of the genre, for syndicated sports documentary series it was a necessary precondition to their production and circulation. Independent producers like Ziv expanded into television and documentaries by relying as much as possible on cost-effective, adaptable production styles that minimized the creation of new content, focusing instead on the reappropriation of previously shot material. In the case of *Sports Album*, this meant utilizing sports newsreels from the Kinograms archive and only adding new opening credits voice-over narration.

After World War II established radio producers were eager to enter television. Ziv recalled that by 1947, "The technical basis had already been established. There had been enough experimental telecasts so that we knew what a set looked like, and what a transmitter looked like, and that a projector could transmit film and that you could receive it in your home."[12] Despite this familiarity with the inchoate medium, the growth of television was slowed when the Federal Communications Commission (FCC) imposed a freeze on all new station licenses in September 1948. The freeze had both benefits and drawbacks for independent producers like Ziv. It prevented Hollywood studios from gaining a hold in the television industry and positioning themselves as both networks owners and program producers.[13] However, the FCC's decision also enabled the established radio networks CBS and NBC to consolidate their control over television and limit the number of stations where independent producers could sell filmed programs. This reduced market compelled Ziv to keep production costs to a minimum in order to stay competitive.

To facilitate entry into syndicated television production in a low-cost, low-risk manner, the Ziv Company purchased two large film libraries.

In February 1948 Ziv acquired the General Film Library of New York for $240,000. The library contained approximately 10 million feet of 16mm and 35mm film. Five months later Ziv purchased the General Film Library of California for $100,000, adding another 3.5 million feet of footage.[14] With these acquisitions Ziv owned the largest motion picture library of any telefilm producer.[15] He acquired these libraries specifically because they were comparatively affordable compared to Hollywood studio features. Eric Hoyt explains that independent distributor Matty Fox paid $15.2 million in late 1955 for the television rights to most of RKO's library of 740 titles. Shortly thereafter Paramount sold its library of 700 pre-1948 features for $50 million, and Warner Brothers' sold 750 sound pictures and its pre-1948 shorts for $21 million.[16] Ziv's acquisition of his film library at a fraction of the price of those sales helped his company keep production costs to a bare minimum by compiling archival newsreels instead of filming original material, which in turn enabled him to lower rates for advertisers and stations.

Ziv was able to purchase the Kinograms archive in part because it was an independent newsreel company. Kinograms has a unique place in American film history because, as Raymond Fielding explains, it was the only prominent newsreel not associated with a major studio for any length of time.[17] The newsreel was distributed by Educational Pictures, which specialized in short subjects. Through its thirty-six exchanges across the country, Educational distributed Kinograms to independent theater chains along with theaters owned by MGM and Paramount, the two vertically integrated studios that did not produce their own newsreels during the silent era.

The majority of the material in Ziv's new film library was originally used for the Kinograms newsreel that ran from 1918 to 1931. Ziv's compilation shows reflected the topics that dominated newsreels during the period. The weekly or biweekly newsreel releases regularly included a sports segment featuring game highlights or post-1927 brief interviews with athletes. The amount of time that news films devoted to sports increased significantly throughout the 1920s and 1930s, as Michael Oriard notes, reaching about a quarter of all footage shot by the late 1930s.[18] Newsreel coverage largely corresponded with the different sporting seasons. Between April and October, for instance, the Kinograms sports coverage was dominated by baseball and regularly featured segments with nationally recognized athletes like Dizzy Dean, Babe Ruth, and Ty Cobb.

The introduction of synchronized sound newsreels in the late 1920s impacted Kinograms more adversely than any of its competitors. MGM and Paramount began producing their own sound newsreels, and Kinograms lost many of its exhibition accounts. By the end of 1931 Kinograms was bankrupt, and all of its assets, including its newsreel library, were put up for sale. Despite the low cultural status of the newsreel genre, many in the industry recognized its commercial potential. Morris J. Kandel, president of Ideal Pictures and owner of the General Film Library, purchased Kinograms' library, laboratory, cameras, and newsreel equipment.[19] The news footage was added to his self-described "largest stock shot library in the industry." Kandel seems to be particularly interested in the sports material, which was frequently advertised in trade publications like the *Film Daily* as containing everything from "dramatic punches" to sports.[20] Kandel planned to use the Kinograms newsreels to produce documentaries, including the six-reel feature "Headlines of Yesterday" and a thirteen-part series, "Screen Biographies."[21] Although these projects were never realized, the adaptability of the newsreel footage was inspiring producers to develop new documentary projects.

Ziv's Television Programming

After purchasing the General Film Library from Kandel in 1948, the Ziv Company first used the footage for the company's initial foray into television, the syndicated *Yesterday's Newsreel*, which ran for 139 episodes from 1948 to 1950. Each fifteen-minute episode compiled short vignettes of historic events or individuals from Kinograms newsreels, accompanied by voice-over narration from Warren Sweeney, Ray Morgan, or Roslyn Green. Other than a longer run time, the structure and aesthetics of the show were identical to *Sports Album*. The scope of *Yesterday's Newsreel* was a direct reflection of the material Ziv acquired, and since Kinograms stopped production in the early 1930s, the material included in the show focused only on the 1910s and 1920s. Like the Kinograms newsreels, each episode contained a few sports segments, typically at the end. For instance, the twentieth episode of *Yesterday's Newsreel* featured segments about international news, U.S. news, celebrities, and women's fashion. The episode ended with two sports segments: on runner Paavo Nurmi (using footage from 1929) and the Stevens brothers bobsledders (from 1933).

The representation of sports in *Yesterday's Newsreel* was shaped by Ziv's plans to develop additional television series utilizing the same newsreels from his film library. The plans to produce additional series meant that the most popular spectator sports of the era, including college football, baseball, horse racing, and boxing, were rarely included here. The most frequent sports segments in the show were golf, automobile racing, and "Olympic" sports, including track and field, swimming, and skiing. The more commonly televised sports were de-emphasized to such an extent that out of approximately 1,400 total segments in the series, college football was featured only twice. Likewise, there were also only three baseball segments during the entire series: "Indians-Dodgers in World Series, 1920," "Giants Win 1933 Pennant," and a profile of Washington Senators ace Walter Johnson. Perhaps most remarkably, *Yesterday's Newsreel* did not include a single boxing match in the entire series. The only boxing-related news films in the show were two celebrity profiles of Jack Dempsey. This suggests that the in-depth coverage of the era's sports was secondary to Ziv's emphasis on quickly expanding his brand into television and bolstering the commercial appeal of his next show, *Sports Album*.

Each episode of *Sports Album* focused on an individual sport, led by professional baseball (fifty-eight episodes), collegiate football (twenty-six), and wrestling (eleven). The show did not seek to develop new approaches to exploring sport history or introduce new themes. Rather, the predominant focus was on star athletes of the 1920s and the most popular professional and collegiate teams. This thematic structure helped Ziv's staff compile the episodes more efficiently, and the star iconography facilitated its sale to television stations.

Ziv sold *Sports Album* to sponsors from industries traditionally associated with sports media. While sports media today is associated predominantly with national or even international brands, a key appeal of Ziv's syndicated programming for these sponsors was that it offered a platform for local and regional companies to reach audiences on a market-by-market basis. Before the show went on the air, Ziv signed up a number of advertisers for

Sports Album, often on a nonexclusive basis, where the show would air on multiple stations in the same market. In New York City the show was sold to both Dodge and Kuppenheimer Clothes. Dodge planned to place the program on the ABC affiliate WJZ-TV and air it prior to New York Giants football games, while Kuppenheimer scheduled it before college football games on WNBT, New York's NBC affiliate.[22]

In an effort to reach the stereotypically male demographic associated with sports media, breweries were the most common sponsors of *Sports Album*. In September 1948 Ruppert's Beer purchased the show to broadcast in a number of large East Coast markets, including Boston, Philadelphia, and New York (to air on the local CBS station).[23] Ruppert's Beer must have been satisfied with the show's reception, since it extended its contract to sponsor the program for three additional years before the original contract expired at an estimated total cost of $170,000. The association of *Sports Album* with breweries expanded as the show entered new markets. Hanley Beer sponsored the show on WNAC in Boston, and Glasgow Brewing bought the show for WTAR in Norfolk, Virginia.[24]

Sports Album found a home on local stations because it complemented the established structures of sports on television, in terms of both the centrality of live event broadcasting and its relationship with breweries. Syndicated sports documentary shows offered breweries a platform to advertise their products within the context of sports during a period when many teams and leagues did not yet permit them to sponsor local or national telecasts. For instance, when Liebmann Breweries offered to sponsor the 1947 World Series, Major League Baseball commissioner A. B. "Happy" Chandler turned down the offer, since he believed "it would not be good public relations for baseball to have the Series sponsored by the producer of an alcoholic beverage."[25] Breweries were able to break into live television sports advertising only in the 1950s, after, Red Barber explains, "Wheaties dropped out of it, and, by and large, beer took over."[26]

Ziv's sales material emphasized to stations the broad accessibility of the show, explaining that television audiences would be familiar with both the subjects and the style of the newsreels in *Sports Album*. This was because like the original newsreels, the show was primarily structured around game highlights and the spectacle surrounding the original sporting events. Though supplemented by the voice-over narration, the program's treatment of sports history relied on audiences' recognition of the athletes and familiar sports narratives, such as the dominance of the Yankees or Notre Dame football in the 1920s.

Ziv's influence on early sports telefilms can be seen in the competitors who tried to imitate his brand. For instance, one of Ziv's competitors was Palm Beach Co., a men's apparel manufacturer that sponsored *Inside Secrets of Baseball*, which ran for thirty-seven episodes in syndication during the early 1950s. Narrated by former pitcher and Cincinnati Reds radio announcer Waite Hoyt, the series featured stars like Ted Williams demonstrating hitting, pitching, and fielding techniques. The filmed shorts were telecast alongside Major and Minor League games in markets such as Chicago, Philadelphia, Atlanta, Dayton, and New Orleans.[27] Palm Beach's next show was the five-minute filmed program *How to Improve Your Golf*, narrated by Harold "Jug" McSpaden, former professional golfer and sales promotion director for the company. Like Ziv, Palm Beach Co. sought to produce its television documentaries as cost-efficiently as possible. To help defray the costs of using well-known athletes in these sports shows, Palm Beach split the production budget with a department store in each of the nineteen markets where the show aired. Ziv's shows were nonetheless able to reach a wider audience because of his production methods and the reuse of archival footage of famous athletes. This allowed him to charge sponsors less for the rights to broadcast *Sports Album* and thus encourage its wide circulation.

Especially compared to more recent sport documentaries, the focus of *Sports Album* was on the spectacle and celebrity cultures associated with sport history, rather than exploring any connection to wider social issues. Accordingly, along with game highlights, *Sports Album* often incorporated newsreel footage of complementary events such as practices, athletes posing for the camera, and game-day activities. The show evoked what Michael Oriard describes as "the calculated heightening of dramatic spectacle" of sports newsreels. Important plays were juxtaposed with shots of cheering fans, sidelines, mascots, bands, and cheerleaders.[28] While the newsreels were restructured to create new narratives, *Sports Album* still employed this familiar juxtaposition by including footage that evoked the game-day atmosphere alongside footage of what contemporary audiences would recognize as conventional sports highlights.

This heightening of spectacle served as a way to uncritically celebrate sports traditions through a nostalgic perspective. Perhaps fittingly, then, the football teams that were most frequently featured in *Sports Album* were the Army and Navy service academies. "The Service Teams in Action" episode does not start with game action but begins with humans dressed as the Army mule and Yale bulldog mascots chasing each other on the Yale field before the game. The episode draws on widely recognized narratives about the history and significance of the Army-Navy rivalry, focusing on spectacle surrounding either team rather than the outcomes of each game. Similarly, the "Army-Navy Classics" episode, which uses footage of the 1922, 1924, and 1926 games, foregrounds the central importance of rituals to the rivalry. The episode opens with a 1922 newsreel segment featuring shots of the (actual) Army mule mascot meeting the Navy goat, Navy Midshipmen marching on the field, President Coolidge acknowledging the crowd, and military officials. All of these pregame shots were followed by only a single shot of game action. A similar structure is used for the episode's next segment on the 1924 Army-Navy game. Amid shots of the crowd, coaches, and Coolidge moving from the Navy side of the field to the Army side at halftime, there are four shots of highlights from the game itself. Spectacle and social rituals were at the center of the show's construction of sports history, with other contexts left aside.

Any context for the archival footage in *Sports Album* came from the voice-over narration. The program did not identify the archival source material used here, and the opening credits simply explained that these were "news shots specially edited for television." The omission of this seemingly significant production information enabled Ziv to de-emphasize historical fidelity by using approximate archival footage from sources in his film library other than the Kinograms newsreels. For example, the third segment of the aforementioned "Army-Navy Classics" episode features a close-up of a smiling Army coach Lawrence "Biff" Jones. The shot came from another source; it was filmed in a grassy, outdoor area, while the rest of the archival footage used in the segment was shot at the game's location at Soldier Field in Chicago, identified by the narrator as 1926. Despite the disparity between the Jones close-up and the rest of the 1926 game segment, the need for efficient production practices took precedence over other aesthetic and narrative considerations. Notably, this same outdoor shot of Jones was also reused in other *Sports Album* episodes. In "Army–Notre Dame Games," the narrator even identifies it as having been shot in West Point in 1928, another example of Ziv's emphasis on efficiency, as he was willing to use the same shot in different contexts instead of finding alternative ways of portraying the past.

The repetition of shots in multiple episodes highlights the different evidentiary function that archival footage served in early sport documentary series compared to contemporary works in the genre. *Sports Album* illustrates what Paul Arthur describes as the "figurative" use of archival footage. Arthur contends that, "many, if not the majority, of illustrative instances in documentary collage are understood not as literal but as figurative representations of their subjects."[29] He cites an example from Frank Capra's *Why We Fight* (1942–45) series in which the same footage of a woman running through a bombed-out street is used in three different episodes to represent three different countries. The shots of Jones in numerous *Sports Album* episodes are likewise not intended to serve as evidence of where Jones was at specific times or connote that his pregame demeanor was somehow linked to the outcome of the game. While the repetition of the shot was undoubtedly a cost-cutting measure, it also evoked a sense of the coach and his personality. As a result, the sequence of specific events in the Army-Navy games bolsters the nostalgic celebration of star athletes and coaches from this period and draws on more familiar narratives about sports.

Temporal Disparity in "Knute Rockne's Training Techniques"

Bill Slater's voice-over narration in each *Sports Album* episode was integral in minimizing viewers' experience of temporal disparity between the time when the footage was initially shot and its reappropriation years later. Although it ultimately further decontextualized the historical newsreels, this minimization helped extend the show's circulation on television since it would not seem outdated in light of recent news.

These could include events such as the death of Babe Ruth, the subject of three different episodes of *Sports Album*, in August 1948. To take another football-focused episode as an example, in "Knute Rockne's Training Techniques" the narration rhetorically diminishes the juxtaposition between sports' past and present. It avoids any reference to events that occurred between the time when Rockne was shot for the newsreels in the 1920s and 1930s and when the show was produced in 1948, including skipping any reference to Rockne's death in 1931 in a plane crash on his way to Hollywood.

Viewers watching *Sports Album* would have undoubtedly been familiar with Rockne's passing. Sports historian Murray Sperber argues that his death was more than a widely known news event, and for many Americans, it "was a riveting moment in their lives, analogous to the responses by later generations to the sudden deaths of John F. Kennedy, Martin Luther King, and Robert F. Kennedy."[30] Rockne's death was front-page news around the world, and his life was commemorated in both newsreels and feature films. To capitalize on the sudden surge in audience interest, newsreel producers mined their archives and rushed compilations of Rockne footage to theaters. Fox Movietone, for instance, drew on its expansive library of footage of the coach shot between 1924 and 1931 for a sixteen-minute newsreel tribute. The piece compiled footage from Rockne's home life, his coaching career, and funeral on the Notre Dame campus. Rockne was additionally memorialized in two popular Hollywood features, *The Spirit of Notre Dame* (Russell Mack, 1931) and *Knute Rockne, All American* (Lloyd Bacon, 1940), with J. Farrell MacDonald and Pat O'Brien, respectively, portraying the coach.

By avoiding contextual information like Rockne's death, the "Knute Rockne's Training Techniques" episode frames the archival newsreel segments as though viewers were watching news footage of events occurring in the present, or at least very recent past. This lack of distinction between sports history and the present was typical throughout *Sports Album* and many subsequent sport documentary series. In this episode this technique is reinforced through the use of both voice-over narration and the selection of particular selections of dialogue recorded at the time the newsreel was filmed. For instance, it opens with Rockne giving a motivational speech at an outdoor team practice. As he addresses the team Slater simply notes via voice-over, "Now Rockne has something to say to them." The narration provides little new information for viewers, except to establish the relationship among the subjects. Later as the team does jumping jacks, Slater again elides any reference to the past, noting, "Rockne personally puts his boys through calisthenics." Though the narration was recorded eighteen years after the original newsreel was produced, no reference is made to this significant gap between the "then" and "now."

Although largely forgotten today, *Sports Album* illustrates how the sport documentary developed the lowly generic status that recent works like *O.J.: Made in America* have actively tried to counter. *Sports Album* emerged from independent producer Frederic Ziv's success in radio, particularly the syndicated *One for the Books* series, as well as his purchase of two large film libraries, highlighted by the Kinograms newsreels of the 1920s and early 1930s. Ziv used this archival footage to expand his brand of syndicated programs into television through compilation shows that could be economically produced and easily adapted to the needs of individual stations. *Sports Album* served as a precursor to sports news shows such as *This Week in Baseball* (syndicated, 1977–98) and *SportsCenter* (ESPN, 1979–present) by introducing viewers to historic athletes and teams. Like these more contemporary news shows, *Sports Album* often served an important industrial role for stations and sponsors as a complement to live sports telecasts. Ziv employed a figurative and nostalgic approach that prioritized celebrity culture and spectacle over the consistently accurate construction of sports history. *Sports Album* suggests that the cultural status of the sport documentary genre in television has been predicated on the engagement of the characteristics that earlier syndicated series avoided, including addressing sport's sociopolitical contexts, the development of in-depth narratives, and nuanced characterizations. *Sports Album* was the first of a long line of syndicated sports documentary series, and the continued exploration of these series can help us better understand the intersecting industrial, economic, and institutional factors that have shaped the cultural status of the genre from the earliest years of TV through today.

1. Michael Z. Newman and Elana Levine, *Legitimating Television: Media Convergence and Cultural Status* (New York: Routledge, 2012), 2.

2. All of the 16mm film prints of the *Sports Album* episodes are preserved at the Wisconsin Center for Film and Theater Research, Wisconsin Historical Society in Madison.

3. Bill Slater had extensive experience with this work, as prior to *Sports Album* he had worked as a sportscaster (including covering the 1936 Summer Olympics for NBC, along with Yankees and Giants baseball games), a radio and television game show host, and Paramount news announcer.

4. Jaimie Baron, *The Archive Effect: Found Footage and the Audiovisual Experience of History* (New York: Routledge, 2013), 18.

5. A sizable body of scholarship has examined the relationship between the studios and the broadcasting industry and the sale of Hollywood features to television in the 1950s. Monographs on the subject include Christopher Anderson, *Hollywood TV: The Studio System in the Fifties* (Austin: University of Texas Press, 1994); William Boddy, *Fifties Television: The Industry and Its Critics* (Urbana: University of Illinois Press, 1992); Michele Hilmes, *Hollywood and Broadcasting: From Radio to Cable* (Urbana: University of Illinois Press, 1990); Eric Hoyt, *Hollywood Vault: Film Libraries before Home Video* (Berkeley: University of California Press, 2014).

6. James R. Walker and Robert V. Bellamy Jr., *Center Field Shot: A History of Baseball on Television* (Lincoln: University of Nebraska Press, 2008); Ronald A. Smith, *Play-by-Play: Radio, Television, and Big-Time College Sport* (Baltimore: Johns Hopkins University Press, 2001); Keith Dunnavant, *The Fifty-Year Seduction: How Television Manipulated College Football from the Birth of the Modern NCAA to the Creation of the BCS* (New York: St. Martin's Press, 2004).

7. Derek Kompare, *Rerun Nation: How Repeats Invented American Television* (New York: Routledge, 2005).

8. John McMillan, "Meet Mr. Ziv," *Sponsor*, August 29, 1959, 32.

9. Ziv sold *Fans in the Stands* to multiple Cincinnati radio stations since the Reds' broadcasts moved around the dial. For example, in 1945 WCKY began broadcasting Saturday Reds games, taking the feed from WPCO, which previously had the exclusive broadcast rights. *Fans in the Stands* aired on both WCPO and WCKY on Saturdays.

10. For more on Sam Balter, see Alex Kupfer, "Sporting Labor in the Hollywood Studio System: Basketball, Universal Pictures, and the 1936 Berlin Olympics," *Spectator* 35, no. 2 (2015): 10–17.

11. Tracy Dodds, "'One for the Book': Sam Balter: He's a Lot More than Just a Broadcaster," *Los Angeles Times*, August 24, 1984, E1.

12. Morleen Getz Rouse, "A History of the F. W. Ziv Radio and Television Syndication Companies: 1930–1960" (PhD diss., University of Michigan, 1976), 99.

13. Boddy, *Fifties Television*, 42–62.

14. "General Film Library Is Purchased by Ziv," *Broadcasting*, July 12, 1948, 28.

15. Rouse, "History of the F. W. Ziv Radio and Television Syndication Companies," 102.

16. Hoyt, *Hollywood Vault*, 168.

17. Raymond Fielding, *The American Newsreel, 1911–1967* (Norman: University of Oklahoma Press, 1972), 154.

18. Michael Oriard, *King Football: Sport and Spectacle in the Golden Age of Radio and Newsreels, Movies and Magazines, the Weekly and the Daily Press* (Chapel Hill: University of North Carolina Press, 2001), 50.

19. "Charles Ritchie Switches," *Film Daily*, April 13, 1932, 7.

20. "Stock Shots: The General Film Library, Inc.," *Film Daily*, November 12, 1924, 5.

21. "1 Feature, 39 Shorts on New Ideal Program," *Film Daily*, April 6, 1932, 1, 12.

22. "Ziv's 'Sports Album' Gets 2 N.Y. Sponsors," *Variety*, September 29, 1948, 44.

23. "Sight and Sound," *Television Digest*, June 25, 1949, 162. The company already had a long association with sports. Jacob Ruppert owned the New York Yankees from 1915 until his death in 1939.

24. "Ziv Programs: New TV Sales Announced," *Broadcasting*, October 16, 1950, 188.

25. "Series to Be Televised; 2 Sponsors Pay $65,000," *New York Times*, September 27, 1947; Walker and Bellamy, *Center Field Shot*, 70.

26. Red Barber, *The Broadcasters* (New York: Da Capo Press, 1985), 182.

27. "Strictly Business," *Broadcasting*, May 21, 1951, 14, 82.

28. Oriard, *King Football*, 51.

29. Paul Arthur, "On the Virtues and Limitations of Collage," *Documentary Box* 11 (1997): 5.

30. Murray Sperber, *Shake Down the Thunder: The Creation of Notre Dame Football* (Bloomington: Indiana University Press, 2002), 352.

10

HBO Sports
Docu-Branding Boxing's Past and Present

TRAVIS VOGAN

The premium cable outlet HBO is best known for its prestigious original series like *The Sopranos* (1999–2007), *The Wire* (2002–8), and *Veep* (2012–19). Scholarship on the outlet has unsurprisingly focused on these productions and their role in building HBO's brand as a site of "quality TV."[1] But sports programming—and boxing in particular—has similarly contributed to HBO's repute by building the subscribership that bankrolls its expensive and renowned original series. "We'll always have our mainstay of boxing that continues to drive massive ratings for the network," remarked former HBO Sports president Ross Greenburg in 2003.[2]

Documentary accompanies boxing as a key contributor to HBO's image that scholarship has mostly overlooked. HBO uses documentary's stereotypical refinement among TV genres to position itself as a journalistically rigorous, artful, and even socially conscious outlet that seeks both to educate and to profit. It also deploys the vaunted genre's edifying repute, as Susan Murray points out, to balance the salacious and tawdry focus of programs like *Real Sex*, *G String Divas*, and *Cathouse*.[3] Boxing and documentary, then, aid the intersecting economic and cultural elements that compose HBO's envied industrial status and shed light on its history.

Moreover, HBO's documentaries promote its boxing coverage, and, just as important, stress the media outlet's importance to the sport—a status the channel's sports division HBO Sports emphasizes by branding it as "The Heart and Soul of Boxing." Beyond its documentaries, HBO participates in a range of activities that similarly mediate boxing's reality and emphasize the media outlet's significance to it. These docu-branding efforts—which include docudramas and brand placements in films, video games, and reality-TV programs—build renditions of boxing's past and present that put HBO Sports at its cultural and economic center. They demonstrate HBO's expansive and documentary-driven efforts to publicize its boxing coverage and promote itself as the historically shady sport's ethically scrupulous guiding force.

Putting the Tuxedo on Boxing

Sports programming drove Home Box Office's November 1972 launch out of Wilkes-Barre, Pennsylvania. The second program HBO aired—after kicking off with Paul Newman's *Sometimes a Great Notion* (1970)—was a live National Hockey League (NHL) game between the New York Rangers and Vancouver Canucks from Madison Square Garden. Live sports broadcasts drew at least modest audiences to the fledgling outlet. HBO's early years included nearly any sporting event to which it could secure rights—professional and college basketball, bowling, gymnastics, wrestling, and the like—as well as some for which it did not have permission. The channel brashly risked censure by taking the liberty of televising NHL and National Basketball Association games that were not otherwise on TV without paying those leagues. "The reaction from the NBA and NHL was a lot of grumbling and grousing," writes media journalist George Mair, "but surprisingly, they decided not to fight with HBO."[4] HBO was presumably too marginal an outlet to arouse enough concern for the sports organizations it was pirating to go to the trouble of filing suit. To be sure, the one constant across HBO's early and eclectic slate of sports programming was that few were watching.

While HBO's early sports programming spanned the athletic spectrum, it soon focused its energies on boxing. At the time TV networks were scaling back their investment in the notoriously corrupt sport. The reduction in televised boxing created a gap HBO used to identify with the sport and distinguish the channel in the budding sports cable TV market. HBO premiered its *World Championship Boxing* programming banner by airing a replay of George Foreman and Joe Frazier's January 1973 heavyweight title bout from Kingston, Jamaica. The fight, which Foreman surprisingly won, was also the first big-ticket match promoted by Don King and marked the beginnings of his intimate and eventually stressed relationship with the premium cable outlet.

HBO amplified its association with boxing when it contracted with Don King Productions to carry Muhammad Ali and Joe Frazier's 1975 "Thrilla in Manila"—their third, final, and most vicious bout. HBO arranged to augment King's closed-circuit broadcasts with a live satellite feed to three of its affiliates. It used the Thrilla in Manila to debut is transition to a continual satellite model. In exchange for the rights HBO gave Don King Productions an undisclosed amount of money and allowed King to use its New York–area microwave facilities to feed nearby theaters with a closed-circuit broadcast, which generated the bulk of the fight's revenues.[5] HBO unveiled its satellite service with a ceremony that included speeches from executives extolling the channel's unique potential among cable outlets to bring subscribers live content from across the globe.[6] Ali and Frazier's high-profile match provided an ideal vehicle to showcase this new feature—and composed a pivotal moment for the emerging cable industry. HBO's subscribership doubled after the fight—reaching two hundred thousand by the end of 1975 and breaking one million by the end of 1976. Those cable providers that carried HBO showed a roughly 20 percent boost in customers—a spike that prompted most major services to begin offering the premium channel by the late 1970s. The benefits of boxing, according to Greenburg, convinced HBO to "claim some ownership of the sport" and create exclusive contracts with promising fighters.[7]

HBO's investment in boxing was also aided by the U.S. Court of Appeals' 1977 decision to vacate network-driven antisiphoning rules that prevented cable outlets from carrying certain popular sporting events. The networks argued that cable sports coverage unfairly limited consumers' ability to view events of public interest. The Federal Communication Commission agreed and imposed restrictions on cable sports TV. Spearheaded by HBO, *Home Box Office v. FCC* (1977) overturned the antisiphoning regulations, which opened the door for HBO to expand its sports offerings and laid the groundwork for the emergence of cable channels like ESPN. HBO finally turned a profit in 1977—a development this deregulation aided.

Seth Abraham boasted that HBO did not "just do boxing, we do boxing that tells a story." The outlet began to inflect its broadcasts with documentary practices influenced by Roone Arledge's narrative-driven and journalistic work at ABC Sports. Greenburg, a former Arledge employee, admitted to "taking the philosophy from ABC Sports and bringing it to HBO" by integrating biographical profiles on participants and using cutting-edge technologies to make its broadcasts more entertaining and widen their viewership.[8] The channel demonstrated this approach with *Boxing behind Bars*, a 1978 *World Championship Boxing* special televised from Rahway State Prison in Woodbridge, New Jersey. The special featured a light-heavyweight match that pitted James Scott—an inmate doing time for a parole violation following an armed robbery conviction—against Eddie Gregory, a title contender who consented to fight his incarcerated opponent within Rahway's sealed walls.

Boxing behind Bars begins with a short documentary about life inside Rahway that opens with a point-of-view tracking shot entering the prison's imposing gates. "Inside these walls and bars," HBO host Len Berman announces, "Scott works out in his own boxing program. But he cannot leave the walls to box professionally. So for the first time in boxing history, an inmate is fighting a professional fight inside a prison." Berman builds further intrigue for the historic occasion by explaining that the fight will occur in an auditorium that "was the site of bloody riots four years ago." HBO and the promoters filled the auditorium with 450 curious customers. Meanwhile, Rahway's roughly 1,100 inmates watched on a closed-circuit feed from the drill hall. The exploitative broadcast—which anticipated Jamaa Fanaka's blaxploitation prison boxing movie *Penitentiary* (1978)—periodically cut to the prisoners watching intently to underscore their enthusiastic support for Scott and to highlight the surveilled sequestration that marks even their leisure time.

The introduction suggests *Boxing behind Bars* will both showcase a live competition and tell a mysterious and revealing tale about life in prison. It focuses in particular on Rahway's vocational program, which includes boxing training for inmates interested in pursuing the sport professionally upon their release. Cohost Larry Merchant interviews Rahway's warden, who argues that the boxing program fosters self-respect, discipline, and job prospects. HBO, in fact, gained Rahway's cooperation for *Boxing behind Bars* because the prison sought to promote its vocational training programs. "Prison authorities think a Scott win will help boost their funds," Merchant divulges.

The documentary segment centers most of its attention on the role boxing played in Scott's life behind bars and his hopes to use the sport to make a fresh start once he leaves Rahway. "This fight," Merchant explains, "could begin another passage of freedom, and a career [for Scott]." *Boxing behind Bars* establishes Scott as a sentimental favorite who is fighting as much for his own personal and moral redemption as he is for victory in the ring. It also compares Scott to boxers who found success in the sport after prison stints, such as Sonny Liston and Ron Lyle. HBO Sports' fight coverage clearly prioritizes Scott's narrative and includes frequent cutaways to his fellow prisoners cheering him on from the drill hall, which erupts in applause when Scott is declared the winner by unanimous decision. The coverage, however, also makes note of the deflating fact that despite Scott's great triumph against Gregory, the exhausted boxer will simply return to his cell—albeit with a bit more pride and hope.

With *Boxing behind Bars* HBO uses its documentary programming and boxing coverage to contribute to the brand of prison reform Rahway has established. It unsurprisingly does not question the Rahway program's decidedly naive assumption that boxing might provide inmates with a realistic or sustainable means for economic betterment. Rather, it uses Scott's story to build interest in an otherwise unexceptional bout and justifies the gimmicky match through the journalistic treatment it provides the unusual prison program. But the documentary-driven experiment paid off. HBO won its first Cable ACE Award for *Boxing behind Bars*—one of the first industry accolades it gathered. The special demonstrates how HBO Sports' "boxing that tells a story" helped institute the media outlet's quality brand.

Building on the success of *World Championship Boxing*, HBO secured its first exclusive rights to a heavyweight title fight with Larry Holmes and Mike Weaver's June 1979 match. ABC was originally slated to carry the bout, which Don King Productions was promoting. The network, however, refused to pay the $1 million that King demanded. Mostly out of spite, King sold the match to HBO for $125,000.[9] The Holmes-Weaver match composed an even more visible statement of HBO's connection to prizefighting than *Boxing behind Bars*. As *New York Times* sportswriter Red Smith commented: "It was Home Box Office's finest hour—finest three hours, to be exact. The big brains of television's three major networks turned down Friday night's boxing show in Madison Square Garden, so Home Box Office bought it for the cable system's two million subscribers and wound up with the best fight card in recent memory while the networks were regaling their viewers with an eight-year-old movie, a warmed-over soap opera and yet another whodunit."[10] Smith, whose opinion carried considerable industrial weight, suggested that HBO was furnishing boxing fans with programming that the networks were unwilling to offer and establishing itself as a new destination for marquee fights. HBO soon consistently began to provide worldwide feeds for championship matches. "Our theory is that HBO Sports should stand for big events," Abraham said. "We were going to try to create dominance in the sport," Greenburg added.[11]

HBO surrounded its increasing slate of boxing programming with documentaries. It partnered with Big Fights, Inc.—a production company owned by William Cayton and Jim Jacobs that held the world's largest collection of boxing films—to create *Boxing's Greatest Champions* and the *Boxing's Best* series. *Boxing Greatest Champions* collaborated with the Boxing Writers of America to rank the best-ever fighters in each weight class, and *Boxing's Best* presented biographical profiles on iconic pugilists. The documentaries presented a mutually beneficial arrangement for Big Fights and HBO. They gave Big Fights an opportunity to repackage its footage, much of which it had used in its theatrically released documentaries such as *Legendary Champions* (1968), *Jack Johnson* (1970), and *A.K.A. Cassius Clay* (1970). The programs also underscore Big Fights' role as boxing's primary visual archive. *Boxing's Greatest Champions* host Curt Gowdy, for instance, calls attention to the documentary's inclusion of "some of the rarest film in all of sports," and a *Boxing's Best* segment on Jack Johnson describes Jim Jacobs as "boxing's preeminent historian" when he appears on camera as an interviewee. Beyond buttressing Big Fights' authority, the documentaries cast HBO as an arbiter of sport history on par with the company that participates in its arrangement of boxing's past.

HBO Sports' boxing documentaries also use the genre's enriching repute to distance the media outlet from the sport's stereotypical seediness. "The politics of boxing are as close to 17th century buccaneering as anything that exists on the planet today," Abraham acknowledged. But HBO, according to Greenburg, possessed integrity that its business associates and competitors lacked. "I think over the years we've been able to professionally handle this sport, conduct business the right way, and really create big events for television and kind of stay above the fray," he explained. "I think there's a certain responsibility that comes with HBO boxing and to carry on that legacy you have to stay on the straight and narrow, so that's always been our kind of way of doing business here." HBO's documentaries helped to construct this scrupulous identity—an image that Showtime's Jay Larkin claims "put the tuxedo on boxing" and gave the sport renewed acceptability among mainstream audiences.[12]

A Cash Register in Short Pants

By 1985 the *New York Times* recognized HBO Sports as television's leading producer of boxing broadcasts. While HBO's documentary-driven practices drew critical acclaim, the network's contracts with star boxers drove its steadily bulging ratings. The middleweight "Marvelous" Marvin Hagler became what *Sports Illustrated*'s Richard Hoffer described as HBO's "original meal ticket" during the early 1980s. He was the cable channel's biggest attraction, and his fights generated larger audiences than even HBO's most popular movies.[13] But the bruising young heavyweight "Iron" Mike Tyson soon eclipsed even Hagler's outsize TV ratings. HBO signed Tyson, who was managed by Big Fights' Cayton and Jacobs, to a limited deal shortly after the undefeated nineteen-year-old registered his nineteenth consecutive knockout in March 1986 by flooring Steve Zouski in the third round.

Around the time Tyson joined HBO Don King began collaborating with fellow promoter Butch Lewis to pitch the channel on a heavyweight unification tournament that would produce a single undisputed champion recognized across the often-bickering International Boxing Federation, World Boxing Association, and World Boxing Council. HBO paid $18 million for rights to televise the eighteen-month tournament that would stretch across 1986 and into 1987. Abraham believed the event would cement HBO's position atop boxing's TV hierarchy and reinforce its role as a virtuous entity set on bringing some order to the messy sport. "The three networks have a presence in boxing," Abraham explained, "but they don't have the big fights. We'd like to be the home of boxing's big fights, and I thought the heavyweights were an interesting way to go."[14] Though Tyson was still establishing his professional credentials, his rapidly escalating celebrity as a merciless knockout artist made him a must for the tournament, which he cruised through to become the youngest-ever heavyweight champion and the first undisputed champ since 1978.

HBO signed Tyson to a $26.5 million seven-fight deal shortly after the tournament. The contract, according to biographer Peter Heller, helped the boxer to earn more in 1988 than Jack Dempsey, Joe Louis, Rocky Marciano, and Muhammad Ali made in their entire careers combined. *Wall Street Journal*'s Mark Robichaux described Tyson as "a phenomenon like none other in boxing television history."[15] He was the sport's biggest star since Ali and had the benefit of a more robust sports media landscape seeking to turn his image into profits. Tyson signed endorsement deals with Pepsi, Kodak, and Nintendo, which made him the focal point of the 1987 video game *Mike Tyson's Punch Out!!* The popular game marketed Tyson to Nintendo's typically younger consumers and traded on his superhuman image by making him the nearly invincible final obstacle who knocked opponents down with a single punch.

These combined factors made HBO home to the biggest star in sports. HBO president Michael Fuchs called Tyson "a cash register in short pants," and Abraham referred to him as the media outlet's "most important employee" and a "walking billboard in black shorts."[16] As *USA Today* succinctly put it, "Mike Tyson made HBO the place for boxing."[17] A 1987 survey found that 40 percent of the men who subscribed to the channel for the first time were doing so to watch Tyson's fights, which were attracting a 35 share of HBO subscribers.

While Tyson's popular matches gained much of their value through their live and "video-proof" status, HBO deepened its investment in its "walking billboard" by making a deal with Big Fights to create a series of home-video documentaries that highlighted his most thrilling moments. Titles like *Mike Tyson and History's Greatest Knockouts* (1989) and *Boxing's*

Best: Tyson and the Heavyweights—an extension of HBO Sports and Big Fights' *Boxing's Best* documentary series—installed Tyson within the pantheon of historic fighters. They also, of course, advertised HBO's place as the boxer's home. HBO Sports bolstered further its association with Tyson in the 1989 special *Boxing's Greatest Hits*, which offered a history of boxing on the channel since its launch. As host Jim Lampley announces, the program covers "seventeen years of great boxing memories on HBO." *Boxing's Greatest Hits* conflates the recent history of boxing with HBO's past and emphasizes the media outlet's centrality to the sport's most important recent moments. The special ends with the emotional soft-rock song "Born to Be Champions" alongside an image of Tyson raising his arms triumphantly, which the HBO Sports logo eventually replaces. In no uncertain terms the special builds a historical narrative that aligns Tyson and HBO Sports with boxing's peak.

Tyson became so important to HBO that the media outlet tried to negotiate a lifetime deal with him—an unprecedented arrangement in sports. But the boxer's once-cozy relationship with HBO Sports began to fray shortly after he lost his first match—against James "Buster" Douglas in February 1990—and faced a variety of legal and personal troubles. He also severed ties with Cayton shortly after Jacobs died in 1988 and hired Don King to serve as his new manager. King sold Tyson on the importance of having African American management to look after his affairs—the strategy he largely used to break into the sport in the 1970s. Critics, however, charged that King simply used race as a wedge to gain access to Tyson.

To combat the increasingly negative publicity he and King were facing, Tyson demanded that HBO run a Spike Lee–directed documentary profile prior to his December 1990 fight against Alex Stewart. Lee also hailed from Tyson's hometown of Brooklyn, New York, and had emerged as a leading voice in African American culture since the release of his breakout hit, *Do the Right Thing* (1989), a film set in Brooklyn that features prominently shots of a Mike Tyson mural that celebrates the boxer's status as a local hero. HBO Sports had no involvement in the segment's production and worried that the documentary's overt bias would compromise the journalistic scruples on which its boxing coverage and documentaries trade. In this case, however, it sacrificed editorial control to pacify its newly disgruntled "cash register." Lampley emphasized that the production was Lee's creation—not a product of HBO Sports—in an interview with the director before it ran. When he asked Lee whether the documentary was "journalism or advocacy," Lee shrugged and called it "a little bit of both." Lee contended that Tyson and King had been unfairly "pummeled in the press" and claimed he sought to show a different side of the misunderstood sports celebrities. "We want to make clear that this was Spike's baby," Lampley said. "We interfered in no way, shape, or form after we gave Spike the opportunity to bring a 35mm camera here and to Brooklyn for this profile of Mike Tyson." A title card emerged with an image of Lee that reads "Spike Lee Presents Mike Tyson." The project, which marked the beginning of a long-standing relationship between the filmmaker and HBO, both exploited Lee's auteur persona and used it to relieve HBO Sports from taking responsibility for the brash perspective it presents.

The profile opens with the same Brooklyn-based mural of Tyson that Lee includes in *Do the Right Thing* and is shot in black and white to accentuate its raw, unflinching tone. In particular, the documentary charges the mainstream sports establishment with racism and attributes Tyson's and King's infamy to these prejudices. King proclaims Tyson a black hero whose success in the ring has profound social import for black Americans. "When he strikes a blow," King says of Tyson in his famously bombastic style, "he strikes a blow for all those who are discriminated against, all those who are segregated, all those who are downtrodden, the underprivileged, and denied." King bluntly continues to explain how Tyson's racial identity makes him suspicious regardless of his many athletic, economic, and personal successes. "If you're a n——, you're a n—— until you die. You're either a poor n—— or a rich n——. But you never get to stop being a n——. And if you get to be educated, you're just an educated n——." Tyson and King, the profile suggests, have banded together to fight against this bigoted system, which HBO Sports belongs to and supports. "They always change the rules when black folks come into success," King defiantly argues. "Black success in unacceptable."

Lee's documentary came under immediate fire for its language and divisiveness. HBO Sports boxing analyst Larry Merchant responded directly after it aired by calling King a "snake-oil salesman" who made his way in the boxing business by "wrapping himself in the emotional flags of race and injustice." Former professional athlete and civil rights activist Arthur Ashe published a critique in the *Washington Post* that accused Lee of "simplifying, compartmentalizing, and unofficially amplifying what is already a social mine field."[18] Lee, Ashe charged, exploited and fanned racial tensions. But the confrontational and controversial documentary skillfully built excitement for Tyson's match against Stewart, which Tyson easily won in the first round, that reinforced his salable reputation as the "Baddest Man on the Planet." It also showed the editorial compromises HBO would make to stay in business with its "most important employee" and the role documentary played in negotiating their relationship.

King eventually steered Tyson away from HBO and toward a deal with its main competitor, Showtime. Tyson attributed the divorce primarily to his distaste for Larry Merchant, who had repeatedly criticized King and the boxer. "I didn't want him commenting on my fights," Tyson told ESPN's Roy Firestone. "They [HBO] didn't back down, so I left." But more than Tyson's enmity toward Merchant, King wanted the deal to include a provision that made him the exclusive promoter for Tyson's television partner. HBO would not make such a concession, so King took his boxer to Showtime with an agreement in late 1991 that guaranteed roughly $120 million for eight to ten fights.[19] King immediately created the pay-per-view service KingVision PPV, to compete with the TVKO pay-per-view outlet HBO launched in 1991. Despite TVKO's potential, HBO lost its biggest star. Tyson, however, was soon forced out of boxing after being convicted of rape in 1992 and spending the next three years in prison.

Docu-Branding Boxing

Tyson returned to the ring—still under contract with Showtime—almost immediately after his March 1995 release from prison. Though Tyson and King had severed ties with HBO, the cable channel's film production unit, HBO Pictures, capitalized on the company's association with the infamous sports celebrities through producing unauthorized biographical docudramas on each that did not necessitate TV rights. Like most "based on a true story" productions, docudramas anchor their tales in the real world and trade on audiences' familiarity with the people and events they depict. They are also routinely subject to the critiques historical films garner. "Commercial imperatives most often fuel cinematic rewrites of history," explains film critic Frank Sanello. "Complex economic and social issues are pureed into easily digestible bits of information intended for consumption by Hollywood's most sought-after demographic: the lowest common denominator." Despite these frequent gripes film scholar Robert Rosenstone defends historical films by contending that they can offer "a new form of history, what we might call history as vision." Derek Paget distinguishes docudramas from other historical films by suggesting they maintain a closer relationship to reality by reproducing events and sometimes even incorporating indexical archival footage. Docudramas, Steven Lipkin contends, furnish a useful, if imperfect, documentary function "when actual documentary materials either do not exist or by themselves are incomplete or insufficient to treat the subject matter adequately." As the historical worlds docudramas build, according to Lipkin, "contribute to a culture's vision of itself," HBO's Tyson and King docudramas build a past that contributes to HBO's self-identification as an authority in boxing.[20]

HBO premiered *Tyson*, based in part on José Torres's book *Fire and Fear: The Inside Story of Mike Tyson* (1989), just after the boxer's release from prison. Directed by Uli Edel and starring Michael Jai White, the production depicts Tyson as a tragic figure who lost his way after the passing of his trainer and adoptive father Cus D'Amato and Jim Jacobs. These guardians' absence, the film suggests, left a vulnerable hollowness that Don King and Tyson's ex-wife Robin Givens exploited. The film begins with Tyson in a courtroom standing trial for rape and reflecting on how he went from a poor kid in Brooklyn to one of the world's most famous athletes to a convicted rapist. The film proceeds from this flashback to chronicle his rise and fall.

As communications scholar Jack Lule observes, popular press representations of Tyson amid his arrest, trial, and conviction commonly depicted him through two similarly dehumanizing tropes. He was either a simpleminded victim of his dire upbringing and malicious crooks like King or a beastly savage who could not abide by society's mores.[21] Both tropes, as Lule contends, perpetuate white supremacist racial hierarchies. HBO's *Tyson* reinforces these practices by portraying the boxer as a dangerous and pitiful man-child who cannot resist turning to violence to solve his problems, has a history of abusing women, and is too naive to see through King's and Givens's different but equally blatant forms of malevolence. Moreover, the docudrama suggests Tyson functioned productively only when under the direction of compassionate white custodians like D'Amato and Jacobs. The docudrama contrasts the critique of boxing's racial politics that Spike Lee offered in his prefight documentary.

The film concludes by returning to the courtroom for the announcement of Tyson's rape conviction and, like many docudramas, ends with text that explains the disgraced boxer's eventual fate: "Mike Tyson was found guilty on charges of rape and criminal deviant conduct and sentenced to six years in the Indiana Youth Center." Police escort the just-sentenced and handcuffed Tyson to prison as the text appears on-screen. The final shot depicts the boxer looking up to the sky—and to a symbolic freedom the onetime champ can no longer enjoy—before being corralled into a police cruiser. The conclusion then notes Tyson's release in March 1995, a little more than three years into his six-year sentence, and his intention to continue boxing before explaining that "Don King will retain his role as Mike Tyson's manager" and adding that "King is scheduled to stand trial for insurance fraud in May of 1995." The production unambiguously positions King as a shady villain who contributed to Tyson's demise and will likely continue taking advantage of the boxer after his release.[22] King's impending trial for insurance fraud is hardly relevant to the tragic tale *Tyson* weaves; however, including the point helps HBO to characterize him as a snake. By extension, it distances the media outlet from King's devious machinations and suggests Tyson was better off before he left for Showtime.

HBO extended this vilification of King in *Don King: Only in America* (1997), a biopic starring Ving Rhames and based on Jack Newfield's exposé *Only in America: The Life and Crimes of Don King* (1996), which at one point likens the promoter to Adolf Hitler.[23] The production—which opens by blaring the O'Jays song "For the Love of Money"—traces King's transformation from a Cleveland numbers runner who once did four years in prison for manslaughter into a wealthy boxing impresario. It repeatedly evokes King's insistence that his remarkable story is possible "only in America," but presents his tale as a perverse version of the American

Dream that single-mindedly pursues fortune regardless of the wreckage it leaves behind. The docudrama's distinguishing aesthetic feature is a series of fourth wall–breaking soliloquies King delivers from a boxing ring—his preferred stage—that share his perspective on sport, race, and money. "I'm the American dream," King hollers from the ring with a smoldering cigar in hand. "I am entertainment. If you didn't have Don King, you'd have to invent him." The docudrama, which won a Peabody Award on the strength of Rhames's performance, presents King as the manifestly unethical ringmaster of a blatantly corrupt sport.

Tyson and *Only in America* build realism by reproducing familiar moments in their subjects' careers and including cameos from recognizable members of the fight world. In particular, they frequently include references to HBO. *Tyson*, for instance, re-creates matches that originally appeared on the channel with HBO Sports personalities calling the action and the organization's cameras and microphones capturing it. The scenes use HBO Sports to lend the fictionalized depictions authenticity while emphasizing the prominent role the media outlet played in Tyson's career. Similarly, *Only in America* uses HBO's contentious relationship with King as a plot point. Two of the promoter's profanity-laced rants single HBO out as an adversary. "HBO? I made those motherfuckers a fortune," King exclaims while venting about his business conflicts with the cable channel. As with *Tyson* the scene accentuates HBO's role in King's career while distancing it from his questionable values. HBO Pictures promised that HBO Sports' rift with King did not inform the docudrama's production or the shape it took. "They were uninvolved and I had a clear path," HBO Pictures' president John Matoian said of HBO Sports. Abraham claimed that HBO Sports provided only a few minor notes and that HBO Pictures had final say over the production's shape. While HBO Sports was not directly involved in *Tyson* or *Only in America*, both docudramas mark HBO's continued efforts to profit on the former business partners while underscoring the media outlet's importance to their careers and separating it from their faults.

HBO Sports had continued making boxing documentaries through the 1990s, such as *Sonny Liston: The Mysterious Life and Death of a Champion* (1995) and *Sugar Ray Robinson: The Bright Lights and Dark Shadows of a*

Champion (1998). The Liston and Robinson documentaries reflect *Tyson* by offering comparable stories of tortured boxers. But the process of creating these films became more challenging in 1998, when ESPN outbid HBO, Fox, the NBA, and Madison Square Garden to purchase the Big Fights, Inc., library for $80 million. HBO continued to produce boxing documentaries, but the prospect of licensing historical footage from a competitor that was attempting to break into the sports documentary genre made the task more arduous.[24]

HBO Sports skirted these challenges with *Legendary Nights* (2003), a historical documentary series made entirely of HBO-owned footage. Branded as part of HBO Sports' *Sports of the 20th Century* series of historical documentaries, *Legendary Nights* commemorated HBO's thirtieth anniversary by creating twelve segments that offer the stories behind the greatest fights the channel covered. As Greenburg commented, "Fifty or 60 years from now when people wonder what boxing was like from 1973 to 2002, they can pull out these 12 documentaries and see that HBO was there in the middle of the ring documenting history." Lampley plugged the documentary series as "testimony to how rich our heritage is and how many great fights and stories we've had."[25] Anticipating ESPN's *30 for 30* series, a project launched in 2009 to commemorate the network's thirtieth anniversary, *Legendary Nights* conflates boxing's recent past with HBO—points it reinforces by using its own footage as the primary historical record and relying mostly on its personalities to serve as expert interviewees. *Legendary Nights* also continues HBO's insistence that it is a rare force for good in the sport. The segment on Meldrick Taylor and Julio César Chávez's 1990 light-welterweight championship fight—a bout the documentary says "had it all" and that *Ring* magazine named the match of the decade—was particularly telling. After recounting their historic brawl the episode ends by commenting on Taylor's ill-advised decision to continue boxing even though he is obviously suffering from dementia pugilistica, now commonly known as chronic traumatic encephalopathy (CTE), and critiquing the boxing establishment that enables him to persist despite the obvious danger. *Legendary Nights* casts HBO Sports as a principal player in boxing's recent history and an advocate for reform that looks after the legends it helped to create once they leave the spotlight.

Aside from its own films HBO makes frequent arrangements to integrate HBO Sports trademarks and personalities into fictional Hollywood productions. Nearly every big-budget film since the late 1990s that depicts a prominent televised boxing match has marked it as an HBO event. The productions use the HBO Sports brand placements to serve a documentary function that suggests the fights they showcase appear as they would were they actually being staged. HBO Sports, in turn, benefits from the brand placements' suggestion that it is the first stop for big-time boxing matches.

For instance, Ron Shelton's *Play It to the Bone* (1999) tells the story of Cesar Dominguez and Vince Boudreau, two aging boxers and best pals who get the unexpected opportunity to compete on the undercard of a Mike Tyson bout that HBO is carrying via TVKO. The rub is that the friends must fight each other. The formulaic comedy follows their harried road trip from Los Angeles to Las Vegas for the bout along with Grace— Vince's ex-girlfriend and Cesar's current flame—who gives them a ride in her flashy muscle car. The movie's combined elements of the road film, buddy comedy, and love triangle reflect Shelton's earlier (and far more successful) sports film *Bull Durham* (1988).

Play It to the Bone situates the HBO Sports bout as a vehicle through which Cesar and Vince hope to revive their languishing careers. Accordingly, Shelton uses HBO and its personalities to stress the match's profile. He also references HBO's credibility in a scene where the promoter—a scheming businessman named Joe Domino—confronts Lampley before Cesar and Vince's fight. He apologizes for the substitute match's seemingly shoddy quality and asks the sportscaster if HBO Sports can "put the best face" on it for the audience. Lampley refuses and begins to ask questions about Cesar and Vince's fitness, potentially damaging queries the slippery promoter dodges. The scene buttresses HBO Sports' journalistic reputation preceding Cesar and Vince's match, which is presented through Lampley, Merchant, and George Foreman's commentary. Their bloody slugfest concludes in a draw, and Lampley dubs the surprisingly engaging bout "an instant classic" and an "epic battle." "Years from now," Lampley continues in his effusive postmatch summary, "the real fight fans will be telling each other they were here to see this bout." It was the kind of match, he implies, that might eventually wind up on *Legendary Nights*.

David O. Russell's *The Fighter* (2010), an inspirational biopic about light-welterweight boxer "Irish" Micky Ward, similarly uses HBO to stress its subject matter's importance and to build realism. The film depicts Ward through a familiar underdog narrative à la *Rocky* (1976), in which the white fighter out of Lowell, Massachusetts, overcomes economic hardship and past failures to find success in the ring and redeem his brother, Dicky Eklund, a onetime pro boxer who became a drug addict. HBO's *America Undercover* documentary series, in fact, used Eklund's transformation from promising boxer to down-and-out junky as the topic of a 1995 episode titled "High on Crack Street: Lost Lives in Lowell." *The Fighter* depicts the *America Undercover* crew following Eklund and uses the poignant but embarrassing documentary to highlight Ward's underdog status and to stress his potential to improve his family's fortunes and reputation.

As HBO explained Eklund's struggles with "High on Crack Street," it helped to make Ward a star through televising a series of three fights against Arturo Gatti. Like *Play It to the Bone*, *The Fighter* showcases Ward's matches through HBO Sports' visual aesthetic and with some of the same talent that commented on his original bouts. But Russell took this quest to build documentary realism further by conscripting the same cameras HBO Sports used to televise Ward's matches. This televisual and branded aesthetic composed a key quality that critics identified in the mostly positive reviews the Academy Award–nominated film gathered. "We had HBO come and shoot the fights for us, use the same cameras that they shot the great Micky Ward–Arturo Gatti fights with," said Mark Wahlberg, who played Ward and served as a producer on the film. "HBO does such a great job of capturing all the action and suspense and drama in a fight. As long as it's there in the ring, they never miss anything."[26] Wahlberg's endorsement positions HBO Sports as the standard-bearer for televised boxing—a perspective *The Fighter* reinforces by mimicking the division's coverage. It also, though indirectly, supports Wahlberg's interest in *Entourage* (2004–11), a comedic HBO original series he produced at the time that shared the channel's mostly male boxing audience.

The 2000 Acclaim Sports video game *HBO Boxing* channeled the brand placements' efforts to advertise HBO Sports' association with boxing toward a younger crowd. Like many sports video games, *HBO Boxing* has participants adopt the avatar of actual fighters and climb the ranks to compete for a championship. Though ostensibly based on reality, the game includes only those contemporary fighters under contract with HBO Sports and excludes its competitors' boxers. Moreover, and like the films, its fights occur as if they are being televised by HBO Sports with the channel's graphics packages and announcers. "The video game accurately reflects the electricity and excitement of what it's really like to fight on HBO," enthused HBO fighter and commentator Roy Jones Jr. while promoting the game.[27] Extending the Hollywood brand placements, the game creates a reality in which HBO Sports is not simply the leader in television boxing but the only perceptible presence in boxing TV.

HBO Boxing's "career mode" most conspicuously markets HBO Sports by having players graduate through the media outlet's increasingly prominent boxing shows. Fighters begin on *KO Nation*, a Saturday-afternoon program geared toward younger viewers that featured less polished professionals. They then work their way up to *Boxing after Dark*, *World Championship Boxing*, and ultimately a TVKO championship bout. "If you work hard," the game's booklet reads, "you can beef up your boxer as you rise to the pinnacle of your career: a chance to have the world watch you fight in a TVKO pay-per-view from HBO." The game advertises HBO Sports' varied boxing programs, which inflect its fights with televisual realism while branding HBO's TVKO pay-per-view events as the sport's apex.

The documentary/reality series *24/7*, which debuted in 2007 to provide viewers an inside view of fighters' preparations leading up to an appearance on pay-per-view, composed a more consistent effort to docu-brand HBO's association with boxing. Narrator Liev Schreiber described the first *24/7*—a four-episode primer to Oscar De La Hoya and Floyd Mayweather's 2007 championship bout—as "an unprecedented, unfiltered look at the lives of two champions as they prepare for an historic showdown." The program continued HBO Sports' traditional commitment to producing "boxing that tells a story" by building narratives that might expand the fight's eventual pay-per-view audience. "The programs we present," Greenburg promised of *24/7*, "will appeal far beyond the hard-core boxing fan."[28] The first season framed the featured combatants as opposites. Mayweather is a trash-talking playboy who resides in Las Vegas. De La Hoya is a soft-spoken family man.

Though their personalities differ significantly, both are single-minded competitors who train unrelentingly in preparation for their fight. The series 24/7 also emphasizes the tensions between Mayweather and his estranged father, Floyd Sr., who previously served as De La Hoya's trainer. Worried that Mayweather Sr. would not be able to train him properly for a fight against his son, De La Hoya replaced the trainer. As a result Mayweather Sr. attempts to reconnect with his son, who is trained by his uncle Roger Mayweather, and become part of his team. The family drama added another layer of intrigue to the prefight buildup.

Depending on the situation, HBO Sports marketed 24/7 as a documentary series and reality program to take advantage of the overlapping genres' different cultural meanings and audiences. "In order to court a particular type of audience identification and set of expectations," writes Susan Murray, "television networks can take a program that has somewhat liminal textual generic identifiers and set it as either a documentary or a reality program by packaging it in such a way as to appear either more educational/informative or more entertaining/sensational, or in some cases both."[29] When asked whether 24/7 was a reality program, for instance, Greenburg curtly claimed to "hate that word. 'Reality' shows to me are manufactured reality," he huffed. "This is dramatic documentary filmmaking." In a separate interview conducted the same year, Greenburg praised Mayweather—whose legal troubles and eventually contentious relationship with HBO recalled Tyson—as a "reality superstar" on par with the cast of *American Idol* and *Survivor*.[30] Greenburg's selective branding practices indicated that 24/7 both participated in trends in reality television and bolstered the "quality" status HBO's documentaries helped to build.

Regardless of 24/7's precise generic designation, the program continued HBO Sports' varied docu-branding efforts to place the media outlet at the center of boxing while publicizing its coverage of the sport. The series, as *New York Times* sports media critic Richard Sandomir points out, "served a dual function as a documentary and infomercial" for an HBO Sports pay-per-view event coursing with the drama 24/7 brought out.[31] HBO Sports even self-reflexively made the 24/7 series into a plot point in its documentation of the lead-up to De La Hoya and Mayweather's match. The second episode shows Mayweather and his team watching the series' first installment. Mayweather is so motivated by the sight of his adversary training that he immediately leaves to do some roadwork. Later in the series Mayweather critiques De La Hoya's *24/7* performance as boring—another indication that he was watching the show carefully and that its production enhanced the fight's stakes. The scenes indicate that HBO Sports does not simply cover boxing matches but composes a cultural hub for the sport and a resource that boxers use to learn about their trade, survey their competition, and even taunt opponents.

The series *24/7*'s first three episodes aired on Sunday evenings after *The Sopranos* and *Entourage*—the most coveted spot on HBO's weekly schedule—and replayed twelve times a week. "It's the first time an HBO Sports product has broke through to get the kind of space," a satisfied Greenburg said of *24/7*'s scheduling. "If we can perform, it takes the stature of HBO Sports up a notch within the building."[32] The final episode aired on the Thursday before the Saturday-evening fight and ended with shots of HBO Sports banners at the event to emphasize the pay-per-view spectacle that was about to unfold—a sort of fifth installment of *24/7* that HBO subscribers would have to pay an extra $55 to see.

HBO's pay-per-view coverage of the Mayweather–De La Hoya match, which Mayweather won by a split decision, gathered 2.5 million purchases to become the biggest selling nonheavyweight title fight ever and the most lucrative prizefight of all time. The show expanded the fight's reach. The series "exposed a lot of young viewers to Oscar and Floyd," remarked HBO Sports spokesperson Ray Stallone. "That's what boxing needs." The series quickly became a standard ingredient of HBO Sports' marquee fights and extended into other sporting events that sought to benefit from its ability to grow their audience.

Like the documentaries, docudramas, product placements, and video games, *24/7* fashions a reality for boxing that indicates the sport could not exist—or would at least be markedly different—without HBO Sports while publicizing its fight coverage. These diverse docu-branding efforts expand on HBO Sports' long-standing combination of boxing and documentary to show the crucial—but mostly overlooked—roles these intersecting genres play in HBO's history. But HBO's reliance on boxing steadily waned along with the combination of the sport's declining popularity and an influx of sports media outlets competing for viewers. In 2018 the media outlet discontinued its involvement in the sport. "We've seen audience research that indicates boxing is no longer a determining factor for our subscribers," said HBO Sports executive vice president Peter Nelson.[33] Despite the recent shift, HBO Sports' "boxing that tells a story" helped to create the infrastructure from which the cable outlet transformed into an esteemed destination for "quality TV" that no longer needs the viewers that prizefighting offers.

NOTES

1. Gary R. Edgerton and Jeffrey P. Jones, eds., *The Essential HBO Reader* (Lexington: University of Kentucky Press, 2008); Marc Leverette, Brian L. Ott, and Cara Louise Buckley, eds., *It's Not TV: Watching HBO in the Post-television Era* (New York: Routledge, 2008).

2. Tom Umstead and Ross Greenburg, interview, Cable Center Oral History Collection, May 2003.

3. See Michael Curtin, *Redeeming the Wasteland: Television, Documentary, and Cold War Politics* (New Brunswick NJ: Rutgers University Press, 1995); Travis Vogan, "ESPN Films and the Creation of Prestige in Contemporary Sports Television," *International Journal of Sport Communication* 5, no. 2 (2012): 137–52; Susan Murray, "'I Think We Need a New Name for It': The Meeting of Documentary and Reality TV," in *Remaking Television Culture*, ed. Susan Murray and Laurie Ouellette, 40–56 (New York: New York University Press, 2004).

4. George Mair, *Inside HBO: The Billion Dollar War between HBO, Hollywood, and the Home Video Revolution* (New York: Dodd, Mead, 1988), 16.

5. "Bird Is In Hand for Pay Cable," *Broadcasting*, October 6, 1975, 26.

6. Mair, *Inside HBO*, 25.

7. Toby Miller and Linda J. Kim, "It Isn't TV, It's the 'Real King of the Ring,'" in *The Essential HBO Reader*, ed. Edgerton and Jones, 217–36, 228; Dean J. DeFino, *The HBO Effect* (New York: Bloomsbury, 2014), 52.

8. Umstead and Greenburg, interview.

9. Richard Hoffer, "A Fistful of Dollars," *Sports Illustrated*, January 15, 1990, 102.

10. Red Smith, "The Big One That Got Away," *New York Times*, June 24, 1979, S3.

11. In Neil Amdur, "For Cable, a Week of Prime Coverage," *New York Times*, February 15, 1983, B9; Umstead and Greenburg, interview.

12. Hal Lancaster, "Despite Big Obstacles, HBO Sports Chief Has Grand Plans for the Cable Network," *Wall Street Journal*, October 15, 1987, 35; Umstead and Greenburg, interview; Hoffer, "A Fistful of Dollars," 102.

13. Hoffer, "A Fistful of Dollars," 99.

14. Skip Myslenski, "HBO Series Tries Cleaning Boxing Mess," *Chicago Tribune*, April 15, 1986, C3.

15. Peter Heller, *Bad Intentions: The Mike Tyson Story* (Boston: Da Capo Press, 1995), 189; Mark Robichaux, "Cable TV Promotes Holyfield-Holmes as It Faces Life after Mike Tyson," *Wall Street Journal*, June 19, 1992, A7.

16. Mike Tyson with Larry Sloman, *Undisputed Truth* (New York: Penguin Group, 2013), 168; Rudy Martzke, "HBO's Multi-million Dollar Deal with Tyson Pays Off," *USA Today*, February 24, 1989, 3C; Norman Chad, "HBO and Tyson: Trying Another Combination," *Washington Post*, July 21, 1989, B3.

17. Brian Donlon, "Increased Options Made Cable a Live Wire," *USA Today*, November 30, 1989, D3.

18. Arthur Ashe, "Spike Lee Can't Have It Both Ways," *Washington Post*, December 15, 1990, D3. Kristen Fuhs explains how several documentaries—including the Spike Lee production *Undisputed Truth* (2013)—brokered Tyson's reintegration into popular culture after his legal troubles and brief suspension from boxing for biting Evander Holyfield's ear in 1997. See Kristen Fuhs, "How Documentary Remade Mike Tyson," *Journal of Sport & Social Issues* 41, no. 6 (2017): 478–92.

19. Larry Stewart, "A Sad L.A. Story: KCBS Last Again for NCAA Field," *Los Angeles Times*, March 8, 1991, C3; Phil Berger, "A Tyson HBO Deal That Wasn't," *New York Times*, December 12, 1990, D23; "HBO and Showtime Climb into the PPV Ring," *Broadcasting*, December 24, 1990, 28.

20. Frank Sanello, *Reel v. Real: How Hollywood Turns Fact into Fiction* (Lanham MD: Taylor Trade, 2002), xiii; Robert A. Rosenstone, *History on Film/Film on History* (New York: Routledge, 2013), 160; Derek Paget, *No Other Way to Tell It: Docudrama on Film and Television* (Manchester: Manchester University Press, 1998); Steven Lipkin, "Defining Docudrama: *In the Name of the Father, Schindler's List*, and *JFK*," in *Why Docudrama: Fact-Fiction on Film and TV*, ed. Allan Rosenthal (Carbondale: Southern Illinois University Press, 1999), 372; Steven Lipkin, *Docudrama Performs the Past: Arenas of Argument in Films Based on True Stories* (Newcastle, UK: Cambridge Scholars, 2011), 91.

21. Jack Lule, "The Rape of Mike Tyson: Race, the Press, and Symbolic Types," *Critical Studies in Mass Communication* 12, no. 2 (1995): 176–95.

22. In James Toback's 2008 documentary on Tyson, the retired boxer called King "a wretched, slimy, reptilian motherfucker. This is supposed to be my 'black brother,' right? He's just a bad man, a real bad man. He would kill his own mother for a dollar."

23. Jack Newfield, *Only in America: The Life and Crimes of Don King* (New York: William Morrow, 1989), 289.

24. See Travis Vogan, *ESPN: The Making of a Sports Media Empire* (Urbana: University of Illinois Press, 2015), 58.

25. Dan Rafael, "HBO Honors Its Bouts of Class; Legendary Nights Highlights 12 Fights over 30-Year Period," *USA Today*, March 13, 2004, C14.

26. Mark Wahlberg, interview with Terry Gross, *Fresh Air*, National Public Radio, January 6, 2011; "*The Fighter*: Why Movies and Boxing Go Together," *Wall Street Journal*, November 18, 2010, D2.

27. "Acclaim Sports' HBO Boxing Shifts to Retailers," *Business Wire*, November 15, 2000, 1.

28. Chuck Johnson, "HBO to Air Four-Part Prelude to De La Hoya–Mayweather Jr.," *USA Today*, January 29, 2007, C9.

29. Murray, "'I Think We Need a New Name for It,'" 44, 49.

30. "Quotable," *USA Today*, January 26, 2007, C3; Chuck Johnson, "Dancing with Success," *USA Today*, December 6, 2007, C1.

31. Richard Sandomir, "Worshipping at the Altar of Pay-per-View," *New York Times*, May 6, 2007, 15; Richard Sandomir, "With *24/7* HBO Refines Winning Formula," *New York Times*, January 2, 2012, D7.

32. Ben Grossman, "HBO Sports Increases Its Reach," *Broadcasting & Cable*, March 5, 2007, 4.

33. George Willis, "Why HBO Is Stunningly Leaving Boxing Behind," *New York Post*, September 27, 2018.

CONTRIBUTORS

SHAUN M. ANDERSON is assistant professor of organizational communication and faculty adviser for the Institute of Business Ethics and Sustainability at Loyola Marymount University. His teaching and research focus on corporate social responsibility initiatives, particularly within the sport context. He has published articles and essays in *Psychology of Popular Media Culture, International Journal of Sport Communication*, and *Huffington Post*.

AARON BAKER is professor of film and media studies at Arizona State University. He is the author of *Contesting Identities: Sports in American Film* (2003) and the forthcoming *Screening Baseball*.

DARIO BRENTIN is a researcher at the Centre for Southeast European Studies at the University of Graz and a PhD candidate at the School of Slavonic and East European Studies at University College London. He has published widely on the nexus of sport, politics, and ideology in the post-Yugoslav region.

EVAN BRODY is assistant professor of media and culture in the Communication Studies Department at the University of Wisconsin, La Crosse. He researches the various ways the LGBT community is represented in, and engages with, popular culture. His work primarily focuses on sports and television studies and has been published in the *Journal of Sports and Social Issues, Journal of Homosexuality, Spectator*, and other venues.

DAVID BROWN is completing his PhD at the Centre for Southeast European Studies at the University of Graz. His research focuses on the intersection of contemporary protest and soccer fandom in the Balkans. He has published on various topics connected to the region, including protest, sports fandom, and race.

BRANDEN BUEHLER is assistant professor in the College of Communication and the Arts at Seton Hall University.

RAY GAMACHE is a retired professor of journalism and media history. When not lost skiing the Maine woods or sailing Casco Bay, he drops anchor and does research in South Portland, Maine. He has published journal articles in *Journalism History, American Journalism, Journal of Sports Media, Studies in Symbolic Interaction, West Virginia Philological Papers*, and elsewhere.

JUSTIN HUDSON is a museum curator at the Smithsonian National Museum of African American History and Culture in Washington DC. Before starting at the museum, he completed his PhD in journalism studies from the University of Maryland, College Park, where his research focused on the intersection of race, sports, and collective memory.

ALEX KUPFER is visiting assistant professor in the Department of Film at Vassar College. His articles have appeared or are forthcoming in the *Moving Image, Spectator, Mediapolis*, and *Casino and Classic Card Games: Communities, Cultures, and Play*. His current book project examines the varied uses of educational and sponsored college football movies during the interwar era.

KORRYN D. MOZISEK earned her PhD in communication and culture from Indiana University. She is the director of integrative learning in the Office of the Vice Provost for Education and Special Faculty in the Department of English at Carnegie Mellon University. She studies the rhetoric of sport in relation to gender, sexuality, and citizenship.

EMILY PLEC is professor of communication at Western Oregon University. Her teaching and research areas include environmental communication, rhetoric, intercultural communication, sport, labor studies, media studies, and prison communication. She has contributed articles and essays on sports media and the rhetoric of racism to several journals and edited collections. She also edited the award-winning volume *Perspectives on Human-Animal Communication: Internatural Communication* and has published dozens of articles in communication journals and anthologies.

SAMANTHA N. SHEPPARD is the Mary Armstrong Meduski '80 Assistant Professor of Cinema and Media Studies in the Department of Performing and Media Arts at Cornell University. Her book *Sporting Blackness: Race, Embodiment, and Critical Muscle Memory on Screen* is forthcoming from University of California Press.

TRAVIS VOGAN is associate professor in the School of Journalism and Mass Communication and the Department of American Studies at the University of Iowa. His most recent book is *ABC Sports: The Rise and Fall of Network Sports Television* (2018).

INDEX

men: emphasis on, 38; female journalists and, 50–51; stereotypical, 184; white, 14, 36; young, 19, 20–21, 26, 36. *See also* gay men; masculinity

men, black: as Bad Buck, 121–24; deaths of, 96–97; families of, 99–100; identity issues and, 118; laws aimed at, 89, 94, 102–3, 104; oversimplifications about, 4, 80–81, 89, 90–94; stereotypes of, 130–31; as Uncle Tom, 117–21; violence and, 94–95

Merchant, Larry, 196–97, 202–3, 208

Meru, 154

metronormativity, 79–80

MGM, 181, 182

Miami OK, 81–82

Michael Sam: The Documentary, 64, 68, 70, 76, 80–81

The Middle of Nowhere, 37, 47

Mifflin, Lawrie, 56, 58

Mihailovic, Dragoljub "Draža," 151n23

Mihajlovic, Sinisa, 142, 145

Mijatovic, Predrag, 142

Mike Tyson and History's Greatest Knock-outs, 200–201

Mike Tyson's Punch Out!! (video game), 200

Miller, Phyllis, 51

Miller, Randy, 51

Miller, Toby, 17

Miller, Warren, 159

Millner, Steven, 115, 122

Mills, Richard, 137

Mills, Sara, 162

Minor League Baseball, 179

MLB (Major League Baseball), 20, 111

Momentum Generation, 24

monarchism, 151n23

Moore, Billy, 102–3, 105

Mordwand, 165, 166, 167–68

More than a Game, 3

More than an Athlete, 131n4

Morgan, Ray, 182

mountaineers, 154, 155, 162

mountain films: environmental issues in, 164–65; filmmaker's responsibility in, 157–58, 159–60; overview of, 7, 153–56, 171–72; techniques used in, 158–59, 160–64, 166–70; themes in, 156–57, 158–59, 161–64, 165–67, 168–71

MTM Enterprises, 14–15

Muñoz, José Esteban, 78

Murderball, 2

Murray, Cori, 45

Murray, Susan, 193, 211

Musburger, Brent, 116

Muslims, 151n23

myth: American Dream as, 92, 93, 102; death and, 105, 171; frontier, 158–59; makers of, 90, 95, 136; social issues and, 176–77; Yugoslav dissolution in, 139–40, 143

narration, 28. *See also* voice-over narration

narratives: ambivalent, 146; binaries and, 66; coming out, 66–71, 73–74; context of, 155–56; counternarratives and, 91, 93, 102, 103, 104–5, 147; emotions and, 42, 43; false, 95, 118, 143–44; familiar, 93, 113, 185–86, 187; heroism in, 154; historical, 137–38, 141, 201; ideology and, 136, 137; individualist, 127, 129, 131; influence of, 112, 113–14; influences on, 172; memory, 137–38; mythologized, 139–40; nationalistic, 148–49; neoliberal, 77; "official," 90, 102–3; overview of, 4, 6; of prime-time television, 11–13; queer, 83–84; simplified, 89, 91–92; of sports television, 16; transcendent, 155, 158; of the urban and the rural, 79, 80–81; whites in, 126

National Association of Black Journalists, 93–94

To order or obtain more information on these or other University of Nebraska Press titles, visit nebraskapress.unl.edu.

CPSIA information can be obtained
at www.ICGtesting.com
Printed in the USA
LVHW051738160720
660877LV00002B/246